Aging and Social Policy

SOCIOLOGY SERIES

John F. Cuber, Editor

Alfred C. Clarke, Associate Editor

Aging and Social Policy

EDITED BY

John C. McKinney
Frank T. de Vyver
BOTH OF DUKE UNIVERSITY

New
York

Appleton-Century-Crofts
DIVISION OF MEREDITH PUBLISHING COMPANY

PREFACE

Under the terms of a grant from the Ford Foundation, a Program in Socio-Economic Studies of Aging was established at Duke University in 1959. The grant made it possible to conduct a series of research projects related to socioeconomic aspects of aging during the period 1959-1964. Major publications of this program include Juanita M. Kreps, (Ed.), *Employment, Income and Retirement Problems of the Aged* (Durham, N. C.: Duke University Press, 1963); Ethel Shanas and Gordon F. Streib (Eds.), *Social Structure and the Family: Generational Relations* (Englewood Cliffs, N. J.: Prentice-Hall, 1965); and Ida Harper Simpson and John C. McKinney (Eds.), *Social Aspects of Aging* (Durham, N. C.: Duke University Press, 1966). All of these volumes are empirically based and reflect relatively specific research problems. Their scope is justifiably and necessarily limited by the research that they represent. As the program neared its termination, a number of the participants felt that it would be desirable to have a capstone volume that would approach aging from a more general point of view and from the perspective of policy implications. The present volume is an outgrowth of that feeling.

In order to implement the decision to have a capstone volume for the program, a symposium on aging and social policy was held at Duke University on March 25-26, 1965. The symposium, and the resultant volume, benefited greatly from the service, advice, and assistance of many people. The basic planning of the symposium was the responsibility of the Executive Committee of the Program, consisting of Professors Frank T. de Vyver, Paul M. Gross, Alan K. Manchester, and John C. McKinney. Miss Frances C. Thomas, Secretary-Treasurer of the Program, managed all local arrangements.

Dr. Ethel Shanas, Professor of Sociology, University of Illinois at Congress Circle; Professor Gordon F. Streib, Chairman of the Department of Sociology, Cornell University; and Dr. Donald P. Kent, then Director of the Office of Aging, U. S. Department of Health, Education, and Welfare, gave valuable advice concerning the selection of topics and authors. Professor Shanas and Dr. John W. McConnell, President of the University of New Hampshire, acted as formal critics of the papers presented at the symposium. Their critical commentary resulted in significant revision of the papers on the part of several authors prior to inclusion as chapters in this volume. Finally, a special acknowledgment must be accorded the editorial assistants for the Program, Mrs. Sandra F. Mascitelli and Mrs. L. Corbin Zeren. Their efforts have made a positive and significant contribution to the quality of the volume.

J.C.McK.
F.T.deV.

CONTENTS

Aging and Social Policy

Introduction

John C. McKinney
Frank T. de Vyver

The beliefs, sentiments, and values present in the social systems of a community and of the society in a general and pervasive sense, specify the roles and statuses of aged persons. While age inexorably advances, one's self-conception does not necessarily keep pace with it. Similarly, as the age structure of a society undergoes change, prevailing attitudes and practices in the society do not adapt in perfect coordination to those changes. It may be safely assumed that attitudes toward the aged, hence definitions of their roles and ascription of their statuses, will vary with respect to several subsystems within a complex society and within a diversified community. It is now a sociological commonplace that such subsystems as age groups, racial groups, religious groups, and occupational and social classes will vary in terms of their beliefs, sentiments, and values. Consequently, the treatment accorded the aged as expressed in role expectations and status ascription will vary extensively within a society and within its constituent communities. We do not know the precise nature of this variance, although research, particularly in the past two decades, has shed some light on this matter. We have a limited knowledge of how the social and intrapersonal relations of the aged are complicated by these factors. Moreover, we have a great deal to learn about the functional consequences for both the individual and the society of the many current patterns of role and status allocation with respect to aging.

Despite these limitations of factual data, it is clearly evident that within the general value system of American society there is an emphasis on youthfulness and remaining young; yet at the same time, individuals are penalized when they aspire to or assume roles which

1

society deems inappropriate to their age. Certainty of one's own status tends to decline as one proceeds toward the termination of the life cycle. In American society it is normatively expected that persons reaching sixty-five (with variations for specific groups and individuals) must generally move from recognized and established social positions into those that are relatively uncertain, ill-defined, and lacking in prestige. This involves relinquishing social roles and relationships typical of the so-called productive years, and accepting social roles and relationships characteristic of the later years. In place of the traditional primary roles of earning a living and maintaining a family, most older persons are faced, often rather abruptly, with the difficult task of discovering and developing different roles and activities. The "life-space" for the older person decreases as his past lengthens, his present undergoes vast alteration, and his future diminishes. Elderly individuals confront these brute facts with greatly varied equipment. Such conditions as occupational retirement, reduced income, economic dependency, loss of an independent household, subordination to adult offspring or institutional control, increased probability of illness and incapacity, loss of positions of leadership and influence, necessary restriction of participation in social affairs, and bereavement are characteristic of the period of the later years. Faced with these difficult and sometimes overwhelming conditions, the elderly person is frequently forced to modify his way of life radically. Some of the elderly manage the discontinuities in the life cycle with varying degrees of successful adaptation and a minimum of stress, while many others experience grave difficulties in coping with the discontinuities and frequently fail to develop meaningful activities and roles in later life.

It is of mounting importance and must be made clear that in discussing the elderly, we are discussing an increasingly large number of people who comprise an increasingly significant component of American society. In 1900, there were 3.1 million persons aged sixty-five and over in the United States, which at that time constituted only 4.1 percent of the population. For the next thirty years the increase of persons in this age category only slightly more than kept pace with the growth of the population in general. Even so, the 1930 census enumerated 6.7 million persons, or 5.4 percent of the population, as sixty-five years of age or over. After 1930, the rise in both the absolute and relative importance of the aged became noteworthy.

In 1940, an estimated 9.0 million persons were sixty-five and over, and in 1963, there were about 17.6 million; these figures represent an annual increase of 367,000 persons of this age group, and a near doubling of the aged population in twenty-three years. The combined effects of the post-Civil War rise in the birthrate, a slight increase in the expectation of life at age sixty-five, the precipitous drop in the birthrate from 1900 to 1936, and the gradual aging of millions of migrants who flocked to the United States just prior to World War I, have fundamentally changed the society's age structure. This demographic change is presently receiving widespread attention, not only in scholarly inquiry, but also in the spheres of policy development and politics.

The following facts further illustrate the magnitude of the change that has drawn this increased attention. Between 1900 and 1950, the number of persons aged sixty-five and over increased 297 percent, whereas the population as a whole gained by only 98 percent. At the start of the century, only one person in twenty-four was in the aged category; at present one person out of every eleven has passed his sixty-fifth birthday. Continued substantial increases in the elderly population are indicated by the Bureau of the Census' projections to 1985, but the rate of growth is expected to diminish. The projections show an increase of 7.4 million during the twenty-two year period after 1963, with an average annual gain of roughly 378,000 persons over sixty-five. The proportion of aged persons in the society may rise or fall from its present level, however, depending on future changes in fertility. At present, about 9.3 percent of the population is sixty-five or over. Projections assuming high fertility for the future suggest that the proportion would fall to 9.1 percent by 1985, but projections based on the assumption of low fertility predict that the proportion will rise to 10.1 percent. In any event the total number of people over sixty-five will approximate 19.6 million by 1970 and will rise to 25.0 million by 1985.

Although both the absolute and the relative increases in numbers of elders give some indication of the magnitude of the change in the age structure of American society, it is the concomitant trend of occupational retirement which emphasizes the nature of that change. Employment and retirement practices call for decreasing participation of elders in the labor force. There has been little assessment of the economic consequences to society, and even less assessment of

the noneconomic consequences, of the retirement of an ever increasing number of people for longer periods of time. The functional
problems of allocation (the problem of proper or optimum distribution of resources among their alternative uses in the satisfaction of
wants of consumers) and integration (the problem of maintenance of
a social system as a going concern with respect to the sharing of common prescriptions and proscriptions for conduct, belief, and valua-
tion), traditionally major problems of society, may be seriously
aggravated by the expanded practice of retirement from the labor
force. The presence in society of more and more people outside of
the work force may put severe pressure upon our present economy
of roles and statuses as well as upon the economy proper. Although
the elderly are normally considered a conservative component of
society and a force for the maintenance of the status quo, it is entirely possible that the elderly as an aggregate may, as a latent function, constitute a powerful force for change simply by their presence
in society. This is because they are now the "newcomers" to an institutionalized role system which historically evolved in terms of an
age-structure population skewed toward youth.

The expanding retirement years may create rising demand
within our economy of roles and statuses for which there is no ready
supply. The relative lack of established expectations and activities
for the aged which are positively valued by society contributes to an
inconsistency and ambiguity of role patterns and hence to a decrease
in stability of social interaction and societal life generally as the number and proportion of aged in society increase. On the other hand,
complex social systems with elaborate divisions of labor, for example, the United States, are characteristically flexible. This flexibility
may, under certain conditions, including policies and practices, permit the acceleration of role development and elaboration. In view of
the characteristic adaptability of complex social systems, the future
accorded any segment of the population, including the aged, is both
problematic and contingent. It is with these facts in mind that we
have undertaken in this volume an exploration of existing and potential social policy with respect to the aged.

For the purposes at hand we pragmatically use the term *policy*
to refer to the complex of individual ideas, organizational postures,
institutional attitudes, operational realities, temporary working arrangements, and practical or necessary compromises out of which

emerge decisions concerning what will be done to, with, and for the aged in society. The idea of an explicit national policy on aging is relatively new, in contrast to economic or foreign policy, because aging has only recently taken on the dimensions of a major problem. Changes in the age structure of society, accompanied by changes that are rapidly taking place in all sectors of societal life, have set the stage for the evolution of a national aging policy. We are not suggesting that a national aging policy is impossible nor that it is different in kind from policy in such established areas as economic activity, foreign relations, and scientific endeavor. To say that a government needs an articulated policy with respect to the aged is merely to note that in recent times there has devolved upon the government a major and continuing responsibility to make choices about issues which involve the aged as a special category of people. This responsibility implies the need for a perspective from which to assess, weigh, and balance the composite national interest with the interest of the elderly. The nation must equilibrate its conflicting internal needs and demands in order to pursue effectively those national goals most appropriate to and representative of the total populace. The pursuit of such goals requires some ability to establish and proceed from a position of consensus (necessarily a moving consensus) with respect to all major areas of social life and to all categories of the population. It is in terms of this definition and view of social policy that the following series of analyses has been undertaken. In effect, the analyses constitute a set of explorations in matters relevant to policy for the aged.

The volume is organized in two sections. The first section is concerned with the macro view of aging and social policy. It consists of three chapters which explore the general relationship of the aging process and the aged populace to the social, economic, and political systems of the United States. Aging as a process and the aged as an aggregate pose different problems for the three systems. In turn, the systems themselves, in terms of established custom and policy, pose different problems for the aging individual. These chapters examine the nature of the impact of the forces of aging on the system and on the individual and attempt to assess some of the prospective changes.

Chapter 1, "Aging and the Social System," was written by a sociologist, Wilbert E. Moore. Professor Moore asserts that man's biological nature has often been minimized or neglected by social scientists. He attempts to take account of this biological nature by focusing upon the interplay between the human life cycle and the social system, with implicit emphasis upon the results of this interplay for the aged. An assessment of demographic changes suggests that the continuing replacement of participants of a system through biological reproduction introduces change in the system, since the new participants will vary from the old both in biological competence and aptitudes and in exact socialization experiences. Apart from other considerations, the rate of replacement should be correlated with the rate of systemic change. This orientation leads to a consideration of two demographic aspects of replacement—"demographic replication" and "demographic turnover"—in terms of their implications for the aged. Professor Moore then turns his attention to continuities and discontinuities in the life cycle. Examples are presented of "somewhat regularized age grading" and "discontinuities in the pace of aging" with reference to the contemporary United States. The problematic impingement of both on the aged are illusstrated. In examining the problem of structural change and the aged, the model of a balanced reciprocity of services between parents and children which works out over several decades is viewed as an inaccurate representation of the flow of services between generations in contemporary American society. An alternative model suggested is that of *serial service,* which pictures the parents as passing services on to their children, not necessarily with the expectation of having these services returned to them at a later date, but with the expectation that their children will behave similarly when they themselves are parents. Moore suggests that the behavior which this alternative model describes is closely associated with the structure of a highly industrialized society, and the effects of this behavior on the aged are implied. As a concluding note, the problems posed for the aged by the rate of continuous change in a system are considered. Four cases in which the rates of change in the system differ are briefly described, and their effects on the aged are assessed.

Joseph J. Spengler, an economist, prepared Chapter 2, "The Aging of Individuals and Populations: Its Macroeconomic Aspects." Using American society as a focal point, this essay considers, from a macroeconomic perspective, the impact on the economy of an increase in the number of aged persons and the effect of prospective technological and socioeconomic changes on the economic situation of aged persons. Illustrative data are presented which show that *collective aging* (increase in the relative number of older persons) is more the result of a decline in the gross reproduction rate, and hence in the relative number of younger persons, than of an increase in life expectancy. But the increase in life expectancy is crucial to the *individual* dimension of aging since it has brought about greater concern on the part of those in younger age brackets for the problems and opportunities facing people sixty and over. Professor Spengler suggests that although the absolute economic condition of the aged is generally better now than it has ever been, there are certain factors which preclude optimum development. The high rate of population growth has absorbed capital which could have been used to improve the economic condition of the aged. The number of job-seekers in their twenties is growing nearly twice as fast as the population in their sixties. Work-life expectancy has been declining, and the average income of older men and women is decidedly below the general average. Several circumstances on which employment of persons beyond sixty years of age depends are mentioned. Increasing bureaucratization of the conditions of employment sets rigid retirement ages, tends to fix the maximum age at which a worker may be newly employed, and retards job mobility for older workers. Decline in the productivity of older persons in the labor force is affected by two sets of factors: factors closely associated with age (health, effectiveness of faculties, reserve capacities) and factors partially associated with age (obsolescence of knowledge and skills). Improvements in medicine may reduce the decline in productivity due to the former, and such things as higher general educational attainment and on-the-job training and retraining may reduce the decline associated with the latter. The aggregate demand for labor does not give a favorable picture for the aged since the demand in general continues to lag increasingly behind its supply. On the other hand, income-eroding factors, such as uncompensated inflation and the older worker's not sharing in the rise in per capita income, may actually increase the need of the older person to work. Although economists have usually viewed leisure and work as alternatives, a temporal perspective calls this view into question since a rise in money income may not entail a rise in the demand for leisure. Applying this concept to the aged, Professor Spengler suggests that the preference for work would be strengthened at the expense of that for leisure if their incomes seemed inadequate to them or if the status decline of retirement was too painful. Finally, the author discusses two arrangements which might lead to an optimal distribution of a person's waking hours between work and leisure and points out the implications of these arrangements for older people.

Chapter 3, "Aging and the Political System," was written by a political-sociologist, Fred Cottrell. Professor Cottrell maintains that the aged in the United States are pressing for more than has traditionally been allotted to them as their fair share. Any policy concerning the aged adopted by our society is seen as the outcome of a power struggle between the aged and their allies on the one hand, and those who oppose them on the other. Two elements affecting the possible outcome of this struggle are examined: the "economic law" perspective, whose supporters hold that "natural" economic laws will be the factor which most determines the economic share which the aged will have; and the "power" perspective, whose advocates take the position that the share the aged will receive is subject to power struggles which transcend the boundaries of the economy and are thus not subject to economic laws. This examination leads to the choice of the "power" perspective and the view of the ensuing power struggle as a useful model for understanding societal and primarily political policies toward the aged. Professor Cottrell asserts that as the relative number of older persons increases, the aged will likely seek a stronger place in the existing power structure and use their increased power to raise the position occupied by their values in the hierarchy of values served by the system. The results will be many changes in the power structure and the ways in which power is used, as well as disturbance in the family, church, market, union, and state, none of which has effectively provided roles for so many elders. Professor Cottrell expresses the view that a realistic approach to governmental policy toward the aged cannot be based on their gross voting power (20 percent of those who voted in the last presidential election were over sixty), since few politicians believe this power can be mobilized except in support of a few limited objectives. On the contrary, any realistic approach involves learning what these limited objectives are and how likely they are to be achieved through government rather than some other organization. Evidence points to the fact that the needs of the aged cannot be basically met through encouragement and voluntary practice of the "old morality"—thrift, profit-sharing plans, private insurance—nor through private agencies. However, the lingering value of this old morality, the hostile objections which private agencies often have to the use of government funds to help the aged, and the resentment of the aged themselves to the connotation of "welfare" that government aid has for them are all seen as obstacles in the path of strong governmental assistance to the aged. Although the image of the aged as a great political ogre about to overturn the structure of power politics does not emerge from this examination, the prognosis of possibilities for power is not hopeless. Professor Cottrell asserts that the aged can threaten the balance among other minorities and force concessions, and that new structures may emerge, providing new bases upon which to organize various segments of the older voting population. Moreover, he suggests that a different image of the aged may develop which will provide a new base for power by means of mass communications.

Following these broad overviews of the relations between aging and the major spheres of social life in Part I, a series of analyses of "critical areas" of social life with respect to the problems of the aged is presented in Part II. The seven chapters in this section bring certain critical problems into focus and examine them with some degree of specificity.

Chapter 4, written by a sociologist, George L. Maddox, focuses on "Retirement as a Social Event in the United States." Economic problems are seen as the most immediate and the most important consequence of retirement. The author argues that since work is becoming less and less the center of life, the greatest sense of loss upon retirement will be economic rather than psychological and social. If these economic problems are to be understood, the distinction must be made between those for whom inadequate income in retirement is constituted by wage loss and those for whom the impoverishment of retirement is only an intensification of a life-long problem. The conceptualization of retirement as a social event with a single meaning for all individuals is criticized. Drawing upon concepts and theoretical formulations from the work of W. E. Moore and H. L. Wilensky, the author suggests that knowledge of the retirement and/or old age of an individual is not sufficient to understand either the degree and nature of his social participation or the kind of self-concept he possesses. Other factors, such as the presence or absence of an orderly career in his past life experiences and the implied correlates of a career, would seem to be crucial and antecedent. Retirement as part of the inevitable and intrinsic process of psychological withdrawal (as it is pictured in the disengagement theory of Cumming and Henry) also comes under attack, not only because of the short shrift this theory gives to intervening variables such as the life style of an individual developed during earlier years, but also because of the inadequate attention it gives to variations in situational constraints. Professor Maddox suggests that the more important efforts at improving the position of the aged are those which deal with future generations of retirees rather than those which deal with current generations. This view is based on the assumption that more education for these future generations of aged and retired will likely give them more adequate resources to draw upon in adjusting to the status of elderly persons. Professor Maddox further asserts that if social life for the elderly is to be meaningful and satisfying, there is no substitute for the continuing experience of social integration in community life, not only in the later years but also during a substantial portion of the earlier years.

Following this discussion of retirement, in Chapter 5, Juanita M. Kreps, an economist, examines the problem of "Employment Policy and Income Maintenance for the Aged." Professor Kreps develops the view that people beyond the age of sixty-five face very poor employment opportunities, due essentially to a rapidly expanding labor force and a decrease in the aggregate demand for labor brought on by the pace of mechanization. This implies that attention will increasingly need to be focused on the maintenance of retirement income for the aged. Policy formulation resulting from this attention must take into account both the short-run situation of wide general unemployment which penalizes the older worker and the long-run trend toward a shortened work life, which requires that one's work-life earnings be spread over a longer nonworking period. Two basic goals of policies directed toward alleviating the economic position of the aged are examined. One is to raise the standard of living of people in general rather than that of any one particular group, such as the aged; but if this goal is achieved, the economic position of aged persons living on fixed incomes gradually worsens relative to that of the economically active population. The other objective is to redistribute the gains from economic growth so that older persons receive a larger share. Implementation of the second goal is discussed in terms of two types of approach. The first type of approach involves the adoption of measures to spread the work among all age groups and thus "share the unemployment," that is, by reducing the number of workweeks per year. Although ideally the long-run consequence would be to lengthen the work life and prevent further lengthening of the retirement period, this possibility is viewed as being rather impractical as far as the immediate economic needs of the aged are concerned. The second type of approach—dealing with the unemployment of the aged by special unemployment insurance, as distinguished from early retirement pay, which in effect dilutes one's later income—comes to grips more readily with the immediate problem and is seen as diminishing the long-run pressure for early retirement.

After mentioning early retirement as a constraint on the maintenance of income for the aged, Professor Kreps discusses two other restrictions which hinder redistributing more of the national product to the aged. One is the level of production of the economy, which must be such as to support massive efforts at redistribution of income to the aged; and the other is the competing needs of other and often more powerful age groups within the society. On the positive side, mechanisms for the implementation of such policies, for example, social security and old-age assistance, are readily available. Professor Kreps concludes that consigning the aged person an increased span of leisure without also allotting him adequate income converts leisure from a utility to a disutility and makes retirement synonymous with unemployment. This suggests that within the overall constraints of total income and total needs, the temporal distribution of both leisure and income should be reappraised.

In Chapter 6, John G. Turnbull, an economist, examines "Federal and State Programming." After briefly discussing the "preventive" approach (preventing loss of income by keeping the aged at work), Professor Turnbull examines at length the "alleviative" approach (permitting job separation but substituting other income to alleviate the aged's economic condition). He elaborates some principles underlying the condition and considers four kinds of alleviative programs—OASDI, other public programs such as public employee retirement and veterans' programs, group plans which are private in nature, and private individual plans. Turnbull emphasizes the following: coverage, qualification for retirement benefits, benefit levels, administration, financing, and operational details. Two other public programs, old-age assistance and general assistance, used as measures to care for those aged not qualifying under any of the above four kinds of programs, are then briefly commented upon. The general outlook for the effectiveness of all of these programs, according to Professor Turnbull, is that progress in income maintenance is being achieved and that as OASDI and private group benefits become payable to more individuals as time passes, the picture will improve still further. When the criteria of freedom and justice are applied as bases of evaluation, these programs are usually evaluated favorably. In reference to the future, Professor Turnbull expresses the view that there is little likelihood of merging the various assistance programs into one universal program because of our cultural notions about the desirability of a pluralistic approach. Also, the continuance of the shift from individual choice to group choice in old-age assistance programs is likely to continue.

A sociologist, Donald P. Kent, deals with the topic of "Social Services and Social Policy" in Chapter 7. Professor Kent develops the thesis that in order to understand services and policies related to aging, it is necessary to consider the social context in which the problems of the aged occur, since these services and policies constitute attempts to deal with such problems as they are defined by members of society. Making up the social context are such things as the increasing interdependence of the members of society with a resultant expansion of social concern, the rather recent notion that it is always possible to do something about problems, and the idea that the cause of most social ills can be known. These factors and others have led to the emergence of social welfare as a major focus of concern in modern times. Social policy toward the aged in America has been almost exclusively concerned with their economic wellbeing. Hebraic social thought, Greco-Roman philosophy, and Christian ethics are seen as laying a basis for the development of social welfare in general; but the specific form it took in the United States was shaped by the belief in individualism, the distrust of government, and the notion that voluntary groups are good. Four goals are posited as being the dominant ones toward which our social policy concerning the aged is directed: *security*—of income, of physical and mental health, and of suitable housing and living arrangements; *recognition*—as a significant member of society and as an individual with a separately identifiable personality; *response and relatedness*—the opportunity to relate to others and to be responded to by them; and *creativity*—to allow fulfillment of the need for exploration and expression of one's capabilities. For each of these rather general goals, a set of specific objectives of social policy is given. According to Professor Kent, responsibility for achieving these goals and the specific objectives associated with them lies with several different groups of people. The elderly themselves have obligations to those who are contributing to their support, such as doing as much for themselves as they can and attempting to make contributions, however small, to society. Although it does not seem wise to force responsibility for financial support of the elderly upon younger generations, these younger generations do have the obligation of voluntarily making such contributions out of love and affection. The government is responsible for guaranteeing sufficient income and providing facilities and services for the elderly. The responsibility for supplementing the governmental and family services to the aged is within the domain of voluntary organizations. Although advances have been made to alleviate the plight of the aged members of society, there is still much to be done. In summary, Professor Kent states that most of the elderly have incomes below subsistence level; most suffer from some chronic physical or mental illness and do not have money to pay for proper treatment of the illness; thirty percent live in housing which is structurally substandard or deficient with respect to normal facilities; their dignity is insulted by many laws, and a significant number are thereby caused to do without the assistance they need. In addition, American society has yet to face seriously the problem of involving elderly people in social activities, and personnel with specialized knowledge of aging are greatly needed.

Psychologists Daniel M. Wilner and Rosabelle Price Walkley undertake an examination of "Some Special Problems and Alternatives in Housing for Older Persons" in Chapter 8. They point to several facts which underlie general discussions of housing for the elderly. Due to an increase in size of the older population, 32 million Americans (the size of the population fifty-five years and above in 1960) are either already thinking about or beginning to think about housing arrangements for themselves as older persons. The great majority of the aged (sixty and above) do not live with relatives but reside independently in their own dwellings, and 20 percent of them live alone. In more than one-half of the households in which those sixty and above reside, the income is less than $4,000 per year; and the housing facilities tend to be relatively old and to some extent in a state of disrepair. The role of housing as it is related to certain physical, social, and psychological aspects of life in later years is examined. Evidence suggests that housing quality is related in a causal manner to infectious and communicable diseases and to accidents, although equally compelling evidence is lacking in regard to its relationship to basic social and psychological factors. Architectural arrangement of dwelling units as a factor affecting social interaction among the aged is briefly commented upon, followed by a consideration of factors which precipitate residential mobility among the elderly. The authors suggest that all of these factors and others must be taken into account in forming a viable policy toward housing for older people.

Three major alternative solutions to problems related to providing housing arrangements for the elderly are observable. The writers maintain that independent living arrangements in unplanned settings will undoubtedly remain the norm for persons in later years, although forces are at work which are making inroads on this as a primary solution. A second alternative, living with children, is not seen as a very workable solution. The third alternative, planned congregate arrangements (retirement villages and the like), is a substantially new development which has been gaining popularity in the past twenty years. The economics of such housing makes necessary the large-scale participation of federal loan and loan protection agencies, the most important of which has been the Housing and Home Finance Agency (HHFA). The principal programs for dealing with congregate housing for the elderly and some of the effects of these programs are described. Some data and findings from the 1964 *California Study of Retirement Housing* pertaining to the housing facilities of the two million elderly persons in California are then presented in summary form. In the final section of the chapter, some arguments and counterarguments concerning the implications of group housing for the elderly are discussed. It is concluded that both the pros and the cons of group housing will need to be debated and weighed in ensuing years before guidance for policy will be unequivocal regarding the priority that should be accorded this form of housing provision.

Following Wilner and Walkley's discussion of housing, Ewald W. Busse, a psychiatrist, presents in Chapter 9 an analysis of "Social Forces Influencing the Care and Health of the Elderly." This essay focuses on social influences which bear on the health and care of the aged. The role society plays in determining who will and who will not receive medical attention is held to be crucial, because limited funds are available for retraining and rehabilitating those disabled by chronic diseases, of whom the aged constitute a large percentage. Dr. Busse asserts that members of the medical and health professions must be cognizant of society's tendency to reject the chronically impaired person who does not overcome his handicap, which is often the case with aged people, since this makes it difficult to restore to his original group the chronically ill person whose functioning has been improved. Dr. Busse then examines the attitudes of physicians and other members of the medical and health professions who deal with the aged person and assesses the effect of their attitudes on the health care he receives. The physician's attitude may well be negative because elderly patients present an attack on his self-esteem when he does not see improvement and because the chronically ill elderly patients will frequently indicate dissatisfaction with his services. In brief, Dr. Busse indicates that to a significant extent physicians and other members of the medical and health professions *share* with society its generally negative attitudes toward the aged. Although no clear relationship between retirement per se and death is seen, Dr. Busse points to some evidence that relocation of the elderly person, primarily through institutionalization in homes for the aged, has an adverse effect upon health and can speed the approach of death. He then argues that the idea that older people are placed in state mental hospitals because they are rejected or because their families are not interested in them is false. He holds that they are sick people who need comprehensive medical care and for whom no other adequate community facility is yet available. Adverse conditions bearing upon the elderly in institutions are briefly discussed, and the point is made that in the ultimate sense it is society which decides whether these conditions will be alleviated.

Within the general context of health, but with a very special focus, the next chapter deals with "Personality and Aging—with Special Reference to Hospitals for the Aged Poor." Chapter 10 was written by a cultural anthropologist, Jules Henry. Professor Henry utilizes cross-cultural materials and the anthropological perspective in a comparative analysis of situations in various types of institutions for the aged. Professor Henry begins with the premise that a large proportion of the aged in the United States are sick and poor and are thus likely to spend a good part of their remaining lifetime in public or inexpensive private institutions. It is necessary, therefore, to understand the extent to which such institutions may destroy the personality. He argues that individuals are persons to the degree that they are attached to a social system, and this involves the acquisition and retention of certain tangible and intangible symbols of attachment. In acquiring these symbols, individuals in all cultures go through certain processes and achieve certain statuses. Taken together, these constitute personality in the sense that a person, by virtue of having acquired all necessary symbols and statuses essential to attachment, has the power to compel deference to himself—in short, to be treated like a person. From this perspective, Professor Henry then undertakes an analysis of the factors involved in depersonalization, which is defined as the process of depriving the individual of the factors that attach him to the social system. The analysis is based on a study conducted in a very large public institution and in a large, low-priced private institution for the chronically ill aged. Depersonalization takes place in various ways: through symbolic means, essentially the generalized loss of communication possibilities and the negative handling of the body; through material means, basically the deprivation of material amenities and the use of material objects in a distorted way; through extinction or violation of the shame and disgust functions; through routinization and deprivation of individuality and protection; through inconstancy and distortion of the human environment; and through staff-centeredness. Professor Henry goes on to say that since society's interest in its poor, sick, and aged does not go beyond material things and the correct performance of tasks of high visibility, humane behavior by the caretakers is left to chance. Since the caretakers in such institutions are poorly paid, poorly educated, and overworked, they have little incentive to humaneness. Professor Henry concludes that the ultimate consequences of depersonalization are mutual hostility, loss of capabilities, and apathy. The role of institutions for the aged in depersonalization is viewed with deep concern.

In the final chapter of the volume "The Social Meaning of Death and the Law" is analyzed by a social psychologist and a lawyer. Kurt W. Back, the social psychologist, and Hans W. Baade, the lawyer, engage in a dialogue which focuses upon the social meaning of death as it is reflected in the legal structure of American society and the implications of this meaning for the aged. They indicate that death in contemporary American society seems to be denied on the one hand and perceived as an intense threat on the other. Factors are examined which may have contributed to this attitudinal ambivalence, and mechanisms through which each attitude is expressed are briefly explored. In order to examine this phenomenon more fully, several considerations related to the meaning of death in contemporary American society as reflected in the legal structure are examined. Workmen's compensation and laws concerning liability and financial responsibility in traffic accidents are discussed as they pertain to the question of why the law protects individual life to the greatest extent while allowing anonymous death to occur. The removal of the immediate symbols of death from constant public view is examined in terms of sanitary legislation and zoning laws. With reference to the law as a help or a hindrance concerning a person's influence over his offspring after death, it is pointed out that, although somewhat hostilely, the law allows the "dead hand" ruling, primarily through the skillful utilization of trusts and future interests. Foundations are seen as an indication of the law's encouraging a person's striving for immortality through the creation of permanent charitable establishments. In relation to the final question of how far the legal order as such provides comfort in the continued existence of society as it was known to the deceased, it is argued that it is primarily the legal profession (basically conservative) rather than the law per se (a tool of change as well as a mechanism to promote stability) which serves as a basis of such comfort. The position of the aged in contemporary society is seen as a reflection of ambivalent attitudes toward death. Since the aged are to a certain extent symbols of death, they are segregated, thus emphasizing their concern with death. Yet as members of society, they have accepted the society's attitude toward death and hence attempt to deny it and to postpone it. From the perspective of the aged, then, they are supposed to be concerned and at the same time not concerned about death. From the perspective of society, the aged become a symbol of delaying death and simultaneously a symbol of its inevitability.

In summation, it is quite evident that the various chapters in this volume have explored selected general and specific aspects of a complex problem related to aging and social policy. The approach has been frankly exploratory and may be thought of as constituting a rough cognitive map of the domain of relevance rather than a definitive statement of what policy should be. We do not presume that our volume is anything more than a preliminary, but perhaps useful, step in the direction of evolving national policy on aging. The multiple authorship and multidisciplinary approach have contributed diversity to the content of the volume. Despite the diversity one consistent theme runs through the work. This theme is exemplified in the following quotations. Professor Maddox has commented, "The formulation of social policy toward the aged should not ignore the heterogeneity of elderly persons nor the importance of distinguishing between the current and future generations of the elderly." In the same vein Professor Spengler has remarked that when devising policies for the aged, the social scientist must "distinguish between transitory problems in need of temporary solution and persisting problems which are avoidable or at least soluble through future-facing instead of backward-facing measures." This is clearly a theme worthy of serious thought and attention in times such as these when the pressure for action is so great.

BIOGRAPHICAL NOTES

JOHN C. MCKINNEY was born in Velasco, Texas, in 1920 and educated at Colorado State College and Michigan State University (Ph.D.). He was a member of the faculty at Michigan State University (Instructor to Associate Professor) 1947-1957. Since 1957 he has been Professor of Sociology and Chairman of the Department of Sociology and Anthropology at Duke University. Mr. McKinney has contributed to many professional journals and symposia and is the author of *Constructive Typology and Social Theory*, coauthor of *Introduction to Social Research*, coeditor of *The South in Continuity and Change,* and coeditor of *Social Aspects of Aging.* In addition to his interest in aging, he has had a long-time interest in macrosociology, the problems of large-scale systems in development, continuity, and change.

FRANK TRAVER DE VYVER was born in 1904 in Mount Vernon, New York, and was educated at Oberlin College and Princeton University (M.A. and Ph.D.). Mr. de Vyver is currently Professor of Economics and Vice-Provost of Duke University. He is a member of the American Economic Association, past president of the Southern Economic Association, a member of the Industrial Relations Research Association and the Board of Trustees of the Joint Council on Economic Education. He has been a Fulbright Lecturer on Economics, a State Department appointee as Lecturer in Economics, and Chairman of the Department of Economics and Business Administration at Duke University. Among his most recent publications are "Arbitration—Its Differences and Its Drawbacks," a Shann Memorial Lecture at the University of Western Australia; "The Transplantation of Trade Unionism to British Africa," in *Transfer of Institutions;* "Grievance Systems in American Industry," in the *Australian Quarterly;* and "The 1920 Civil Service and Teachers' Strike in Western Australia," in *The Journal of Industrial Relations.*

I

THE MACRO VIEW OF AGING AND SOCIAL POLICY

1

Aging and the Social System

Wilbert E. Moore

In his quest for intellectual distinctiveness and s
exclusiveness, man has often minimized or neglected his bic
nature. In this he has been abetted by many social scientists,
attempting to evade biological determinism and to avoid havir.
man behavior become merely a special branch of mammalian
ogy, the social scientists have tended to deal with cultural man i
than with biological man. The two, of course, can scarcely be
tinguished analytically, and certainly not concretely.

Human evolution is a complex biosocial process. There is
reason to suppose that biological adaptation ceased with the eme
gence of "culture,"[1] which, after all, is coextensive with the huma
species in time and space. As long as man does not control the me
teorological and geophysical forces around him, but remains subjec\
to the discipline of his own mortality, he cannot be said to have mas-
tered the nonhuman environment in order to live in an environment
solely of his own creation.

The social scientists' neglect of biological man has been selective
rather than total. Human sexuality has not been left to the exclusive
attention of poets and novelists; it figures in not a few scholarly
treatises—especially those of psychologists and sociologists. And children enter the picture in those disciplines also. They almost never
appear in economics or political science. In all of these disciplines,
most of the more abstract analytical and theoretical systems of the
social scientists appear to deal exclusively, if implicitly, with normal
adults. Even if attention is paid to the implications of biological recruitment in the continuing necessity for incorporating the recruits

[1] See Theodosius Dobzhansky, *Mankind Evolving* (New Haven: Yale University Press, 1962).

into an ongoing system, this process of *socialization* is most commonly treated as being of short duration in early childhood, leading to a one-by-one and nearly instantaneous conversion from savagery to civilization.

A rather different perspective on social organization and social process results from dealing with the entire human cycle as if it were a necessary biological dimension of continuing social systems. Indeed, age as a kind of neutral and continuous variable, which manifests itself in both continuous and discontinuous changes in behavior, is relevant for most forms of social discourse and social structure. Our task here is to examine the interplay between this unavoidable basis for individual change and the social system that comprises the ordering of behavior according to values and norms, and allocates activities to actors in terms of positions and roles.

The conception of social system entails the notion of interdependence among constituent elements. The concept does not require the assumption that "everything fits together." Within the temporal and spatial boundaries of any social system identified and specified, there may be acts that are discordant and acts that are simply indeterminate. These become empirically determinable dimensions or characteristics of systems, neither impossible by definition nor necessarily destructive of other systemic qualities if discovered. The concept also does not require the assumption that systems remain static. At the minimum, functional relations are rarely instantaneous. But the relations among elements may be sequential as well as merely reciprocal, and how systems change is as legitimate a query as how they persist.

The title of this essay will be taken seriously in the following discussion, in that we shall deal in part with life-cycle phenomena and not solely with the aged, those persons at later parts of the cycle. The ultimate cause of death is birth, and aging is a process that starts at conception. This elementary biological fact is intrinsic to social systems, though it may be neglected for various analytic purposes. It can scarcely be left out of account if we wish to attend to the facts of systemic change, or to inquire about the way life-cycle phenomena affect the operation of the social order. Our procedure will be to deal first with the implications of the fact that immortal systems are inhabited by mortal men. We shall then examine continuities and discontinuities in the life cycle. Since culture and social organization in large part flow between generations and along age lines, we shall attend to the differences between true reciprocities and what we shall call "serial service." Finally, in an era when the pace of many social changes is accelerating, we shall note the additional strains that arise between the cumulative experience of the aging individual and the collective experience of social systems.

I

A society as a whole or any continuing social organization is perforce faced with a succession of actors or role-players. Man's mortality assures the necessity of recruitment. Ultimately that recruitment rests on biological reproduction, but various positions require prior socialization, or at least the achievement of some testable or arbitrary degree of "maturity." Typically, various social positions have some kind of age-specificity, though the age grade may be rather broad and not always defined in precise, chronological time: for example, infancy, childhood, youth, adulthood, and, perhaps, old age. Transition from one broad age grade to another thus entails some discontinuity in the life cycle, a subject to which we will turn in the following section. But it also entails replacement as individuals leave an age grade, whether they leave by "graduating," or, sooner or later, by death.

In all societies there may be considerable periods in the life cycle when aging is gradual and expected role-relationships essentially constant. During these periods, cumulative experience or even physical vigor may count for little in differentiating younger and older members of the category, so that there is little sense of either progression or retrogression. This appears to be most often true of the broad age grade of adulthood, and even in a highly graded society such as our own, many of the powers and responsibilities of adults have little variability according to either exact chronological age or social seniority in the position.

Yet the succession problem remains. And for any social role— that is, any role beyond the passive one of the newborn infant—there are two interacting sources of variability among recruits: biological competence and aptitudes, and differences in exact socialization experience. I have accordingly argued elsewhere[2] that vagaries and uncertainties in the socialization process must introduce flexibilities and change potentials in any continuing system, and that these potentials are increased by the associated necessity for adult role requirements to constitute tolerable ranges rather than highly precise specifications. The replacement of those who move through and out of a system by recruits moving in will introduce some change in the system itself, however small that change may be. Obviously the rate of replacement should be correlated with the rate of systemic change, apart from all other considerations.

We thus encounter the paradox that life expectancies are low and social succession high precisely in the underdeveloped areas of the world where the social order is commonly supposed to be traditional and relatively unchanging. Although the latter assumption no doubt has been exaggerated, two countervailing sources of stability may be noted. First, the risks of mortality do not bear equally on all ages. The average expectation of life is greatly affected by the mortality of the very young. Adults may not have death rates radically higher than those in more economically advanced societies.[3]

There is a second source of stability in "traditional" societies, despite somewhat higher turnover through adult mortality. For those who reach adulthood, the social structure is generally much less finely differentiated than it is in modernized societies. This lack of detailed differentiation is especially true of the system as it bears on the individual, although, for the structure as a whole, status and other distinctions may be rather extensive. The Indian structure of castes and subcastes, for example, is wondrously complex, but the individual is not subject to their distinct demands either simultaneously or *seriatim* through a career. Once the individual is placed in the system, the role demands and skills may be relatively simple, standardized, and easily acquired. Mortality that is merely "high" but that does not literally wipe out a standardized segment of the system may have little gross impact on the way the survivors play out their roles. (Differential mortality between status segments would, of course, have consequence for their relative positions.)

[2] Wilbert E. Moore, *Social Change* (Englewood Cliffs, N. J.: Prentice-Hall, 1963), especially Chapter 1, "The Normality of Change."
[3] See the data and sources in the paper by Joseph J. Spengler in Chapter 2 of this volume.

We are dealing, then, with mortal men occupying and passing through positions in a system that is in principle immortal. The magnitude of the succession problem depends on the way age-specific mortality rates intersect with the age-grading characteristic of a society and its various subsystems.

Let us assume (probably correctly) that age-specific mortality actually has the greatest relevance for succession and accompanying structural change where many people move through a somewhat graded career; and this would primarily be the situation in modernized societies. Let us also assume that the structure is more or less adapted to relatively stable or slowly changing mortality conditions within and among the various age grades. Then we should expect the greatest structural dislocation by sharp changes in mortality conditions. As a concrete illustration, substantial war losses among young men in military service leave gaps in the "recruitment cohorts" for subsequent civilian employment, improve the competitive career chances of the survivors and those just younger, and incidentally damage the marital chances of their female contemporaries. Conversely, to take a hypothetical situation, a substantial reduction of mortality rates of men over, say, fifty years of age, would impair the promotional prospects of younger men and postpone the demise of persons in lifetime positions. (One cannot avoid noting the parallel at the individual level of the impatient heirs of a wealthy but long-lived ascendant or the watchful suspense created by an overage hereditary ruler.)

Different age cohorts in a population represent different "environmental histories," including differing mortality conditions. When we add structural changes that are at least somewhat independent of current age-compositions, for example, variations in employment opportunities for new entrants to the labor force, it is clear that age cohorts have differential "life chances" as they move through a social order. It goes without saying that life chances are also differentiated by sex, by "class," and by other variables; but our focus here is on the intersection of age and social patterns.

In general, changes in proportional age distributions are much more a reflection of changes in fertility than of changes in mortality. After a careful examination of the evidence, Coale concludes that ". . . the rising fraction of the aged in western countries has not resulted from lowered death rates but almost wholly from a long his-

tory of declining fertility."[4] He also notes[5] that the substantial variations in fertility in the United States over recent decades have
produced a highly irregular age distribution.

Persons now (in 1965) aged sixty-five and over are, of course,
the survivors of birth cohorts before the turn of the century, when
fertility rates had not gone far in their downward slope. The growing
proportions of aged persons in the population and the prospect for
those proportions to continue increasing are largely a function of
subsequent fertility declines prior to World War II. Persons now in
their early thirties are the survivors of small birth cohorts during the
Depression, and as Spengler's paper[6] shows, the smallest proportional increase over the period of 1960-1985 will be the "mature"
segment of the population, twenty to sixty-five. A little before the end
of the century, in the absence of major declines in mortality rates at
older ages, American society will have a temporary respite from the
swelling number of oldsters as the Depression babies finally reach
retirement age.

Since we are dealing with succession to social positions as individuals age (that is, move through the life cycle), and since we are
concentrating for the moment on the demographic components of
succession, we need to note two other points. One relates to the lack
of what we may call "demographic replication," and the other relates to the average length of generations.

With regard to demographic replication I have noted elsewhere
that ". . . a precise total and differential control of fertility and mortality is extremely unlikely. Thus the exact size of a population cannot be expected to remain stationary through time, and it is even less
likely that births and deaths will exactly maintain existing distributions among various social categories."[7] This means that the social
system must permit some mobility between generations, even if
placement is nominally hereditary. That implication leads to another,
namely, that socialization into prospective future roles in the life
cycle must be uncertain or improper for some people in any society.
Of course, these problems are much more severe in modernized so-

[4] Ansley J. Coale, "How the Age Distribution of a Human Population is
Determined," *Cold Spring Harbor Symposia on Quantitative Biology*, 22
(1957), 83-89; quotation from p. 88.
    [5] *Ibid.*
    [6] Spengler, paper in this volume, Table 2-3.
    [7] Moore, *op. cit.*, p. 14.

cieties, where mobility is the necessary norm and where the future is cloudy and uncertain because of rapid structural changes. To these points I shall return in another context.

The rapidity of demographic turnover (with its implications for social succession) is also affected by the length of generations. If we define generational length as the average age of parents at the birth of their children, it is almost certainly higher in underdeveloped than in modernized societies. This holds true despite the practice of very early marriage and childbearing in many societies, for in the absence of contraception mothers who remain alive and fertile continue childbearing until menopause. The present and recent situation in modernized societies, even during the "baby boom," is characterized by relatively early marriage, early childbearing, and early termination of childbearing. In the United States relatively few babies are born to mothers over the age of thirty. If these shortened generations continue—and there is every reason to suppose that they will—the multigenerational lineage will be increasingly common, with most children having all their grandparents alive until the children themselves reach maturity.

We have been examining the demographic flow of recruits to social positions relative to age. The succession problem is somewhat more than the flow of birth cohorts through age-distribution tables or life tables. We must also bear in mind variations in time and space of the social significance of age and aging. Various systems set minimum and maximum ages for types of social participation: labor market entry, marriage, voting, holding office, or, later in the cycle, compulsory retirement. Other rights and privileges or their termination are made functions of time rather than age as such: years of qualifying experience, terms of office, length and thus seniority of service. When coupled with age minima, these temporal patterns may be viewed as a further aspect of succession.

It is a commonplace that different social systems place differing values on various stages of the life cycle and allocate differing privileges and responsibilities to the older ages. Yet, whether most individuals experience a gradual and steady rise in relative position as they age until the time that they die or become unmistakably senile, or go through an ascent and descent only partially parallel to their physiological capacities, the age curve of social participation is irretrievably cyclical in view of man's mortality. The temporal order of social systems[8] must somehow accommodate the temporal order of biological man.

II

Let us examine age grading and life cycles in a little more detail, and narrow our field of vision to modernized societies and particularly to the contemporary United States.[9]

With the growth of a highly standardized educational system which is compulsory to ages ranging from fourteen to eighteen, most of the children and youths of the society are caught up in a system involving rather precise age grading. This grading involves orderly progression from year to year, interspersed by somewhat sharper transitions between broad types of schools, for example, primary, secondary, college, and postgraduate. Though some individuals may be advanced or retarded according to the age-grade norms, there is a marked tendency in educational organization to accommodate individual differences *within* grades. Thus an individual's place in this formal organization can be inferred with high probability from knowledge of his age alone. When membership in the system becomes competitive and optional, as is generally true at higher levels, cohorts become depleted and age grading tends to become looser for those remaining.

The adult breadwinner is also subject to age grading, though of a somewhat looser sort. Particularly for those in administrative careers in the military, civil service, or large private bureaucracies, such as universities and corporations, there are always norms or standards for advancement with age. Careers will of course be affected by market demands for levels and types of skills—witness the ambivalence of today's senior professors when they compare their own slow advancement with the quick achievement of full professorial rank by men a few years beyond their doctoral studies.

[8] See Wilbert E. Moore, *Man, Time, and Society* (New York: Wiley, 1963). See also R. M. MacIver, *The Challenge of the Passing Years: My Encounter with Time* (New York: Trident, Simon and Schuster, 1962).

[9] For a perceptive but essentially static view of age grading in the contemporary United States, see Talcott Parsons, "Age and Sex in the Social Structure of the United States," in his *Essays in Sociological Theory: Pure and Applied* (New York: Free Press, 1949), Chapter X.

Careers are also affected by the inconsistency between permanent tenure until formal retirement and the pyramidal shape of administrative hierarchies. Even if age, or its organizational equivalent in seniority, is a major requirement for promotion, it cannot be an exclusive one, for some members of an age cohort must be left behind when the positions thin out faster than the ranks of eligibles.

The adjustment problems of aging clearly are not confined to persons in retirement.[10] The age grading of achievement, even if loose, presents adjustment problems throughout adulthood, particularly for regular members of the labor force. Keeping up with, falling behind, or forging ahead of one's age peers provides a constant or periodically recurrent opportunity for comparison.

A somewhat different problem is presented by the interrupted career. Married women who enter or reenter the labor force after the youngest child has reached adolescence have dual careers in the sociological sense, with a temporal ordering in their respective primacy. Their adjustment problems include loss of time (and its experiential equivalents) as compared with potential competitors with singular careers. They also find themselves in competition with current or recent labor-force entrants among the young. Apart from the preferences of employers for youths, which may be nonrational, the young may have a distinct and sensible advantage in this competition: they may have both a superior basis of knowledge and skills, either because of secular improvements in educational levels and standards or because the housewives' former competence has deteriorated, and they may have superior habits conducive to continuous learning and adaptation.

Remarkably little is known of career patterns or of the forms of career building in later maturity. There is a good deal of folk wisdom, of untested reliability, concerning crucial periods in age and achievement. Some organizations, such as the military, formalize age-grade relationships, with the man who falls behind his contemporaries ("overage for rank") being required to retire early or to resign. In other careers, the competitive system encourages occasional reappraisals, for example, when a man is passed over for promotion, thus closing his last opportunity for access to very high

[10] On the varying significance of retirement, see the chapter by George L. Maddox, "Retirement as a Social Event in the United States," in this volume.

positions. I have elsewhere[11] discussed speculatively the complex interplay among aspirations, expectations, and achievements in graded careers. The frustration intrinsic to career competition is commonly commented on, although again we have little exact knowledge of the levels or significance of such frustration and the relative success of various coping mechanisms. Yet the man who exceeds his own earlier expectations, if not his wilder dreams, is also worthy of note, for he too has adjustment problems: living up to his unexpected success and quieting his misgivings concerning his own relative merit.

Not much progress is going to be made in our understanding of aging in later maturity until we develop the underlying data on career sequences and analyze those data in terms suitable to their complexity. One model is that of the Markov chain, whereby reaching certain points (due regard being taken of age and rate of prior movement) establishes probabilities for reaching later points in the chain. Unfortunately, few social scientists are methodologically equipped to handle this kind of analysis.

Despite the abundance of examples of somewhat regularized age grading, some of it annual, there are discontinuities in the pace of aging. Some of these are formally marked off and honored by passage rituals. Others are more subjective, although still real and important. MacIver[12] notes that adults experience "indifferent intervals," often whole decades, interrupted by sharp realizations of aging as the ages of thirty, forty, fifty, sixty, and so on, are reached.

The past when matters were better synchronized and coordinated may be largely mythical, but it is certainly true that the unequal rate of contemporary changes adds new degrees of problems if not new kinds. The shortened generation that derives from earlier cessation of childbearing does not correspond to the lengthened expectation of life and its implications for living to and beyond retirement age. Thus mothers tend to "retire" from their major social role some twenty years before their husbands retire from work. The mothers whose youngest child has reached secondary school have the alternatives of entry or reentry into the labor force or some form of leisure-time activity. They also comprise the bulk of what may be

[11] Wilbert E. Moore, *The Conduct of the Corporation* (New York: Random House, 1962), Chapter XIII, "Climbers, Riders, Treaders."

[12] MacIver, *op. cit.*, Chapter XII, "The Indifferent Interval and Other Protections."

called the volunteer labor force, upon which many community and welfare programs depend for services. If they choose economic activity, they must somehow make adjustments for their lack of continuous activity and accumulated experience. They may need to join technologically displaced males in adult retraining. If the women do not enter the labor market, they must find a use for unaccustomed leisure. They may be, in effect, in early retirement, and the rising rate of female alcoholism attests to some failures in adjustment.

Thus women tend to retire much earlier than men, despite their greater life expectancy. Many spend nearly half their lives in not performing their "primary" female role, though in a sense they may continue to play an "integrative" role, both within the family system and in the neighborhood and community. Alienation is less surprising than its comparatively low incidence. By the time their husbands retire, the wives have had considerable practice in filling up time in some sort of secondary roles. There is no assurance at all that the wife becomes an appropriate role model for the retired male, as leisure may be as sex-differentiated as are primary adult roles.

The extended experience that many women have in use of leisure before they reach old age may stand them in good stead, as they may be unwittingly preparing for widowhood, which is their eventual, probable lot. The offphase cycle deriving from higher female life expectancy is exacerbated by the conventional practice of women marrying men a year or two older than they, and in the event of a remarriage, the age differential is likely to be considerably greater. The aged population thus comprises a disproportionate number of widows, who are not only cut off from children and grandchildren in varying degrees, but have also lost the marital companionships that may have previously substituted for maternal responsibilities.

III

Most human populations are recruited biologically. The exceptions, such as migratory resettlement or celibate religious orders, are either temporary or parasitic. The truism about biological recruitment takes on significance with the additional fact that the human infant at birth is quite unable to sustain life unaided. There is thus an intrinsic flow of "services" from older to younger members of a population, at least until the younger ones are able to fend for themselves. In all societies the overwhelmingly predominant structure for assuring the support and primary socialization of the young is the family. Although the family is rarely the exclusive agency of socialization, it is temporally primary and always important even where other formal and informal mechanisms operate.

Now the usual view is that the services between the generations in premodern societies begin to balance into complementarity as children take on various tasks, and finally change directions as parents who have lost productive vigor are supported by their mature offspring. Children thus become economic assets for the family as a productive unit by their added labor, and then become old-age insurance for the parents. When things work out according to the model, there is a kind of balanced reciprocity which achieves balance only after several decades.

Such intergenerational reciprocity assumes that the young actually survive to add substantial effort to common activities and to become the primary source of economic support. With high infant and child mortality rates prevalent in premodern societies, the initial support by the parents often must be unrepaid. The reciprocity also assumes that parents live to an unproductive old age requiring support by their children, and that too, somewhat less often, is not the case. Nevertheless, long-term reciprocity exists frequently enough to constitute a kind of standard.

The usual view of the family in modernized societies and particularly in the United States is that the social separation of the generations (and of siblings) at the maturity of the children cuts off the repayment. Services then run in one direction only, and from the point of view of a kind of hedonic calculus, parenthood becomes sacrificial.[13]

It is clearly true that the social mobility requisite to an industrialized society establishes a separation of the generations in terms

[13] I expressed this view, without qualification, some years ago. See Wilbert E. Moore, "The Aged in Industrial Societies," in J. Douglas Brown and others (Eds.), The Aged and Society (Champaign, Illinois: Industrial Relations Research Association, 1950), pp. 24-39. I now regard the view as partially mistaken, as the discussion in the text indicates. For a more extended discussion of an evolutionary view of contemporary kinship, see my The Impact of Industry (Englewood Cliffs, N.J.: Prentice-Hall, 1965).

of social function and status, and it is most consistent with a nuclear, conjugal family system that permits adult siblings also to find their ways separately in competitive placement. But I believe that the scattered evidence now at hand is consistent with a somewhat different view, by adding a temporal perspective to structural arrangements. It appears that the initial impact of economic modernization is the most damaging to laterally and vertically extended kinship reciprocities. The traditional patterns are commonly undermined not only by the residential separation of new recruits who leave the countryside or village to find new opportunities in modernizing cities, but also by the fact that the new recruits (typically youths and young adults) operate in radically novel structural and institutional settings. Between the old ways and the new there may be very little basis for mutual understanding, to say nothing of uniformity of social position.

As most of the population becomes caught up into a modernized socioeconomic system, the separation of the generations and siblings in terms of the *kinds* of systems they participate in is partially reduced, although continuing rapid change means that some generational differences in social experience are intrinsic and an enduring feature of modernized societies.[14]

It appears, then, that the contemporary American kinship system has been able to survive the social inequality of its constituent primary families. Many kinship duties have become optional rather than mandatory, with consequent strains in attempting to honor competing claims. In most American legal jurisdictions, mature children are not responsible for the support of indigent parents, though this does not, of course, remove the claims of conscience.

If one asks, "Where does the American family turn first in time of trouble?" the modal answer is almost certainly, "To kinsmen." One might have to make exception of rather standardized professional services available from physicians, school teachers, and clergymen. But illness that requires home nursing and family care, many types of financial emergencies, and bereavement, certainly, commonly call for use of kinship bonds. If residential propinquity permits, even such services as shopping and baby-sitting may be rendered unilaterally, traded in kind, or traded with crude complementarity. Of

[14] On this point I *was* correct in the paper cited in the preceding note.

course, the reestablishment of kinship ties has been aided by improved transportation and communication.

From the scattered evidence, services and simple visiting are most likely to link the female kindred, and financial assistance to link the males (except for financial help to widows, which may be regarded as the primary duty of sons).

In the broad perspectives of comparative social change, the partial restoration of kinship ties after the shock of modernization is one of a somewhat limited range of instances of structural continuities in modified form after a substantial and discontinuous structural change. Such instances occur only once in each system, but recur in social space (time being incidental) as successive systems undergo a somewhat standardized transformation.[15]

More to the present point, the strains in the modernized kinship system are intrinsic. (Since in every kinship system separate lineages are linked by marriage, there are always intrinsic strains between primary families and other kinsmen, but that is another matter.) Given the intimacy of intrafamilial relations and the primary functions of affectivity and normative socialization directed at the young, it would be unlikely that adults emerging from this structure should treat one another as strangers. The links between generations are likely to endure, apart from all considerations of property transfers or other economic attributes of lineage.

If a society is viewed as a system that not only persists through time but also accumulates physical capital and "cultural heritage," it is clear that the young can scarcely repay their inheritance. There is therefore a kind of unilateral flow of goods and services from generation to generation, or at least from predecessors to successors. In addition to true reciprocities, there is a kind of *serial service,* the initial beneficiaries "passing it on" rather than "passing it back."

The occurrence of serial service is by no means unique to the temporal order of generations. Much of the division of labor in modern manufacturing, though complementary in the grand design of the organizational plan seen in cross section, is not strictly reciprocal. The workman at later stages in continuous assembly does not reciprocate the prior services of his fellows; his duty is to render services for those still later in the sequential pattern. An even closer parallel

[15] See Wilbert E. Moore, "Predicting Discontinuities in Social Change," *American Sociological Review,* 29 (June, 1964), 331-338.

is offered by Whyte[16] in his description of suburban communities inhabited more or less briefly by young corporate executives subject to administrative transfers. Residents render all kinds of initial services to newcomers, thereby passing along benefits earlier received from *their* predecessors. Again, the obligation incurred by the newcomers is not to repay their benefactors, but to render like services to later arrivals. It is probably because sociologists have been exclusively preoccupied with models of self-balancing systems that so little attention has been given to serialization.

One aspect of serial service from generation to generation that was briefly alluded to above deserves some comment, namely, patterns of property inheritance.[17] The widespread practice of some form of inheritance in kinship lineages usually has been neglected by those who viewed traditional obligations between generations solely in terms of delayed reciprocities. At least for those prosperous enough to accumulate some kind of an estate beyond their own needs for support, which in some places becomes a kind of *quid pro quo* for their old-age support by heirs,[18] the sequential flow is clear.

In contemporary society, however, we encounter some further dislocations of what had previously seemed to be normal patterns. The increased longevity of the old may substantially reduce the size of the prospective inheritance by the needs for current support, and in any event postpones the transfer. (The ambivalence of heirs may be rather acute, but they can scarcely admit, let alone express, their impatience.) The effects of increased longevity are reinforced by the effects of shortened generations. Thus, by the time the last surviving parent (usually a widow) dies, the heirs are probably well beyond the middle of their own careers, that is, at a time much too late for their life chances to be greatly affected.[19] In this situation, expenses for higher education of the young may be taken as a kind of "hidden capital transfer" or preinheritance, and more or less nominal loans for home purchase serve a similar function. Although I

[16] William H. Whyte, Jr., *The Organization Man* (New York: Simon and Schuster, 1956), Part VII, "The New Suburbia: Organization Man at Home," especially Chapter 21, "The Transients."

[17] See Chapter 11 in this volume by Kurt W. Back and Hans W. Baade, "The Social Meaning of Death and the Law."

[18] See, for example, Conrad M. Arensberg, *The Irish Countryman* (New York: Macmillan, 1937), especially Chapter III, "The Family and the Land."

[19] This discussion is based on Moore, *Man, Time, and Society, op. cit.,* pp. 80-84.

know of no evidence on this, it seems probable that lifetime distributions to immediate heirs are increasingly common, with posthumous transfers skipping a generation and running to grandchildren, who are at a more propitious stage of the life cycle to benefit from an inheritance.

Lest we get carried away, however, by the not very gripping problems of very well-to-do families, we should return to more statistically normal patterns. Here there is little question that most parents make genuine sacrifices for their children, both for current levels of support and especially for providing educational and similar bases for competitive opportunity. And these sacrifices are, I believe, not made with an eye toward future, reciprocal benefits.[20] Rather, the parents precisely expect serialization, that is, that the children will behave similarly in providing services and opportunities to the following generation. To be alliterative, serial service becomes sacrifice *seriatim*. And the rewards, if mundane at all, must be satisfaction in conscientious performance, not the expectation of reciprocal return. This may not be tragedy, as I once characterized it,[21] but it will serve until the real thing comes along.

The sacrificial elements in the flow of services between generations are not completely unrequited. Some financial support and various services are provided by children for aged parents directly. And since support of the aged on the basis of need or on the quasi-insurance principles of Old-Age and Survivors Insurance has become a matter of public policy, the young *do* support the old. This is a nice example of the "loss of family functions," but the function of old-age support, I have argued, often has been either irrelevant or poorly performed within the world's range of kinship systems.

The adjustment problems of aging in contemporary society would be severe enough if we attended only to the demographic changes that have increased the proportions of the aged and the basic structural changes associated with economic modernization. But a simple before-and-after comparison is inadequate for appraising current and prospective problems. A society does not become quiescent once it achieves a modern demographic balance and mod-

---

[20] I owe my conviction on this point mainly to conversations with Professor Matilda White Riley, who is engaged in a series of studies on intergenerational family functioning.

[21] See Moore, paper cited in note 13.

ern forms of structural differentiation. On the contrary, the reverse is more often true.

It is particularly to the problems posed by the pace of continuous change that this concluding section attends. The procedure will be to compare individual change in the course of experience during a life cycle and collective change as wrought by a multiplicity of individuals in a social system. We shall examine briefly four typological cases of the interplay between aging individuals and social systems.

First, let us take the situation, typical of so-called traditional societies, where most structural changes are relatively minor, and aggregate change is relatively slow. In these circumstances the view of the individual "passing through" a system is approximately accurate. The individual in the course of his life may essentially replicate the lives of his predecessors. And since generations properly go by lineages and cannot be applied cross-sectionally to entire populations, all ages coexist. Thus, even in the improbable event of very fine age grading, prior role models are constantly at hand. The inevitable slippage in training between true generations may thus be partially offset by the existence of "collateral intermediaries" who serve to smooth out the generational gap. The frequency with which this situation occurs in the contemporary world should not be exaggerated, in view of the universality of radical structural changes, but it has some interest as a kind of limiting case with extensive historical importance.

If structural change is somewhat more rapid, the adjustive individual may be able to keep current—the microcosm in effect replicating the macrocosm. The individual in the course of aging adds experience at about the pace that events are taking place. As a small example of this, an artisan or other technically trained producer may be able to keep up with developments as they are introduced by the aggregate of practitioners.

A third situation is one widely prevalent in newly modernizing societies. Structural change may be so rapid and so radical that it is essentially discontinuous with precedent. Here both the innovators and the adherents are likely to be young, with role models that are doctrinal and borrowed from other social systems. The aging person has no role models consistent with prior experience and values, and may be unable to adjust to novel arrangements. Indeed, he com-

40

WILBERT E. MOORE

monly suffers a loss of authority, for he is no longer the exemplar and instructor for his children or others who traditionally might have emulated him. He becomes a pathetic figure, treated with indifference or contempt by the young revolutionaries.

A fourth situation is that of contemporary modernized societies, including the United States. With extremely rapid change, the pace of collective experience becomes too rapid for the individual to keep current; he falls behind. Generational succession gives way to dependence on a steady supply of new entrants to the labor force, bringing fresh skills and capacities for creative adjustment; but the young innovators are quickly threatened in their turn. Again, if we take the example of the person technically trained, his rate of accumulated experience is far less rapid than the rate of innovation produced by the aggregate of experts. He may be able to protect himself by specialization—to know more and more about less and less. He may be able to restrict access to his specialty, enforce employment security through seniority or tenure provisions, or become an administrator because he is no longer technically competent. He may, however, become plainly obsolete, and require a period of retraining if he is going to continue a productive career.[22]

In a society in which social change is organized and institutionalized, "stopping progress" for the sake of a privileged position is not highly regarded. The alternatives are poorly developed, because the problem is generally seen as special rather than endemic. One alternative, and probably a bad one in view of poorly developed use of leisure in constructive ways, is something like a creative but short-lived participation in the labor force—say, fifteen years. Another alternative is for adult retraining, on a cycle that is likely to become increasingly frequent during a normal career. But that will require genuine attention to needful skills and intellectual habits, rather than (or in addition to) contract bridge, bookbinding, flower arrangement, Shakespeare, current events, and ballroom dancing. A third alternative, which does not exclude the others, is a radical revamping of the educational system as a preparation for adulthood. The capacity for continuous learning, continuous adjustment, and continuous creativity must supersede the capacity for repetition and recall.

[22] See Juanita M. Kreps, "Employment Policy and Income Maintenance for the Aged," and John G. Turnbull, "Federal and State Programming," both in this volume.

Creative adjustment will not solve all problems of aging. The notion of an ideal solution is a mischievous myth. But the beginning of wisdom would be preparation for an uncertain future, and thus the abandonment of the notion that individuals simply flow through a stable order.

This is probably the best and worst time in world history to be old—or to be young.

BIOGRAPHICAL NOTE

WILBERT E. MOORE was born in Elma, Washington, in 1914 and was educated at Linfield College, University of Oregon, and Harvard University (Ph.D.). Mr. Moore is now Sociologist, Russell Sage Foundation, and Visiting Lecturer with the rank of Professor at Princeton University, where he has spent twenty-one years, thirteen as Professor. Among his extensive list of published essays and books, the greater part deals with relations between economy and society, including demographic studies, industrial sociology, and social aspects of economic development. Two of his most recent books are on more theoretical themes: *Man, Time, and Society* and *Social Change*. He is past president of the Eastern Sociological Society and President of the American Sociological Association.

2

The Aging of Individuals and Populations: Its Macroeconomic Aspects

Joseph J. Spengler

Ah nothing is too late
Till the tired heart shall cease to palpitate.

— HENRY WADSWORTH LONGFELLOW

Grow old along with me!
The best is yet to be.

— ROBERT BROWNING

Yet joy is as naught
Alloyed by the thought
That youth slips away and that old age is coming.

— SHIH TSUNG (LIU CH'Ê), 2nd century B.C.*

But cannot bring myself
In pensioned idleness to rot.

— WEI YING-WU, 8th century A.D.*

This essay has to do with the economic aspects of two interrelated kinds of change: (a) the impact upon the economy of the increase in absolute and relative numbers of aged persons; and (b)

---

* These two quotations are from H. A. Giles' translations, in his *Gems of Chinese Literature: Verse*, 2nd ed. (Shanghai: Kelly and Walsh, 1923), pp. 25, 118.

the impact of prospective technological and socioeconomic changes upon the economic situation of aged persons. While the essay is focused upon these two kinds of change as such, its illustrative content is drawn largely from American data and experience.

I

Our fundamental concerns being the macroeconomic dimensions of the changes noted above, their microeconomic dimensions will be examined only insofar as such examination is essential to explanation of macroeconomic outcomes. The term *aged* is truly an objectionable antiphrasis when one may, with Joseph S. Davis, speak of "the youthening of the elderly," and of old age as beginning at seventy-five or eighty. As used in this paper, the term will ordinarily refer to persons aged sixty or more years, on grounds both of statistical convenience and of the fact that the sixties currently constitute the most crucial decade for analysis of employment aspects of these changes. Here used to denote the cumulation of years at the individual level, together with economically oriented concomitants of such cumulation, the term *aging* will relate principally to post-sixty cumulation.

We shall conceive of the economy as an analytically and empirically distinguishable subsystem of an all-inclusive societal system.[1] The primary function of this subsystem is to make provision for the material needs of a society's membership and thereby permit a fairly broad range of choice to both its individual members and the various collectivities formed by these members. We may also think of this economy in terms of the world of economic space and time within whose boundaries individuals plan and move to maximize their own and their collective welfare, though always subject to a variety of constraints. Proceeding in this manner permits us to focus attention upon enlargement of the individual's world of space and time, upon his perception of this enlargement and his reaction thereto, and upon the constraints to which his reaction may become subject as he ages.

We shall attempt to isolate the several types of supply and demand functions, the manner of whose equilibration bears signifi-

[1] See Talcott Parsons and Neil J. Smelser, *Economy and Society* (New York: Free Press, 1956).

cantly upon the economic well-being of the aged. Circumstances affecting the economic mobility of the aged will be examined in conjunction with our analysis of these equilibrating processes. Account will also be taken of relevant technological and socioeconomic changes now in prospect.

II

As defined in this essay, aging has two dimensions: the collective and the individual. The former is dominated by the movement of fertility; the latter, by forces affecting life expectancy.

Collective aging—increase in the relative number of older persons—is associated with decline in fertility and, hence, in the relative number of younger persons. Illustrative data for males are presented in Table 2-1. In column 1 gross reproduction rates (GRR) are given, and in column 2, average future lifetimes, or expectations of life at birth ($°e_0$). When the GRR and the $°e_0$ on a given line are combined, the age composition of the population that eventually results will correspond to the percentages reported on the same line in columns 3 through 5. Thus, according to line 1, combining a GRR

TABLE 2-1

AGE COMPOSITION OF MODEL STABLE POPULATIONS
CORRESPONDING TO GIVEN FERTILITY AND
MORTALITY RATES

GRR	$°e_0$	PERCENTAGE OF STABLE POPULATION		
		0-14	15-59	60 and over
3.0	30	41.3	54.5	4.1
2.5	30	36.9	57.6	5.5
1.5	70.2	29.3	57.7	13.0
1.0	70.2	19.5	58.6	21.9

Source: United Nations, *The Aging of Populations and Its Economic and Social Implications,* see footnote 2.

of 3.0 with an $°e_0$ of 30 gives rise to a stable population made up of 41.3 percent of persons (in the present case, males) under fifteen years of age, 54.5 percent aged fifteen to fifty-nine, and 4.1 percent aged sixty or more years. With $°e_0$ remaining unchanged at 30 and the GRR declining to 2.5, the percentage aged sixty and over rises to 5.5, and it would rise to 18.7 if the GRR declined to 1.0. When, as on the last two lines, GRR of 1.5 and 1.0, respectively, are combined with an $°e_0$ of 70.2 years, the percentages formed by persons sixty and over in the resulting stable populations approximate 13.0 and 21.9, respectively. This percentage would be only 4.8 in a stable population based upon a GRR of 3.0 and an $°e_0$ of 70.2 years. In short, collective aging is the result of decline in the GRR rather than of increase in $°e_0$. In fact, if the GRR is held constant, increase in $°e_0$ from thirty to 70.2 years increases the percentage aged sixty years only from 4.1 to 4.3.[2]

While the age composition of the population of any given advanced country reflects the past incidence of migration, war, heavy mortality, and so forth, its evolution is always in keeping with what has been said above. For example, between 1850 and 1950 the fraction of the population aged sixty-five or more rose roughly about 60-100 percent in Western European countries and over 200 percent in the United States. In the United States the percentage of the population aged sixty or more rose from about 4.1 in 1850 to about 8.4 in 1930 and 13.2 in 1960; it will approximate 12.8 in 1985.[3] In high-fertility, underdeveloped countries, collective aging has not become a problem. Around 1950 when 11-12 percent of the population of Europe, North America, and Oceania was aged sixty or more years, the corresponding percentages in Africa, Asia, and Latin America were only 4-6, much as in the United States around 1850.[4]

It should be noted that the percentage of the population of working age in a stable population may not be materially affected when *both* fertility and mortality decline. Let this percentage be

[2] This paragraph and Table 2-1 are based upon United Nations, *The Aging of Populations and Its Economic and Social Implications*, ST/SOA/Series A, Population Studies, No. 26 (New York: United Nations, 1956), pp. 26-27.

[3] *Ibid.*, p. 17; U. S. Bureau of the Census, *Current Population Reports*, Series P-25, "Population Estimates," No. 279 (February 4, 1964); W. S. Thompson and P. K. Whelpton, *Population Trends in the United States* (New York: McGraw-Hill, 1933), p. 109.

[4] United Nations, *The Future Growth of World Population*, ST/SOA/Series A, Population Studies, No. 28 (New York: United Nations, 1958), p. 35.

represented by that of persons aged fifteen to fifty-nine. The percentages reported in column 4 of Table 2-1 remain close to 58, given a GRR of 2.5 or less. Had mortality remained unchanged as the GRR fell from 2.5 to between 1.0 and 1.5, the percentage fifteen to fifty-nine years old would have increased about one-tenth. Thus, decrease in mortality has largely offset the decline in fertility; had fertility remained unchanged, the percentage aged fifteen to fifty-nine would have fallen about 7-10 percent as ^oe_o rose from 40 to 70.2 years.[5]

While prolongation of life has not materially affected the percentage of the population aged sixty or more years, it has affected the situation of individual persons in and beyond the fifties and thus influenced the view which persons below fifty form of their post-sixty economic prospects. One-and-a-half to two centuries ago death remained at the center of life, even though infant and child mortality contributed greatly to the lowness of the expectation of life at birth;[6] indeed, somewhat earlier, so great were parents' subjective expectations of the early death of their children that their passing occasioned no more grief than that of a pet dog would today.[7] Today, by contrast, it is expected not only that virtually all newly born children will live but that most of them will live to retire from gainful employment at, say, the age of seventy. Nor is this expectation unreal; given today's mortality, about 98 out of 100 newly born persons live to the age of ten, and of this 98 about 75 percent will reach the age of seventy. Given the mortality of the early nineteenth century, when the expectation of life at birth was in the neighborhood of thirty to thirty-five, only 60-66 of 100 newly born babies attained the age of ten, and of these only about 16-22 percent, many of whom probably were unfit for work,[8] reached seventy. This increase in the objective statistical probability of survival at particular ages, especially among

[5] United Nations, *The Aging of Populations, op. cit.,* p. 26.

[6] See J. Fourastié, "De La Vie traditionelle à la vie tertiaire," *Population,* 14 (1959), 418; compare Shakespeare's many comments on age, assembled by George Rylands in his *The Ages of Man* (New York: Harper & Row, 1963), Part III.

[7] Philippe Ariès, *L'Enfant et la vie famille sous l'ancien régime* (Paris: Plon, 1960), pp. 29-34. So long as expectation of life at birth fell within a range of twenty-five to thirty-five years, only 57-71 percent of those born alive attained the age of five; today about 98 percent attain this age. See United Nations, *Methods for Population Projections by Sex and Age,* ST/SOA/Series A, Population Studies, No. 25 (New York: United Nations, 1956), pp. 76-77.

[8] In his *Rasselas* (1759), Samuel Johnson suggests how men then viewed old age—as a period few attained, and many of these "dismissed by age and diseases from the more laborious duties of society" (Chapters 45 and 47).

those below seventy, has been accompanied by a somewhat corresponding change in the subjective probabilities men assign to survival—especially in the estimates which individuals put upon their own chances of survival—and their views regarding the comparative appropriateness of various time horizons, time-discount rates, etc.[9]

Table 2-2 is intended to summarize trends in longevity over the past 150 years and to suggest implications of these trends.[10] In the early part of the nineteenth century, when life expectancy at birth often was in the neighborhood of thirty-five (as in the Dutch sample), only about 29 percent of the females born alive were expected

TABLE 2-2

REPRESENTATIVE LIFE-TABLE VALUES FOR FEMALES

AGE X	EXPECTATION OF LIFE AT AGE X			NUMBER SURVIVING TO EXACT AGE X WHEN $\overset{\circ}{e}_0$ IS:		
	Holland 1816-25	Latvia 1929-32	United States White 1962	35	60.4	74.4
0	35.12	60.10	74.4	100,000	100,000	100,000
10	45.03	58.42	66.2	66,151	89,160	97,612
50	18.70	25.38	28.3	38,437	77,105	92,562
60	12.84	17.63	19.9	28,937	69,302	86,421
70	8.01	10.93	12.5	16,860	53,770	72,786
80	4.76	6.26	6.8	5,076	27,082	45,509
85	3.92	4.65	4.8	1,660	13,726	27,037

Source: Columns 2-3, Dublin et al., *op. cit.*, p. 350; Columns 4, 7, *Vital Statistics of the U.S. 1962,* II, Tables 5-3, 5-4; Columns 5, 6, United Nations, *Methods,* pp. 76-77.

[9] Subjective estimates may be more optimistic than objective probabilities warrant, especially in a society in which objective probabilities have been improving rapidly.

[10] For fuller accounts see L. I. Dublin et al., *Length of Life,* Rev. Ed. (New York: Ronald, 1949); United Nations, *Methods,* cited in note 7 above; and United Nations, *The Determinants and Consequences of Population Trends,* ST/SOA/Series A, Population Studies, No. 17 (New York: United Nations, 1953), Chapter 7; U. S. Department of Health, Education, and Welfare, *Vital Statistics of the United States, 1962,* Vol. 2, Sec. 5, "Life Tables."

to reach the age of sixty, and of these only 58 and 18 percent, respectively, were expected to reach the ages of seventy and eighty. In 1962, 86 percent of the American white females born alive were expected to attain the age of sixty, and of these 84 and 53 percent, respectively, the ages of seventy and eighty. These figures indicate that while life expectancy at ages sixty and seventy was only about five-ninths higher in the United States in 1962 than in Holland 140 years earlier (see Table 2-2, columns 2 and 4), the number attaining age sixty and enjoying this increased life expectancy was about 200 percent higher.[11] Today, in other words, of the total number of years of life that will eventually be experienced by a cohort of 100,000 newly born persons, a much larger fraction than formerly will be spent in and beyond the sixties, though not perhaps as large a fraction as optimists anticipate. In order to rule out the disturbing influence of the high infant and child mortality of former times, let us suppose that our cohort has reached the age of ten. Of the total number of years it would still live before all of its members died, only around 9 percent would be spent in and beyond the sixties, given an expectation of life at birth of only about thirty-five years; but, given life expectancies in the sixties to the middle seventies, this percentage moves upward into a 24-27 range.[12] Thus we should expect that today the problems and opportunities facing people in and beyond the sixties would be of concern to a much larger number than formerly (say sixty to one hundred years ago) of those in younger age brackets.

[11] The figures in columns 2-4 and 7 of Table 2-2 are based upon actual life tables; those in columns 5-6, upon synthetic life tables. All the figures are too low in that, as time passes, mortality falls below the levels on which the life table values were based. See P. H. Jacobson, "Cohort Survival for Generations Since 1840," *Milbank Memorial Fund Quarterly,* 42 (July, 1964), 36-53. When, however, as in the United States, mortality has descended to quite low levels, future reductions in mortality, unless through control of cardiovascular-renal diseases and malignant neoplasms, or through a very great diminution of mortality from all other causes, will not increase longevity after age sixty very significantly. See unsigned, "Outlook for Gains in Longevity After 60," *Statistical Bulletin,* Metropolitan Life Insurance Co., 41 (November, 1960), 1-3. Although scientific discoveries could extend life expectancy at birth to ninety to one hundred or more, many decades will pass before such level is achieved, given the high degree of dependence of length of life on man's experience in his youth and early adulthood. See G. A. W. Boehm, "The Search for Ways to Keep Youthful," *Fortune,* 71 (March, 1965), 139 ff.

[12] The relevant data may be obtained from the T_x columns in life tables with appropriate $^0e_0$ values.

III

The economic setting of the aged, along with those in lower age brackets, may be defined in terms of space and time. K. Lewin's concept, "life-space," may be combined with S. C. Pepper's concept, "purposive structure." By giving it more restricted meaning, this can be converted into "economic life-space," or more simply, "economic space," within which are situated the interrelated economic means and ends available, as well as the methods enabling choice from among these means and ends.[13]

While the economic life-space varies from individual to individual and from group to group at any given time, it is evident, even though no simple indicator is available, that the economic life-space of most individuals and groups has increased remarkably over time, and with it multiplicity of choice and hence man's capacity for the peaceful resolution of conflict. The range of means and ends available to individuals is much greater than formerly and so is the amount of ends, of nonobsolete means, and of "income" available per capita. The absolute economic condition of the aged is generally better, therefore, than it ever has been. However, it is not nearly as good as it might be, mainly because of socially created conditions and constraints (some of which are treated below) and because of the content of contemporary sociocultural "space" and "time."[14]

The expression "economic life-space" is not entirely timeless;

[13] For Lewin's and Pepper's conceptualizations, see Pepper, *The Source of Value* (Berkeley: University of California Press, 1958), Chapter 16. I have used the term "available" instead of "given" to allow for the fact that ends and perhaps also means are *creatable*. For, as G. L. S. Shackle observes, "ends, so long as they remain available and liable to rejection or adoption, must inevitably be experienced by imagination or anticipation and not by external occurrence. Choice, inescapably, is choice amongst thoughts, and thoughts, we suppose are not *given*." See *Decision, Order and Time in Human Affairs* (Cambridge: Cambridge University Press, 1961), p. 273.

[14] See P. A. Sorokin, *Sociocultural Causality, Space, Time* (Durham, N.C.: Duke University Press, 1943), Chapters 3 and 4. What I have called "economic life-space" is much more narrowly defined than Sorokin's "sociocultural space," though conditioned by content of the latter even as my "economic space-time" is conditioned also by the content of Sorokin's "sociocultural time." See also W. E. Moore, *Man, Time, and Society* (New York: Wiley, 1963). How contemporary American culture penalizes the aged is described by Jules Henry in *Culture Against Man* (New York: Random House, 1963), and in Chapter 10 of the present volume.

means and ends may have significant time dimensions, with the result that time must be taken explicitly into account and "economic life-space" becomes "economic space-time." It is true, of course, that while almost all decisions respecting means and ends are future-facing, uncertainty sets limits to the decision-governing time horizons of individuals.[15] It is also true that the greatness of the probability that those attaining, for example, the age of twenty will also attain ages sixty and seventy, together with the likelihood that most individuals believe that their chances of survival surpass the objective probability for their cohorts, must have significantly extended individual and family time horizons.[16] Several changes have helped to produce this outcome. Today families are much less subject than formerly to dissolution through death of a spouse, and nearly all children survive to marry if they wish to do so. Moreover, even when death removes the male spouse, the wife will remain in need of support for a number of years; life expectancy of females exceeds that of males by several or more years at most ages.[17] Husband and wife are early under pres-

[15] Shackle, op. cit., Chapter 26. The horizon may be very short. It is said that the ancient Canaanites "were never quite sure whether spring would really follow winter." See Ivar Lissner, The Living Past, translated by J. M. Brownjohn (New York: Putnam, 1963), p. 41. I owe this reference to Royall Brandis.

[16] Moore, op. cit., p. 22. He draws attention to the paradox that "time is perceived as scarce in measure that it becomes plentiful," a paradox whose explanation lies in the growth of two concomitants of the forces making for life extension, namely, emphasis upon refined measurement and intensity of role and other forms of specialization. Ibid., p. 18. Some information on the current use of time, "the third dimension of welfare," is supplied in James N. Morgan et al., Income and Welfare in the United States (New York: McGraw-Hill, 1962), Chapter 21.

[17] Given 1962 United States white mortality, of 100 females attaining age twenty, 89 would attain age sixty, and 75, age seventy. Given 1900-1902 mortality, these percentages become 64 and 45. Corresponding male percentages are 79 and 56 for 1962, and 61 and 40 for 1900-1902. In 1962, at age sixty female and male life expectancy approximated 19.9 and 16 years; at age seventy, 12.5 and 10.3. See "Life Tables," cited above in note 10. In 1950 the median age at the death of one spouse was 64.1 years for husbands, 61.4 years for wives; the corresponding ages in 1890 were 57.4 and 53.3. See Paul C. Glick, American Families (New York: Wiley, 1957), p. 54. These ages are somewhat higher today, although the ratio of widows to widowers (about 4 to 1) is nearly double what it was fifty years ago. "Of the widows bereft of their spouse at age 65, somewhat more than half can expect to live 15 years longer, and about a third still have 20 years of life before them." See unsigned, "The American Widow," Statistical Bulletin, Metropolitan Life Insurance Company, 43 (November, 1962), 2. In an excellent paper read in 1961 ("The Economic Position of the Elderly and the Problems of Their Later Years"), Joseph S. Davis indicates that we now look upon old age as beginning at seventy-five or eighty, whereas

sure, therefore, to enter into long-term contractual or institutional arrangements for the adequate maintenance of income after the main family-supporter retires or dies, and there is widespread demand for economic and related security in old age.[18] It may be said, therefore, that the economic space-time which environs those who are, or will become, aged and thus shapes their economic means, ends, and procedures has been greatly enlarged in the past sixty to one hundred years.

Prospective changes in the age composition of the American population are not likely to affect the economic space-time of the aged very adversely. The percentage of the population aged sixty-five or more years will remain close to 9.2 for several decades or more.[19] Meanwhile, the percentage of the population aged twenty to sixty-four years, perhaps the best index of the relative size of the potential labor force (about 58 in 1950 and 52.3 in 1960), will decline somewhat by 1985, probably to between 49.2 and 50.7, with the level depending upon whether age-specific fertility remains unchanged or declines somewhat.[20] Even though this decline could reduce potential per capita output by 4-5 percent, increased employment of women might prevent such an outcome. Moreover, under

George Washington and Robert Browning thought of it as beginning in the early fifties. S. Kuznets points to the lengthening of the decision span produced by the taking of a family point of view. See his *Capital in the American Economy* (Princeton: Princeton University Press, 1961), pp. 46-47. In an age of three- and even four-generation families, the decision span can encompass fifty to seventy-five or more years.

[18] While the origins of this demand are multiple, careful analysis would almost certainly show that a major source of this demand is the great increase in the relative number of persons in post-retirement age brackets. Walter Firey points out that the realization of values remote in time "is contingent upon their becoming institutionalized—upon their becoming so articulated with social relationships that individuals feel (1) that they have to conform to such values anyway . . . and (2) that such conformity is for the well-being of the group." See his "Conditions for the Realization of Values Remote in Time," in E. A. Tiryakian (Ed.), *Sociological Theory, Values, and Sociocultural Change* (New York: Free Press, 1963), p. 153. Presumably, similar conditions make for the realization of values less remote in time. On the time dimensions of social change, see also Max Heirich, "The Use of Time in the Study of Social Change," *American Sociological Review*, 29 (June, 1964), 386-397.

[19] The corresponding percentage for females, 10 in 1960, will approximate 10.8 in 1985; it will be higher if fertility declines and could rise to close to 16 if fertility approached the population-replacement level.

[20] The corresponding percentage for females, 52.5 in 1960, will fall to between 49.1 and 51.3 in 1985; this is below what one finds in a stable population with a GRR of 1.5 and an $^{0}e_{0}$ of 70.

given conditions it should slightly reduce pressure against the employment of workers sixty-five or more years old and thus cause more of these to be enrolled in the labor force.

Although demographic trends in 1960-1985 will differ greatly from those in 1950-1960, the net effect of this difference upon the economic status of the older population is not easy to assess. Relative population changes are summarized in Table 2-3.[21] The high rate of

TABLE 2-3

INCREASE BY AGE GROUP, 1950-1985 (IN PERCENT)

AGE GROUP	PERIOD			
	1950-60	1960-70	1970-85	1960-85
0-19	35	11-22	19-36	36-65
20-24	−5	54	12-26	85-93
25-29	−12	26	50	90
25-64	9	7	28	37
60-64	18	18	24	46
65-69	25	10	26	39
65 and over	35	17	28	56
Total	19	14-17	23-34	41-53

Source: See footnote 21.

population growth (about 1.8 percent in 1950-1959 and 2.0 in 1960-1963) has absorbed a great deal of capital—probably between $20 and $30 billion per year—a considerable proportion of which might have been used to improve the economic condition of the aged. At the same time, the demand for labor associated with this capital absorption, together with the fact that population in the early adult

[21] This table is based on U. S. Bureau of the Census, *Current Population Reports*, Series P-25, "Population Estimates," No. 279, cited in note 3 above, and *ibid.*, No. 265 (May 21, 1963); also No. 276 (November 19, 1963), and No. 278 (January 29, 1964). Also see Sophia Cooper and Denis F. Johnston, "Labor Force Projections for 1970-80," *Monthly Labor Review*, 88 (February, 1965), 129-140.

years (twenty to forty-four) increased less than 2 percent in the
1950's, must have helped to sustain the demand for the labor of older
workers and thus offset the great increase in the population in and
beyond their sixties. While it is not likely that the overall rate of population growth will decline much in the next twenty years, members
of the labor force in and beyond their sixties are nonetheless likely to
be under increasing economic pressure, for the number of actual and
potential job-seekers in their twenties will be growing over 2 percent
per year, or nearly twice as fast as the population in their sixties.

Despite the seeming favorableness of the employment situation
confronting older workers in the 1950's, this situation has become
less favorable. Work-life expectancy, which had been declining, continued to decline; at age sixty it was lower in 1960 than in 1900, and
at age twenty it was lower in 1960 than in 1950; it is likely to decline
even more. As S. L. Wolfbein's studies show (see Table 2-4), although expectation of life at age sixty had been rising for the entire
male population until in 1960 it was about 1.5 years above that for
white males in 1900, the average number of years of working life remaining at age sixty had declined from 11.5 in 1900 to 8.5 in 1960;

TABLE 2-4

LIFE AND WORK-LIFE EXPECTANCY FOR MALES
AT AGE 60

YEAR	AVERAGE NUMBER OF YEARS REMAINING AT AGE 60			EXPECTED YEARS OF WORKING LIFE PER YEAR OF RETIREMENT AT AGE 20	NUMBER LIVING OUT OF 100,000 LIVE-BORN MALES AT AGE:	
	Life	Working Life	Retire-ment		60	70
(1)	(2)	(3)	(4)	(5)	(6)	(7)
1900	14.3	11.5	2.8	14.1	46,452	30,640
1960	15.8	8.5	7.3	6.1	73,502	51,645
1900-1960	1.5	3.0	5.5	–	27,050	21,005

Source: Wolfbein, *op. cit.,* (in footnote 22), pp. 9, 12. The data in Column 7 were
supplied by the author.

meanwhile the average number of years of retirement had risen from 2.8 to 7.3 years.[22] Of the males aged fifty-nine in 1960, 87 percent still remained in the labor force (as compared with 95 percent of those aged forty-nine to fifty-one), but this percentage was scheduled to decline to 56.3 among those attaining age sixty-five (along with age sixty-four, a year of high retirement rates), with about seven-tenths of the separations due to retirement. By age seventy only 36.8 percent were scheduled to remain in the labor force, with about six-tenths of the separations since age sixty-five due to retirement. After age seventy the fraction remaining in the labor force declines more slowly, more slowly even than it did in 1950, moving to 16.8 by age eighty; however, just slightly over half the separations are due to retirement, presumably because retirement is less compulsory among those aged seventy or more years. Post-age-sixty-four labor market participation rates were roughly 20-30 percent lower in 1960 than in 1950, and in the future they probably will be even lower. Somewhat similar tendencies are manifest in the more developed economies, but not in the economically underdeveloped parts of the world.[23]

As Juanita Kreps shows elsewhere in this volume, average income among older men and women is decidedly below that of all

[22] Whereas *total* work-life expectancy for males rose from 32.1 in 1900 to 41.9 in 1950 and then fell to 41.4, that for women rose from 6.3 in 1900 to 15.2 in 1950 and 20.1 in 1960. Data presented in this paragraph are based upon Wolfbein, "Changing Patterns of Working Life," issued by the U. S. Department of Labor, Office of Manpower, Automation and Training, for presentation at the Sixth International Congress of Gerontology, Copenhagen, Denmark, August 12-16, 1963. See also S. H. Garfinkle, *The Length of Working Life for Males, 1900-60*, Manpower Report No. 8 (Washington: U. S. Department of Labor, Office of Manpower, Automation and Training, July, 1963).

[23] Labor-force participation is much higher in agricultural and semi-industrialized countries among those under twenty and beyond sixty-four than in industrialized countries, declining quite rapidly in the latter after age sixty-four. At age fifteen male life expectancy is 54.5 years in industrialized countries, of which 45.3 will be economically active and 9.2 inactive; in agricultural countries, the corresponding figures are 46.1, 41.5, and 4.6; in semi-industrialized countries, 49.5, 43.1, and 6.4. See United Nations, *Demographic Aspects of Manpower* ST/SOA/Series A, Population Studies, No. 33 (New York: United Nations, 1962), pp. 12-17, 20-21; also on females, pp. 22, 38, 49. See also pp. 49-51, where it is shown that relatively high fertility is associated with and may be making for relatively low female labor force participation and favoring relatively high male participation. In the United States in 1960-1980 labor force participation is not expected to fall much among females sixty-five and over, though it may fall about one-third among males. By 1980 females are expected to form 36 percent of the labor force as compared with 31 percent in 1960. See Cooper and Johnston, *op. cit.*, p. 130.

men and all women. In 1963, for example, the median income of families with heads sixty-five and over, $3,352, was only 54 percent of the median for all families; 26.2 percent received less than $2,000 at a time when the modest needs of an elderly couple may have cost $3,000 or more. Lowness of the incomes received by families with heads sixty-five and over is attributable largely to their lack of full-time employment, for the median income of those with year-round full-time employment (unfortunately only 14.6 percent of all families with heads sixty-five and over) was $6,279, or 84 percent of the median for all families with heads fully employed.[24] The current relative income position of families with heads sixty-five and over is inferior to that reported for 1947, since their average income (then 60 percent of that for all families) has risen only about 75 percent, while that of families with heads twenty-five to sixty-four years has nearly doubled.[25] Were older workers as fully employed in 1960 as in 1945, the income they derived from labor might have been about two-fifths higher than it was, even though their employment probably would have added only something like 1.5 percent to the na-

[24] U. S. Bureau of the Census, *Current Population Reports*, Series P-60, "Consumer Income," No. 43 (September 29, 1964), pp. 5, 8, 22-23. The median income of males sixty-five and over, 36.2 percent of whom received less than $1,500, was only $1,993, or 44 percent of the median for all males. *Ibid.*, p. 36. The corresponding figure for fully employed older males was $4,661, or 77 percent of the median for all fully employed males. See also, *New Directions in Health, Education, and Welfare* (Washington: U. S. Department of Health, Education, and Welfare, 1963), pp. 204-209, 216-219. In their 1964 report the Council of Economic Advisers put the cost of an "economy plan" budget for a family of four at around $3,000. See *Economic Report of the President*, 88th Congress, 2nd Session, House Document No. 278, p. 58. Of the 6.8 million families with heads sixty-five years and over, 3.2 million are described as "poor"; these make up 34 percent of all "poor" families. *Ibid.*, p. 61, also p. 79. Rose D. Friedman puts at about $2,200 the income needed to keep a family of four above the poverty line. *Poverty: Definition and Perspective* (Washington: American Enterprise Institute, 1965), Chapter 3.

[25] As noted above, in 1963 the median for families with heads sixty-five and over was only 54 percent of that for all families. Lowness of income prompts some older persons to work part-time. For example, in 1960, of 1,596,000 nonfarm male workers sixty-five and over at work, 32.8 percent were part-time workers, 26.4 percent for voluntary reasons and 4.3 for economic reasons. The corresponding percentages for 801,000 female workers sixty-five and over were 42.4 and 4.2. See R. L. Stein and J. L. Meredith, "Growth and Characteristics of the Part-Time Work Force," *Monthly Labor Review*, 83 (November, 1960), 1166-1175, especially 1172; also *idem.*, "Unemployment Among Full-Time and Part-Time Workers," *Monthly Labor Review*, 87 (September, 1964), 1009-1013.

tional income. Even in 1960, however, workers sixty and over still comprised about one-tenth of the labor force and probably contributed about one-tenth of the nation's gross product.[26]

IV

The employment prospect of persons in and beyond their sixties depends upon a number of circumstances, including the continually increasing degree of bureaucratization of conditions of employment, the sometime tendency of the productivity of older workers to decline, the behavior of the aggregate demand for labor, the incidence of income-eroding forces upon the income of older workers, and the institutionalization of arrangements for the temporal distribution of leisure. In this section I shall touch upon all but the last, reserving its discussion for the next section.

Both labor-supplying organizations (mainly trade unions) and labor-employing organizations (mainly corporations) are becoming increasingly bureaucratized, indeed, quasi-militarized. Hence they are subject to inflexible rules which freeze decision power, feudalize economies, and rule out that very adaptability and change whereon intelligent government and management rest. In consequence, conditions of access to an increasing fraction of total employment are becoming subject to impersonal and essentially individual-disregarding rules. This tendency is being reinforced, moreover, by governmental and administrative rules and regulations and sometimes also by guild and similar regulations. Increasingly, as a result of these forces, retirement with pension at or near age sixty-five (when life expectancy is 16 years for white females and 12.9 for white males) is being in-

---

[26] The 1.5 percent figure is a very rough estimate. In 1960 about 30.5 percent of the 7.5 million males sixty-five and over were in the labor force; in 1945, the percentage was 48.8, a figure considered by some to approximate the currently employable maximum (though as late as 1930, 54 percent were in the labor force). In 1960 the labor force included 49.5 million males and 23.6 million females. Had the labor force participation rate of males sixty-five and over in 1960 been 45 percent instead of 30.5, about 1.1 million more would have been employed, or about 1.5 percent of the 1960 labor force and about 35 percent of the 3.2 million men and women over sixty-five in the labor force in 1960. On earlier labor force participation rates, see H. D. Sheldon, *The Older Population of the United States* (New York: Wiley, 1958). On 1960 labor force participation see Cooper and Johnston, *op. cit.*, p. 130.

stitutionalized, and provisions facilitating even earlier retirement are being regularized.[27] Arrangements of this sort not only set a retirement age (or age range), but also tend to fix the maximum age at which a worker may be newly employed, particularly when employees' pension claims are not appropriately vested and portable if they change employers. Nonvesting also tends to reduce a worker's inclination to change employers, thus operating to reduce labor mobility even as do seniority and fringe-benefit arrangements which prevent both job-quitting and ease of access to new employment and which can reduce the flexibility of a regional economy.[28] The subjection of retirement age to bureaucratic regulation is currently being

[27] See *Digest of 50 Selected Pension Plans for Salaried Employees, Spring, 1963*, U. S. Department of Labor, Bureau of Labor Statistics, BLS Bulletin 1373 (Washington: 1963); and *Digest of One-Hundred Selected Pension Plans under Collective Bargaining, Spring, 1961*, U. S. Department of Labor, Bureau of Labor Statistics, BLS Bulletin 1307 (Washington: 1962); Juanita M. Kreps, "A Case Study of Variables in Retirement Policy," *Monthly Labor Review*, 84 (June, 1961), 587-591; unsigned, "Pension Plans for Salaried Employees," *Monthly Labor Review*, 87 (January, 1964), 44-47; *A Report on Manpower Requirements, Resources, Utilization, and Training* (Washington: U. S. Department of Labor, 1963), pp. 62-65; and *Mobility and Worker Adaptation to Economic Change in the United States*, Manpower Research Bulletin No. 1 (Washington: July, 1963), pp. 49-53. Typical of arrangements permitting workers to retire before reaching age sixty-five are those achieved by the United Auto Workers Union, among them one allowing retirement with full pension at age sixty (if not earlier) to workers with thirty years of service. See unsigned, "Will There Be a Rush for Early Retirement?" *U. S. News and World Report*, September 28, 1964, p. 106.

[28] See R. L. Stein, "Unemployment and Job Mobility," *Monthly Labor Review*, 83 (April, 1960), 350-358, especially 351-354; Hugh Folk, "Effects of Private Pension Plans on Job Mobility," *Monthly Labor Review*, 86 (March, 1963), 285-288; Gertrude Bancroft and Stuart Garfinkle, "Job Mobility in 1961," *Monthly Labor Review*, 86 (August, 1963), 897-906. On effects of seniority, see Albert Rees, *The Economics of Trade Unions* (Chicago: University of Chicago Press, 1963), Chapter 8. Although there is little likelihood that the use of seniority in promotion will be abandoned, its adverse influence upon mobility may be partially reduced, Rees suggests, through "the development of multiemployer seniority units . . . in some industries, especially those having many employers in the same locality." *Ibid.*, p. 158. On the impact of seniority in the Pittsburgh region, see E. M. Hoover, "Pittsburgh Takes Stock of Itself," reprinted from *Pennsylvania Business Survey* (January, 1964). Mobility is much lower among older than among younger workers. See H. R. Hamel, "Job Tenure of American Workers, January, 1963," *Monthly Labor Review*, 86 (October, 1963), 1145-1152. Two out of three private pension plans covering about three out of five workers were vested in early 1963; see W. W. Kolodrubetz, "Vesting Provisions in Private Pension Plans," *Monthly Labor Review*, 87 (September, 1964), 1014-1021.

facilitated by decline in the relative number of self-employed. However, it should be noted that although many of the occupations with the highest percentages of workers sixty-five and more years old are now growing relatively slowly, this trend probably does not greatly offset the prospects of older workers, for the age composition of these occupations is associated with their slow growth.[29]

Given technological progress and shifts in the demands for specific goods and services, considerable labor mobility is essential to the maintenance of both full employment and economic growth. Much of the change required in occupational structure is accomplished through intergenerational mobility. In 1962, for example, only 23 percent of male workers aged twenty-five to sixty-four years were in the same occupational group as their fathers, with the percentage ranging from 41 for professional, technical, and kindred workers to 5 for clerical workers.[30] In addition, there is need for continuous interoccupational mobility. As has been indicated, institutional arrangements hold down mobility on the part of older workers; at age sixty, on an average a worker has one job change left. Yet there is a great deal of mobility in the United States, 10.1 percent of the people working in 1961 having changed jobs one or more times that year, or nearly as many as in 1955 when 11.1 percent changed; indeed, in a lifetime a worker will average 6.6 job changes. As it was, many older workers changed jobs in 1961, 8.2 and 3.4 percent, respectively, of the male workers forty-five to sixty-four and over sixty-five. For these changes loss of job was often responsible. Four

[29] On occupational age structure, see H. D. Sheldon, *op. cit.*, pp. 53-61 and Chapter 5; Wolfbein, *op. cit.*, pp. 6-7. Self-employed workers, 13.5 percent of all workers in nonagricultural employment in 1940, had declined to 10.1 percent by 1962. Meanwhile, self-employed agricultural workers declined 52 percent. See J. E. Bregger, "Self-Employment in the United States," *Monthly Labor Review*, 86 (January, 1963), 37-43, especially 38. Self-employed persons in nonfarm occupations (whose absolute number increased about 5 percent between 1948 and 1961) have been averaging close to forty-eight hours a week, or about eight more hours than wage and salary workers. *Ibid.*, pp. 40-41.

[30] U. S. Bureau of the Census, *Current Population Reports*, Series P-23, "Technical Studies," No. 11 (May 12, 1964). See also E. F. Jackson and H. J. Crockett, Jr., "Occupational Mobility in the United States: A Point Estimate and Trend Comparison," *American Sociological Review*, 29 (February, 1964), 5-15. On trends, see Max Tirzick and Sol Swerdloff, "The Occupational Structure of U. S. Employment, 1940-60," *Monthly Labor Review*, 85 (November, 1962), 1209-1213; and *A Report on Manpower Requirements* (cited in note 27 above), pp. 15-32, 143.

percent of the males aged fifty-five to sixty-four changed jobs, 56 percent of them because they had lost their jobs; the corresponding percentage for job-changers aged twenty-five to fifty-four was 41.[31] The need for mobility is reduced somewhat by the fact that there is always a reservoir of temporary as well as part-time workers to meet seasonal upsurges in labor requirements.[32]

While increase in the mobility of labor will raise national income (there being less mobility than is required for optimum resource use), increase in the mobility of older workers will find its justification mainly in the economic and noneconomic benefits these workers experience as a result.[33] As will be indicated, much of this immobility on the part of older workers is associated with inadequacy of education and training, with nonportable private pension and welfare plans, and with seniority plans which prevent the worker's carrying an earned status with him.[34] Apparently immobility is not markedly associated with need for change in geographical location, since even among males forty-five and over about 2.5-3.0 percent change county or state every year; about 7.5 and 2.7 percent, respectively, of unemployed and employed males aged forty-five to sixty-four make such a change every year.[35] An older person may be at a disadvantage compared with a younger person, however, if changing employment entails a capital loss (e.g., through sacrifice sale of his residence) or considerable retraining costs, since he has

[31] Wolfbein, op. cit., pp. 18-19; Bancroft and Garfinkle, op. cit.; also R. L. Stein, op. cit., and H. R. Hamel, op. cit.; see also Mobility and Worker Adaptation to Economic Change in the United States, U. S. Department of Labor, Manpower Bulletin No. 1 (Washington: July, 1963).

[32] In 1961, for example, the number who reportedly worked exceeded the regular labor force by about 11 percent. See Bancroft and Garfinkle, op. cit., for the number who worked. In May, 1960, 18.1 percent of the 59.4 million persons at work were reported to be part-time workers; they could, therefore, work longer hours if necessary. Stein and Meredith, op. cit., p. 1172.

[33] Given something like optimum labor mobility, E. F. Denison estimates, the rate of economic growth would increase about 0.01 percent. See The Sources of Economic Growth in the United States and the Alternatives Before Us (New York: Committee for Economic Development, 1962), Chapter 18 and p. 279.

[34] On mobility trends, see ibid., pp. 201-208.

[35] U. S. Bureau of the Census, Current Population Reports, Series P-20, "Population Characteristics," No. 127 (January 15, 1964), pp. 4-5, and No. 134 (March 25, 1965), pp. 3-6, 16-17, 19-21, 34-42. Also Samuel Saben, "Geographic Mobility and Employment Status, March 1962-March 1963," Monthly Labor Review, 87 (August, 1964), 873-881.

fewer years within which to recapture his loss and outlay.[36] However, countervailing action to diminish the impact of such loss may
be undertaken by the state or by a private collectivity.

Although the association of productivity with age varies from
occupation to occupation and with level of education and age-earn-
ing profiles, some tendency on the part of productivity per hour to
decline among workers in or beyond the sixties can often be coun-
tered by reducing rates of remuneration and associated costs of
employment accordingly, thus making the employment of older
workers as profitable as that of younger workers. Such action, of
course, tends to be resisted by trade-union leaders and may have to
be supported by state sanction, a force that may grow as older workers and voters recognize that they have a common interest therein.
Productivity itself depends upon many factors, some fairly closely
associated with age and others only partially associated therewith.
In the former category fall health, effectiveness of the faculties, and
the reserve capacities of the body which condition man's capacity to
readjust to change as well as the degree to which he finds a job
burdensome; these decline with age, in part because the number of
body cells declines. Impairment rates, therefore, increase with age as
does the number of workdays lost. However, it is likely that, although this relationship will persist, improvements in medicine may
reduce the gradient of increase appreciably, especially among those
under seventy.[37]

[36] See Larry A. Sjaastad, "The Costs of Human Migration," *Journal of Political Economy,* 70 (October, 1962), Supplement, Part 2, pp. 80-93. Where
the need to move is the result of economic progress and when both social gains
and individual costs attendant on movement are great, a case may be made for
distributing some of the costs incurred by adversely affected individuals. See
T. W. Schultz, "A Policy to Redistribute Losses from Economic Progress," in
Earl Heady (Ed.), *Labor Mobility and Population in Agriculture* (Ames: Iowa
State University Press, 1961); also other essays in this volume.

[37] Health aspects are discussed in R. H. Williams, Clark Tibbitts, and
Wilma Donahue (Eds.), *Processes of Aging* (Boston: Atherton, 1963), I, pp.
273-276, II, pp. 329-378. In 1960-1961 work-loss days per currently employed
male rose from 4.3 among those aged twenty-five to forty-four through 6.8
among those forty-five to sixty-four to 9.8 among those sixty-five and over. A
less sharp upward trend was found among female workers. Comparable trends
are reported for 1961-1962. See *Vital and Health Statistics,* National Center
for Health Statistics, U. S. Public Health Service, Series 10, No. 2 (Washington: July, 1963), p. 9, and Series 10, No. 4 (October, 1963), pp. 21-23; also
ibid., Series 10, No. 10 (June, 1964), p. 20, where it is reported that days lost
from work in 1962-1963 because of acute conditions number 4 per male aged

In the second category of age-connected factors affecting productivity fall uncorrected obsolescence of knowledge and skills as well as degree of education, increasingly important as brain power supersedes muscle and mechanical power. In the 1950's and early 1960's the median school years completed by males sixty-five and over was about 8; the medians for males fifty-five to sixty-four and forty-five to fifty-four, respectively, 8.6-8.9 and 9.6-11.0. In 1950, R. S. Eckaus estimates, something like 22 percent of the labor force could get along on less than 8 years of education, about 45 required 10 years, and about 25 required 12; only 7-8 required a college education or better.[38] Older workers were at some disadvantage, therefore, relative to younger workers with a higher median of school years completed of nearly 12.5. Insofar as productivity is associated with education and is higher among more educated than among less educated workers, downward shifts in demand functions for particular kinds of labor render the less educated economically unemployable before the more educated are affected. This disadvantage is reflected in the facts that long-term unemployment is highest among older workers, and that among both males and females in age groups fifty-five to sixty-four and sixty-five and over, labor force participation rates rise and unemployment falls with the median number of years of school completed. This pattern may be accentuated with the

---

forty-five and over and 3.3 per male aged seventeen to forty-four. On impairments see *New Directions* (cited in note 24 above), pp. 112-115, 198-203. It must be remembered that even in the seventies chronic conditions limit the activity of only about half the population, and that with the development of geriatrical medicine this number may be reduced. Sheldon's data suggest that about one-third of males aged sixty-five to seventy-four are employable without restriction and that those not employable do not exceed one-third. Reasons of health account for about one-half of voluntary retirement. *Op. cit.*, pp. 42-53. On the physiological decline associated with aging, see N. W. Shock, "The Physiology of Aging," *Scientific American*, 206 (January, 1962), 100-110. The importance of investment in health is suggested by the fact that it amounts to about 38 percent of investment in educational capital. See S. J. Mushkin and B. A. Weisbrod, "Investment in Health: Lifetime Health Expenditures on the 1960 Work Force," *Kyklos*, 16 (Fasc. 4, 1963), 583-598.

[38] See Eckaus' paper in Selma J. Mushkin (Ed.), *Economics of Higher Education*, OE-50027, Bulletin 1962, No. 5 (Washington: 1962), pp. 120-122, and his "Economic Criteria for Education and Training," *Review of Economics and Statistics*, 46 (May, 1964), 181-190. On the current situation, see U. S. Bureau of the Census, *Current Population Reports*, Series P-20, "Population Characteristics," No. 121 (February 7, 1963), p. 3; Morgan et al., *op. cit.*, pp. 83-84, 206-212, 226-232.

progress of automation and the advent of the computer.[39] Presumably, lack of education makes it more difficult for older workers to master new job requirements, especially when, having become unemployed, they must find jobs with new employers and in new lines of activity. The cumulating experience and wisdom that in former times were associated with cumulating years are no longer deemed of so great importance as Cicero assigned them in his celebrated oration.[40] However, given the greater amount of education most individuals now require before entering the labor force, together with the large provision being made for both on-the-job education and manpower training and retraining in general, it is likely that the educational lag of older behind younger workers, together with its apparent adverse effects, will be reduced.[41] This increase in education, along with its cumulative effect upon the educational and aspirational environment of the home, should also operate to reduce appreciably the incidence of poverty among older persons insofar as it is associated with lack of education.[42]

[39] See D. F. Johnston, "Educational Attainment of Workers, March, 1962," Special Labor Force Report No. 30, reprinted in part from the *Monthly Labor Review*, 86 (May, 1963), 504-515; V. C. Perrella, "Marital and Family Characteristics of Workers," *Monthly Labor Review*, 87 (February, 1964), 149-160; Wolfbein, *op. cit.*, pp. 17-18; R. A. Gordon, "Has Structural Unemployment Worsened?" *Industrial Relations*, 3 (May, 1964), 53-77, especially pp. 58-61, 70-75. See also papers by C. C. Killingsworth and J. R. Bright, in *Exploring the Dimensions of the Manpower Revolution*, compiled for the Subcommittee on Employment and Manpower of the Committee on Labor and Public Welfare, U. S. Senate, 88th Congress, 2nd Session, Vol. 1 of *Selected Readings in Employment and Manpower*, pp. 209-217, 558-579. On the effects of education upon employability, see Gary S. Becker, *Human Capital* (New York: Columbia University Press, 1964), pp. 24-29; Walter Y. Oi, "Labor as a Quasi-Fixed Factor of Production," *Journal of Political Economy*, 70 (December, 1962), 538-555.

[40] No longer do men subscribe without qualification to Cicero's statement (*De Senectute*, XIX), "Intelligence, and reflection, and judgment, reside in old men, and if there had been none of them, no states could exist at all." In his delightful *The Rise of Meritocracy 1870-2033* (Baltimore: Penguin, 1961), Michael Young describes the rise of "meritocracy" as bringing about the dissolution of "gerontocracy" in the factories and elsewhere; *ibid.*, Chapter 4.

[41] Jacob Mincer estimates that the aggregate cost of on-the-job training for males approximates that of their formal education. See "On-the-job Training: Costs, Returns, and Some Implications," *Journal of Political Economy*, 20 (October, 1962), Supplement, Part 2, pp. 50-79. The factory's pride does not, of course, reflect the school's shame, but differences in educational purpose associated in part with continuing technical change. Cf. Young, *op. cit.*, p. 82.

[42] While 24 percent of the families with heads sixty-five and over and

Estimates of the relative changes in the major occupational categories between 1960 and 1975 indicate that the required level of education is rising. Those belonging to occupational groups with a median number of school years completed of about 8.5 in 1960 are expected to decline by about one-fifth; those with medians of about 12.5 and 16.2, respectively, are expected to increase about 65 and 34 percent; those with medians of 10-11 are expected to increase about 31 percent.[43] If educational levels should rise commensurately, and they are likely to rise even faster (with median school years completed by males sixty to sixty-four expected to advance from 8.5 in 1960 and 8.7 in 1965 through 10.4 in 1975 to 12.1 in 1985), the older members of the labor force may be at somewhat of a disadvantage a decade hence. But in yet another decade this disadvantage will be reduced to an almost negligible level, with median school years completed 12.7 and 12.1, respectively, for males twenty-five to twenty-nine and sixty to sixty-four.[44] In short, given the educational

---

more than twelve years of school completed were in the "poverty" category in 1959, this percentage was less than half as high as that reported for families with heads of similar age but less than twelve years of school. A family with less than $3,000 per year from all sources is described as in the "poverty" category. The overall proportion among families with heads sixty-five and over was lower in 1962 than in 1947. See *Annual Report of the Council of Economic Advisers* (Washington: January, 1964), pp. 58, 71, 83; also Morgan et al., *op. cit.*, Chapter 16. On the perpetuation of inadequacy of education from one generation to the next, see *ibid.*, p. 70; Florence Campi, "Educational Attainment and Family Background," in *New Directions* (cited in note 24 above), pp. 168-169; also Morgan et al., *op. cit.*, pp. 206-212. Unemployment as well as non-participation in the labor force is associated with an index of socioeconomic status based upon education, income, and occupation. See U. S. Bureau of the Census, *Current Population Reports*, Series P-23, "Technical Studies," No. 12 (July 31, 1964), pp. 1, 5.

[43] See unsigned, "Employment Projections to 1975," *Monthly Labor Review*, 86 (March, 1963), 240-250; Carol A. Barry, "White-Collar Employment: Trends and Structure," *Monthly Labor Review*, 84 (January, 1961), 11-18, and "White-Collar Employment: Characteristics," *Monthly Labor Review*, 84 (February, 1961), 139-147.

[44] By 1962 about 69 percent of the whites and 42 percent of the nonwhites twenty-five to twenty-nine years old had completed four years of high school or more; in 1940 the corresponding percentages were 41 and 12. In 1962 about 27 percent of the whites and 13 percent of the nonwhites had completed one year of college or more; in 1940, about 14 and 4. See Denis F. Johnston, "Educational Attainment of Workers, March 1962," *Monthly Labor Review*, 86 (May, 1963), 506. In 1962 the median number of school years completed by persons twenty-five to twenty-nine was 12.5, or slightly above the median in the age group thirty to forty-four, but it was just over 11 in the group aged forty-five

as well as the health improvements in prospect for older workers, their relative position in the labor force may improve above what it has been in recent years, even if the rate of laborsaving technical progress is high.[45]

The future economic position of the older actual or potential workers will depend in marked degree upon the progress of the aggregate demand for output and the rate of decline in the input of labor per unit of output. The immediate prospect is not very sanguine, given that about 3.6 million jobs per year will have to be provided in the near future to absorb both displaced workers and those newly entering the labor force. Since 1957 the unemployment rate has averaged about 6 percent, or two points in excess of a somewhat hypothetical full-employment goal of 4 percent; in 1963 a $30 billion increase in GNP would have been necessary to reduce unemployment to a 4 percent level, efforts to attain which might have generated some inflation.[46] Since 1957, the last recent year of low unemployment, the number of wage and salary workers employed in manufacturing, mining, and transportation has declined, as has aggregate employment in agriculture; only in services, government, and trade has there been a quite large absolute increase. Mechanization and automation have permitted great increases in output per worker in recent years and will continue to do so for some years to come; they have thus served markedly to reduce real cost per unit of

---

to fifty-four and slightly below 9 among those fifty-five and over. See U. S. Bureau of the Census, *Current Population Reports*, Series P-20, "Population Characteristics," No. 121 (February 7, 1963), p. 7; also *ibid.*, No. 132 (September 22, 1964), on "Educational Change in a Generation"; and U. S. Bureau of the Census, *Current Population Reports*, Series P-25, "Population Estimates," No. 305 (April 14, 1965), on educational projections to 1985.

[45] Eventually, of course, the contribution that improved education of the older worker can make will decline in relative importance. See E. F. Denison, "Education, Economic Growth, and Gaps in Information," *Journal of Political Economy*, 70 (October, 1962), Supplement, Part 2, pp. 127-128.

[46] *The Annual Report of the Council of Economic Advisers* (January, 1964), p. 171. In 1963 unemployment fluctuated between 5½ and 6 percent; it declined somewhat in 1964. See S. S. Holland, "Labor Force and Employment in 1963," *Monthly Labor Review*, 87 (June, 1964), 645-653. Employment of workers fifty-five and over continued to decline. *Ibid.*, p. 652. When unemployment falls below around 5-6 (say 5½) percent, its further reduction is likely to generate rising prices. See P. A. Samuelson and R. M. Solow, "Analytical Aspects of Anti-Inflation Policy," *American Economic Review*, 50 (May, 1960), 177-194, especially pp. 191-193. Also G. L. Perry, "The Determinants of Wage Rate Changes," *Review of Economic Studies*, 31 (October, 1964), 287-308.

output. However, they have not, so it appears, brought in their wake new goods and services, or cheapened "luxuries," the availability of which increases the aggregate demand for goods and services in terms of work or effort, as did the advent of rail or motor transport. The age of computerized automation has not yet become an age in the sense of the railroad age or the age of the internal combustion engine, nor, despite the multiplication of products, has it yet been accompanied by such an age.[47] Nor, so it seems, is such a transformation likely as long as so much of our national expenditure on research and development is devoted to space and military matters and so little to search for job-generating discoveries.[48] If, therefore, the demand for labor lags increasingly behind its supply and the pressure of job-seekers upon employment opportunities increases, it will prove more difficult for displaced older workers to find new jobs and for still-employed older workers to resist efforts to retire them prematurely, especially if the ratio of the cost of their employment to their productivity is much higher than alternatives available to employers.

Two conditions are likely to increase the "demand" for employment on the part of older workers, especially those in and beyond their upper sixties. The first is uncompensated inflation, the income-eroding influence of which is heaviest upon those whose incomes are relatively fixed, as are the incomes of most persons sixty-five and over.[49] Given such reduction of their real incomes, older persons who

[47] On the impact of new products on the demand for work, see my "Product-Adding Versus Product-Replacing Innovations," *Kyklos*, 10 (Fasc. 3, 1957), 249-280.

[48] "The shortage of jobs for other workers may be partly due to the shortage of scientists and engineers working on problems that lead to new industrial growth." See editorial, "The President's Manpower Report," *Science*, 140 (April 5, 1963), 15. See also National Academy of Sciences, *Toward Better Utilization of Scientific and Engineering Talent—A Program for Action* (Publication 1191, 1963); and *Convertibility of Space and Defense Resources to Civilian Needs: A Search for New Employment Potentials*, compiled for the Subcommittee on Employment and Manpower of the Committee on Labor and Public Welfare, U. S. Senate, 88th Congress, 2nd Session, 1964. Paul D. Foote, "Government-Financed Research, Basic and Applied," *Proceedings of the American Philosophical Society*, 109 (April 9, 1965), 57-62.

[49] In the 1950's price changes affected all American families, young and old, in substantially the same measure, Helen H. Lamale reported to the Sixth Congress of Gerontology, Copenhagen, August 12-16, 1963. As has been indicated elsewhere, it is possible for older persons to resort to political means to curb some inflation-producing practices. See Juanita M. Kreps (Ed.), *Employment, Income, and Retirement Problems of the Aged* (Durham, N.C.: Duke

66 JOSEPH J. SPENGLER

are able to work and can find access to employment, part-time or
full-time, would be more inclined to do so. A second condition is the
psychic income-eroding influence of nonparticipation in the fruits of
technical progress. Suppose that real income per capita rises 1.5-2.0
percent per year in the nation at large, but that the retired older
worker shares in this rise little or not at all because his monetary retirement income is essentially fixed. At the end of ten years of retirement his real income will be lagging 16-22 percent behind the incomes of those who, though originally recipients of money incomes
similar to his, now receive 16-22 percent more. One may say, therefore, that the psychic significance of his income has been devalued
by 14-18 percent. Those older persons whose incomes are so devalued, or who, before retiring, anticipate such devaluation, will be
more inclined to seek or retain employment than those who are not
so affected.[50]

V

Man's major concern, after he has taken on peremptory roles
associated with the assumption of mature responsibilities,[51] is to
make optimal use of time—according to Benjamin Franklin, "the stuff
life is made of." His sensibility of this concern increases with both
his years and his wisdom, even as William Hazlitt and Dante observed long before a sociology of time had been elaborated. Perhaps man's only other main and proper concern is that dealt with in
Chapter 11, the achievements of a speedy and painless exit when it
has become "better not to be," an achievement which, however, is
even more difficult to attain than optimal use of time.

University Press, 1963), 228-229; also J. C. Leggett, "Economic Insecurity and
Working-Class Consciousness," *American Sociological Review*, 29 (April, 1964),
226-234, for a type of analysis that may be used to support the view that "anti-
inflation consciousness" can develop and unite older persons.

[50] As Mrs. Kreps and I have suggested elsewhere, this threat to the psychic
security of the aged can be met through provision of a Social Credit for the
Aged. See Juanita M. Kreps (Ed.), *op. cit.*, pp. 221-229; also her chapter in
this volume and my chapter in Ida Harper Simpson and John C. McKinney,
Social Aspects of Aging (Durham, N. C.: Duke University Press, 1966).

[51] While the onset of maturity of responsibilities is commonly dated to the
individual's entry into the labor force (or comparable nonpaid situation), it had
best be dated, in the modern world, from some point in his educational career
since much of this consists in the incorporation of productive knowledge into his
psychophysical system.

Let us distinguish between work time—the time devoted to work or occupation, together with travel to and from place of work—and leisure time—the waking hours not spent at work, or, phrased differently, the "discretionary time." The individual has some option over the disposition of the latter, though it is subject to his enmeshment, great or little, in "the network of social life."[52] Leisure was slow to be treated as an economic good, first being described as a part of national income by Walras and Barone. Perhaps economists considered leisure to be of zero or negligible value as in an overpopulated, unemployment-ridden country where Durkheimian theory of division of labor is most applicable.[53] It is essential to think of a set of roles associated with each category of time, work and leisure. In the former set the occupational and perhaps closely related roles are dominant, while in the other a variety of roles, some complementary and some competitive, may be found. There is no hard and fast division of waking hours between these two sets of roles, as the division varies with individuals and occupations.[54] The input of time into the two sets of roles may be competitive, provided that all of an individual's waking hours are committed to role fulfillment; or it may be complementary if a role in one set reinforces roles in another, or if the output of roles in one set facilitates the fulfillment of roles in the other.

Economists usually treat leisure as a "superior" good and an alternative to work in an exhaustive market dichotomy.[55] The result

[52] See Moore's perceptive observations in *op. cit.*, Chapter 2, on "the temporal location of activities," especially pp. 30-39; also Morgan et al., *op. cit.*, pp. 324-326; also Moore's chapter and George Maddox' chapter in this volume. Availability of time is essential to consumption of various sorts.

[53] See Nicholas Georgescu-Rogen, "Economic Theory and Agrarian Economics," *Oxford Economic Papers*, 12 (February, 1960), 29-32.

[54] An individual may, of course, fill two or three occupational roles as do "moonlighters" who usually make up 4-5 percent of American workers. See Jacob Schiffman, "Multiple Jobholders in May 1962," *Monthly Labor Review*, 86 (May, 1963), 516-523. In May, 1963, however, multiple jobholders made up 5.7 percent of all workers, 7.4 percent of all male workers, 2.4 percent of all female workers, and about 6.3 percent of all male workers over forty-four. See F. R. Bogan and H. R. Hamel, "Multiple Jobholders in May 1963," *Monthly Labor Review*, 87 (March, 1964), 249-257. For a theoretical analysis of moonlighting, see Moses' paper cited in note 59 below.

[55] See Jacob Mincer's analysis in "Labor Force Participation of Married Women: A Study of Labor Supply," in National Bureau of Economic Research, *Aspects of Labor Economics* (Princeton: Princeton University Press, 1962), p. 65; also T. A. Finegan, "Hours of Work in the United States: A Cross-Sectional Analysis," *Journal of Political Economy*, 70 (October, 1962), 452-470.

68   JOSEPH J. SPENGLER

is that an increase in worker money income consequent upon an increase in output per worker may cause him to increase his leisure consumption, even though the real price of labor time (alternative to leisure) has risen with its rise in productivity. This analysis is in keeping with what has taken place in the United States from 1900 to 1963—a 300 percent increase in output per man hour and a decline of 25 percent or more in the workweek—and implies the likelihood of a further decline of 25 percent in the annual number of hours worked over the next forty to fifty years.[56] Indeed, as I suggest below, it is the number of workweeks per year rather than the number of hours per week that may be cut, as increasing output and income per worker augment his demand for leisure and a shortened workweek or work year.

Labor time and leisure time are not clear-cut alternatives over time. In the closing paragraph of the preceding section I touched upon situations in which inflation had reduced real income and thus tended to increase the demand for work. Even if money income remains unchanged, its lagging behind rising incomes may increase the demand for work. Indeed, even should real income rise appreciably, the demand for leisure might not rise, and for reasons other than increase in the labor cost of leisure. For tastes may change, with the result that the demand for work and income rises and entails a downward shift in the demand for leisure. This may happen if many new products come into being, or if consumers become able to purchase essentially new lines of goods (e.g., boats), or if wants increase in consequence of emerging complementarities and anabolic processes.[57] The set of roles associated with work may demand more rather than less time in many instances. The capacity to enjoy leisure may be conditioned by output (i.e., income) received from work and essential to role fulfillment within the leisure sector, or by the periodic pursuit of nonleisure activities,[58] as well as by the capacity of a retired person to find functional equivalents of work.

[56] Ethel B. Jones, "New Estimates of Hours of Work Per Week and Hourly Earnings, 1900-1957," *Review of Economics and Statistics*, 45 (November, 1963), 374-385.

[57] "In a dynamic society . . . new wants are created in the process of satisfying existing ones, and . . . complex consumption patterns spring from simple innovations, 'as if increase of appetite had grown by what it fed on.'" See Paul Streeten, *Economic Integration* (Leyden: A. W. Sythoff, 1961), p. 105, also pp. 106-108; also note 47 above.

[58] More than two centuries ago David Hume wrote, "Leaving nothing but indolence . . . you even destroy the relish of indolence, which never is agree-

In the preceding paragraph I expressed myself in general and nonspecific terms. The labor force on the verge of conventional retirement ages is not homogeneous, however. For example, H. L. Wilensky finds that long-hour workers predominate among those who have wide discretion in the length and use of their work time; these include higher bureaucracy (e.g., types of professors, firm lawyers), intellectuals and professionals, the middle bureaucracy (e.g., managers, officials), high income blue-collar workers (e.g., skilled craftsmen, foremen), independent professionals (e.g., solo lawyers), nonprofessional entrepreneurs (e.g., small proprietors), and agriculturalists. He finds short-hour workers common among engineers, semiprofessional employees, clerical and sales personnel, craftsmen, operatives, service personnel, and nonfarm laborers. He estimates, furthermore, that long-hour agricultural and nonagricultural employment will decline slightly until in 1970 it will embrace only 32.8 percent of the labor force, instead of 35.7 as in 1950.[59] In short, Wilensky shows that changes under way in the occupational composition of the labor force strengthen the aggregate preference for leisure rather than work, even though one's occupation is a fundamental index of status as well as a source of self-respect in Western society.[60] Changes in the nature of the work role or in the essentiality of income to the performance of leisure roles could offset this compositional change. Moreover, should the cumulating experience of persons retiring at or before sixty-five reveal their relatively low retirement incomes to be inadequate, or the status decline consequent

---

able, but when it succeeds to labour, and recruits the spirits, exhausted by too much application and fatigue." See "Of Refinement in the Arts," in Eugene Rotwein (Ed.), David Hume's *Writings on Economics* (London: Nelson, 1955), pp. 21-22.

[59] "Life Cycle, Work Situation, and Participation in Formal Associations," in R. W. Kleemeier (Ed.), *Aging and Leisure* (New York: Oxford University Press, 1961), Chapter 8, pp. 234-235; *idem*, "Work, Careers, and Social Integration," *International Social Science Journal*, 12 (Fall, 1960), 18-20; and *idem*, "The Uneven Distribution of Leisure: The Impact of Economic Growth on 'Free Time,'" *Social Problems*, 9 (Summer, 1961), 37-45. See also M. S. Myers, "Who Are Your Motivated Workers?" *Harvard Business Review*, 42 (January-February, 1964), 73-88; and Moore, *op. cit.*, pp. 33-39, and his chapter in this volume. On the circumstances that affect the standard workweek, see L. N. Moses, "Income, Leisure, and Wage Pressure," *Economic Journal*, 72 (June, 1962), 320-334.

[60] Edward Gross, "The Occupational Variable as a Research Category," *American Sociological Review*, 24 (October, 1959), 640-649; also I. R. Yoshino and G. L. Buck, "Satisfaction with Life for the Retired," *Arizona Review*, 13 (March, 1964), 14. See also George Maddox' chapter in this volume.

upon sudden retirement to be unduly painful, their preference for work would be strengthened at the expense of that for leisure.[61] Increases in the attractiveness of the set of roles associated with leisure, often achievable through education, would produce an opposite effect.[62] Should those favoring short hours win the ear of legislators, they might, as Ethel Shanas has suggested, seek to generate a legal structure unfavorable to those who prefer longer hours.

What each worker requires, if he would maximize his welfare subject to certain constraints, is a temporally optimal distribution of his fixed resource (waking hours) between work and leisure. Such a distribution could be sought in one of two ways. (1) Through a collective stipulation every member of the labor force could be assigned a right to a minimal number of hours of work in his lifetime, say, seventy to eighty thousand, some of which might be reserved for his post-sixty-five years. Of course, an arrangement of this sort would be very difficult to administer, particularly since it is impossible to foresee a future of forty to fifty years which early entry into such an arrangement implies. (2) If discrimination against capable older workers, whether as a result of trade-union policy or of employer policy, were prohibited, and if it were made possible for older workers to offer their services at slightly substandard rates should their productivity be at all in question, older workers would be free to divide their time optimally between work and leisure, particularly in an economy in which over 12 percent of the labor force voluntarily works only part-time. The effect of the latter is to remove socially created constraints upon the would-be older worker's use of his time, whether through denial of employment when he is able to work, or through the imposition of retirement contracts which deny him the right to recontract should he find experience with the contract unsatisfactory.

The latter arrangement would not assure older persons of work in the absence of relatively full employment, particularly if, given

[61] On this last point see Arnold M. Rose, "Mental Health of Normal Older Persons," *Geriatrics*, 16 (September, 1961), 459-464. See also A. C. Clarke, "Leisure and Occupational Prestige," in Eric Larrabee and Rolf Meyersohn (Eds.), *Mass Leisure* (New York: Free Press, 1958), 205-214; also R. W. Hodge et al., "Occupational Prestige in the United States, 1925-63," *American Journal of Sociology*, 70 (November, 1964), 286-302.

[62] "More than four-fifths of all workers who have retired, did so either because they became unable to work or because of involuntary retirement programs." Morgan et al., *op. cit.*, p. 437. But see Yoshino and Buck, *op. cit.*, pp. 13-14.

current tastes for leisure, continuing increase in output and income per hour should produce an upward shift in the demand for leisure. This demand would, therefore, have to be met. Heretofore it has been met through a gradual reduction in the length of the workweek (e.g., in nonagricultural activities from about fifty-six hours in 1900 to about forty at present). However, the time has come to reduce the number of workweeks per year, since this arrangement would allow a worker to make better use of his leisure time than would a further shortening of the workday or workweek. Similarly, in the past, reduction of the number of days worked per week from 5.5-6.0 to 5 enabled the worker to make better use of his increased leisure than would a further reduction in the average number of hours worked per day. Given that the number of hours worked per year will decrease 20-25 percent in the next forty to fifty years, and that the standard work year now is (say) fifty weeks, workweeks per year might be reduced by one every five years. Industry and company work schedules could be reorganized accordingly, though in ways allowing for continuation of a high rate of use of capital equipment. Provision for adjustment in hours worked per week would always be essential to permit the meeting of transitional or other shortages of output.

Whatever arrangement is adopted should enable a worker, in the course of his working life, to provide adequately for the support of his household in retirement. Premature retirement, whether compulsory or voluntary, prevents this. In 1900 (see Table 2-4, column 5), a cohort of males, having reached age twenty, could be expected to work an average of 14.1 years for each year of retirement. By 1960 this average had declined to 6.1 years, and by 2000 it may decline to 5. Accordingly, if we assume with F. Modigliani and R. Brumberg[63] that the only motive for saving is the provision of enough retirement income to allow the saver to maintain a level annual expenditure over his lifetime, or at least that level which he had attained in his later working life, then the representative individual must save a larger fraction of his post-tax income today than he did fifty years ago—perhaps 2 to 2½ times as large a percentage.[64] Yet

[63] "Utility Analysis and the Consumption Function: An Interpretation of Cross-Section Data," in K. K. Kurihara (Ed.), *Post-Keynesian Economics* (New Brunswick, N.J.: Rutgers University Press, 1954), Chapter 15.

[64] See Kuznets, *op. cit.*, pp. 101-103. Let us ignore interest accumulation and suppose that an income earner wishes in retirement to enjoy an income half that which he enjoyed when in the labor force. Then, if he works forty years

many individuals are saving much less than this, often because they think they can get along on much less income when retired.[65] Inasmuch as pension income usually is much below what the pensioner was earning, he must accumulate considerable assets to make up the difference.[66]

Arrangements for a more optimal distribution of work and leisure time within each year, while they can be made to facilitate the employment of older workers, do not assure full employment and thus may not affect at all the number of hours actually worked per year. Here the major concern will probably continue to be the maintenance of an adequate aggregate demand for labor inputs, and the minor concern, a minimization of conditions giving rise to structural and other unemployment not closely connected with dearth of aggregate demand. Full employment is more easily attained, and some kinds of unemployment are more easily avoided, when an economy is flexible and labor is mobile. At present this necessary flexibility is partially denied by the imposition of certain union and other work rules, of seniority provisions, of minimum wage requirements, and of various bureaucratic rules to which reference was made earlier in this paper. These rules and provisions must be made more flexible, in order to make it easier to employ older workers than it is under present conditions.[67] Note needs to be taken particularly of the requirement, should an older worker's full-time earnings be found below so-called minimum approved levels, that corrective action consist in supplementing the wage, not in raising rates of remuneration unless worker productivity warrants such action. Supplementing

---

and expects to spend ten in retirement, he must save (10/40) (1/2), or 12½ percent of his earnings. If the retirement-employment ratio is 15/40, he must save 3/16 of his earnings; and so on. Current savings rates are not compatible with these requirements in many occupations. Whether a retirement income of one-half the average earned would be "adequate" is doubtful, since tastes are formed by a worker's expenditures in his forties and fifties when his earnings are relatively high and his outlay upon the support of children has become negligible.

[65] Morgan et al., *op. cit.*, pp. 441-443.

[66] See unsigned, "Will There Be A Rush for Early Retirement?" (cited in note 27 above). Graduated retirement plans are described by Harland Fox and Miriam C. Kerpen, "Special Retirement Provisions in Industry," *Monthly Labor Review*, 87 (July, 1964), 781-785. See also note 64 above.

[67] On the impact of minimum wage rates and unionization of wages, see for example, Yale Brozen, "Minimum Wage Rates and Household Workers," *Journal of Law and Economics*, 5 (October, 1962), 103-109.

wages, though usually a questionable procedure, does not generate unemployment; but elevation of remuneration levels above productivity levels does generate unemployment.

VI

While it is not my intention to draw further conclusions from the materials presented, one inference may be drawn. The major disadvantages currently associated with aging—especially relative poverty and lack of access to employment—are not necessary concomitants of aging, even in a technologically dynamic age. They usually are sequelae to initially defective education and to subsequent failure to retrain workers as conditions of work change. Accordingly, given effective education and retraining, these disadvantages are likely to be markedly reduced. It follows, therefore, that the social scientist, when devising policies for the benefit of the aged, must not emulate the Colonel Blimps who prepared for the next war in terms of its predecessor. Instead, he must distinguish between transitory problems in need of temporary solution and persistent problems which are avoidable or at least soluble through future-facing instead of backward-facing measures.

A case in point is relief for aged too old or too poorly educated to be employable. The need for this sort of relief, while never entirely absent from a modern society, should prove largely avoidable in the future through education, retraining, social security, and better planning of adjustment to labor-displacing innovations. Until recently, those unemployed twenty-seven or more weeks have numbered about 500,000, of whom about half are forty-five or more years old. If most of these are considered unemployable, together with half the remainder, the number of unemployables approximates 375,000. It would be much cheaper to support them at some acceptable level, say for a family of four at a rate of $2,300 per year, than to try, by macroeconomic devices, to set them to work. Even if a precedent were thereby established, the number affected fifteen to twenty years hence should be very much smaller. Other devices may,[68] of course,

---

[68] See Ying-Ping Chen, "Income Tax Exemptions for the Aged as a Policy Instrument," *National Tax Journal*, 16 (December, 1963), 323-336; Milton Friedman, *Capitalism and Freedom* (Chicago: University of Chicago Press,

be combined with some provision for direct financial assistance to the needy, compatibly with a great reduction in current direct welfare payments.[69]

What constitutes poverty is a subjective as well as an objective phenomenon, of course. It is always possible, therefore, that definition of poverty in prodigal terms, coupled with ostentatious though ineffective anti-poverty programs, will convince many families of their poverty even though they never before had looked upon themselves as poverty-ridden. Here we are confronted with a social mechanism described effectively by Molière in his play *Le Médecin malgré lui*. This mechanism, unless properly constrained, could disadvantage underprivileged persons by diverting to other purposes those public funds which might have been available for their partial support.

What should constitute policy as well as what is the prospect of older people fifteen or more years hence turns partly on present objective estimates of the future behavior of the American economy and the impact of this behavior upon older people. Thus in 1980, according to the President's Council of Economic Advisers, 10-13 percent of the nation's families, perhaps close to one-third with heads sixty-five years and over, will have incomes under $3,000. Given a median family income growth rate at 1947-1956 levels, however, the number of families with incomes under $3,000 could descend to close to 6 percent, or near a minimum ineradicable level. This estimate by L. E. Galloway suggests, therefore, that even though there presently exists a large hard core of poor families, particularly in our older population, economic growth can greatly reduce this core, especially if complemented by appropriate refresher training under industry auspices.[70]

1962), Chapters 11-12. In 1961 direct welfare payments by all governmental units amounted to about $33 billion, or nearly $3,000 per consumer unit to the 20 percent with lowest incomes, or $600 per each of the 57 million consumer units. *Ibid.*, p. 193.

[69] W. H. Locke Anderson finds that most of the "poor" families headed by an aged person are "isolated from economic growth." He includes in this category about three million families. See "Trickling Down: The Relationship Between Economic Growth and the Extent of Poverty Among American Families," *Quarterly Journal of Economics,* 78 (November, 1964), 959. This number turns out to be much smaller given Friedman's estimates of requirements. *Op. cit.*

[70] "The Foundations of the 'War on Poverty,'" *American Economic Re-*

One form of "poverty" not touched upon in this paper should be noted in a general review, even though it is not treated. That is the seeming scarcity of attractive positions for the relatively younger members of a slowly growing population—together with a possible corollary, an unduly large number of quite old, strategically situated decision makers. This form of poverty reflects the fact that whereas the age composition of the labor force is determined by demographic trends, a society's job composition is determined by technological and market trends. For expositive convenience, let all jobs be divided into relatively Attractive (A) and relatively Unattractive (U), and all members of the labor force into Older (O) and Younger (Y) individuals. If a population is growing slowly or not at all, the ratio O/Y will be higher (say one-fourth or one-third higher) than if it is growing appreciably. It follows that the ratio Y/A will be lower *ceteris paribus* in the slowly growing than in the rapidly growing population, with the result that conflict between older and younger workers could emerge in respect of the allocation of jobs in the A category. This problem can be met, however, by rendering job milieus as agreeable as economically feasible and by allowing free play to market forces which tend to eliminate age-connected discriminatory aspects of job allocation, arising not out of differences in performance but through noneconomic ascriptive rules imposed by the state or by trade union-employer agreements. Then, even though the Y/A ratio necessarily remained lower than in a more rapidly growing population, it would become acceptable as a part of "the scheme of things."[71]

The related problem of gerontocracy is easier to deal with, especially in a society largely composed of corporate forms in which responsibility for initiating innovation and solving problems (if not always for final decision) is diffused. A leadership responsible for final decisions may behave suboptimally if dominated by a quite old or by a quite young membership. Possible ankylotic or Struldbruggian tendencies of the sort which could be associated with a pre-

---

view, 55 (March, 1965), 122-131. For the Council data see report cited in note 46 above, pp. 60-61. See also R. C. Wilcock and W. H. Franke, *Unwanted Workers* (New York: Free Press, 1963), especially Chapters 1 and 7.

[71] For an early discussion of the subject of this paragraph, see my "Some Effects of Changes in the Age Composition of the Labor Force," *Southern Economic Journal*, 8 (October, 1941), 157-175.

dominance of very old individuals in strategic decision-making roles are easily averted, however, by limiting the fraction of these roles allocable to such individuals.[72]

BIOGRAPHICAL NOTE

JOSEPH J. SPENGLER was born in Piqua, Ohio, in 1902 and was educated at Ohio State University (Ph.D.). Mr. Spengler, now James B. Duke Professor of Economics at Duke University, has published a number of essays on Southern economic and demographic problems and ante-bellum Southern economists. He has also published books and articles on the demography of France, economic development, population problems, and social and economic theory and its history. Mr. Spengler's publications include coeditorship of *Population Theory and Policy* and *Essays in Economic Thought: Aristotle to Marshall*. He is a past president of the Population Association of America and the immediate past president of the American Economic Association.

[72] *Ibid.*, pp. 169-175. Susceptibility to fatigue increases with age and this may reduce performance, as in the case of master chess players whose chess ability does not decline with age. See N. R. Draper, "Does Age Affect Master Chess?" *Journal of the Royal Statistical Society*, 126 (Part 1, 1963), 120-127.

3

Aging and the Political System

Fred Cottrell

My intention in this chapter is not so much to tell potential policy makers what I think they ought to do; it is rather to show
them where they might look if they want to see more clearly some
of the forces shaping politics in our society. Perhaps this will permit
them to predict a little more accurately what will happen if they
make a given choice. I refrain from making recommendations not
in the interest of preserving an ivory tower of objectivity; I willingly
renounce my right to shape events simply because it has long since
become apparent to me that few things in the universe are much
altered by my wishes.

Politics has been defined as the art of the possible; since policy
must itself represent an adjustment to reality, one could declare that
the two are one and the same thing. But what is possible usually
seems to represent a wider array of events than those that actually
occur. Policy represents an ordering of choice within those limits.
To understand how policy is made we must discover how it is decided, in a given situation, whose values are maximized and whose
are served late or not at all. In order to discover emergent policy we
must look carefully at what is happening; we must examine and
analyze practice. But we seldom do that at the moment it is going
on, or if we do, we find ourselves as observers confused by the same
situation as that in which the policy maker is having to work. This
often resembles chaos more than established order, and generalizations about the way decisions are arrived at will be much more apparent with the advantage of hindsight. When with the perspective
supplied through the passage of time one seeks to characterize the
major trends, he has to choose what tools he will use and what concepts he will develop. If he so decides, he may take the policy maker

himself as the focus of attention. He will study the man's past, the bent given him by the peculiarities of his own upbringing, his value system, his affiliations, and similar sources of his values. Or he may examine the conditions which prevail in the society and shape the choices of the voter, the buyer, or others who have the power to sanction or deny what the policy maker has proposed. But whatever categories he uses, the analyst will deal with only a small part of what affected the choices of the putative policy maker or of the client whose support he is attempting to secure. In this chapter the primary emphasis is given to factors that affect the people generally, rather than to those that operate primarily through the personality of the decision maker.

We have to explain why a person in a system acts in expected ways. One effective way to do this is to show how he receives the goods and services that are necessary to permit and induce him to do what is required by the norms of his society. Wilbert Moore has categorized these norms into four classifications: the particularistic, the market, the public fisc, and impersonal philanthropy.[1] The particularistic type of distribution is perhaps best illustrated by relationships within the family. Specific norms, inculcated through socialization (much of it taking place within the family itself), prescribe specific kinds of claims one person has on another and the sanctions that are to be imposed upon those who fail to abide by them. In the first chapter of this book Moore emphasizes how these norms alter serially during the life of the person; he also attends to the way the norms imposed on specific age groups are themselves being changed. Particular emphasis was laid on the serial character of normal obligations in modern times as contrasted with the reciprocal relationships generally regarded as having been characteristic in the past. There have also been many changes in other forms of particularistic rights and duties, for example, the specific distributive functions attached to the church and its membership.

Long ago Maine emphasized as a major historical process the shift from "status to contract." Today the same general line of reasoning emphasizes the growth of the price system, the expansion of what Veblen called the pecuniary nexus and of what others called free private enterprise. Allocation through the market is supposed

---

[1] Moore introduced this classification into an informal discussion during the "Symposium on Aging and Social Policy" at Duke University in March, 1965.

to relate effectively distribution and production as measured by the price system. Spengler has enlarged on this system as a means of allocating rewards to the aging, and much of what we shall have to say deals with the way this is affected by and affects the allocation of goods through the use of taxing power.

Moore's fourth category, impersonal philanthropy, distributes a considerable segment of the goods and services produced, but the area is relatively new and not well enough explored to give it more than passing mention.

For some time it has been generally accepted among sociologists that the family has lost much of its significance as a means of creating the goods and services needed and sought in modern urban society and of distributing them in such ways as to preserve a system in which the family continues to serve as a major agency. At first sight the tremendous increase in the use of the price system itself seems to provide a sound basis for making such a conclusion. A large part of the values learned by the child is derived from or through the mass communication agencies thought to be dominated by the advertiser and others who regard interference with the free operation of the price system as anathema. But closer examination shows that while allocation *to* the family is in large part derived from a relationship with price-sanctioned activity, allocation *within* the family continues to derive in great part from its own dynamics. Moreover, careful research only now beginning to be made public shows that a very large part of the care of the aging still rests on successful inculcation of family-centered piety. But it is not necessary to cry havoc in order to call attention to the changing character of the relationship of older family members to younger ones. Even with a considerable part of the burden being carried within the family, the rising demand of the middle-aged parent that he be relieved of some of his particularistic obligations is apparent. The absolute refusal of children to assume the responsibilities prescribed by ideal norms is sufficiently frequent to create a need for new institutional means rather than the imposition of ineffective sanctions on adult offspring.

In regard to Moore's four categories, we see some general decline in the use of the family and other particularistic means for reward and punishment, a new and as yet not clearly seen influence being brought to bear through impersonal philanthropy, and a sharply intensified struggle centered around the use of the market with its necessity to sell to justify its existence as contrasted with the state, which, at least in democratic society, derives its ultimate sanction from the polling place.

In the previous chapter, Spengler outlined some of the effects the changing age makeup of our population has had on our economic activities. He also outlined the changing economic position of the aging. He and Juanita Kreps have ably shown that, given the retention of our present economic institutions, it is possible to work out what the future economic position of the aging is likely to be. But if we are to look realistically at fact in making policy, we must also ask whether, in response to what is happening and is likely to happen to them, the aging will accept the finality of our economic setup. If they think they can and should try to change these economic arrangements, what changes are they likely to propose and what is the likelihood that they will succeed? These are questions we must try to answer here.

A great deal of evidence supports the proposition that the aging, along with younger Americans, are questioning the justice of our way of life. They are not content to accept as their fair share what is being assigned to them by traditional means. Some are attempting to improve their own personal position in traditional, "individualistic" ways; many are pressing to gain a more favorable position for older people generally through exercise of their economic strength, for example, through exerting control over the policy to be pursued by their unions in collective bargaining. If the pollsters are correct, many others want to use political means to improve their lot.

Any policy adopted by our society concerning the aging will result from the strength of various sets of aging people and their allies as compared to the strength of others who for various reasons oppose either the ends they pursue, the means they are using, or both. The strength of these groups is changing, and as a result, most observers agree that things are not likely to remain as they have been. But there is no consensus about what is likely to be the outcome of the struggle to alter what will happen to the aging. The prognosticators are divided into two general camps. On the one hand, there are proponents of the position that "economic law" governs, that in the long run the propositions concerning the relationships between production and distribution delineated in our traditional system cannot be avoided or changed. On the other hand, there are those who take the position that economic behavior is merely one kind of human behavior, governed by the same general laws as those relating to familial, religious, and political behavior. In this view the analysis of power is the essential element. A particular institution through which power is brought to bear on conduct can be understood only after one has learned how the whole system which generates and distributes power operates. Economic arrangements have no particular priority over others. If those who control power find other institutions more effective in the furtherance of their values, economic considerations will be subordinated and economic institutions altered accordingly. In this view, it is also quite possible that groups that find their values threatened by the operations of those who control economic institutions will seek to alter drastically the present power position of those who control the marketplace. They will try to direct power through other institutional channels in order to avoid the consequences required by the "economic laws" cited by their opponents.

Obviously, there is no proof as to the validity of the position taken by the proponents either of economic law or of the preeminence of power. But we cannot say much about the political future without exposing at least some of the premises on which various forecasts are being made. We need a clear understanding of the concepts of "power" and "economic law." Such understanding alone will not necessarily solve anything, but without it we have no scientific way even to approach the problem.

Proponents of both schools accept the idea that a large part of the reason for changes in power, wealth, and income derives from the accomplishments of science and technology. Everyone is aware of the magnificent achievements made in these areas. Demographers have been able to show definitively that these gains are being accompanied by an equally revolutionary change in the number and locations of people and the proportions of given ages. Although social scientists are also beginning to learn about the way human values and institutions are being modified in interaction with these scientific, technological and demographic changes, what they know is not so extensive, incisive, or well established as in the physical and biological sciences. Moreover, because knowledge of this kind is intimately connected with the inner life of the individual, it is more difficult to accept than facts that offer more immediate and tangible

rewards in return for their application and pose less of a visible
threat to sacred elements of our civilization. For this reason there is
not much favorable feedback from research into the relations between change in values and institutions and change in other elements of our environment, and in turn, research into resources
devoted to increasing the rate at which we can learn about these relations. In consequence, we have little scientific knowledge about the
ways science and technology are involved in social change. To a great
extent, we must rely on ideology and other forms of word magic. It
is true that social scientists now know a great deal more than practitioners are using. But it is also true that if the difference between
the results secured by using and not using social science principles
was as great and as obvious as that between using, for example,
Aristotle's alchemy rather than modern chemistry, there is little
doubt about what the rate of the spread of the use of these principles would be.

All this is by way of explaining why, when we go into the analysis of power, we enter a quaking bog in which only a few firm step-
ping stones exist. The most advanced students in the field find
difficulty in reaching agreement on even the meaning of the word
power.[2] Usage extends all the way from limiting the meaning to "the
ability physically to coerce" to making it almost synonymous with
influence of any kind on future events. Little wonder that students
of such a wide range of fact come up with different ideas about the
way power originates, how it is customarily supplied, and whether
or not its use is moral or immoral, increasing or decreasing, and so
on.

In spite of the uncertainties created by using a term with such a
wide range of referents, it has become almost universal to identify
politics with the mobilization and allocation of power; there is an
almost equally widespread tendency to equate politics with the
operations of the state. Unless the terms *state* and *society* are identical, the above statement indicates that neither politics nor power
is used by anyone except those who govern. That is, of course,
absurd. Power and politics are aspects of the operation of every
human institution. Yet there is a difference between power wielded
by a businessman or a priest and the power of a general or a bureau-

[2] J. A. A. Van Doorn, "Sociology and the Problem of Power," *Sociologia
Neerlandica*, 1 (Winter, 1962-1963), pp. 3-47.

crat in the civil service. We will have to examine that difference carefully if we are to know anything significant about (1) why the aging are likely to attempt to change the institutional arrangements that serve them and (2) the probability that they will succeed.

It may help to clarify matters if, for the moment, we reduce the meaning of the word *power* to one single attribute characteristic of all the situations denoted by various users of the concept. Operationally, there is no way to deal with "potential power" as such; but in all forms of action, conversion of energy is taking place. Of course, this includes sections that involve the exercise of power. This is true whether dealing with the achievement of ends through the explosion of a nuclear bomb or with controlling the conversion of energy in the bodies of human beings. In the latter case, we may be more involved in the analysis of communication in all of its social and psychological aspects than in the mechanical energy being converted, but communication, too, involves the conversion of energy.

The kind of reductionism represented by making the minimal meaning of power synonymous with "energy conversion" may be of little value in the analysis of much that we want to explain. But, on the other hand, awareness that we are dealing with energy conversion whenever action is involved may provide a way to articulate otherwise fragmented knowledge about how various kinds of power impinge upon one another.

The kinds and amounts of energy available to anyone at any time set limits on what he can do.[3] The fact that only a given amount of energy in a given form is available to any man at a given time also affects the choices he makes. A change in the amount and cost of the energy required to achieve a particular goal reduces or increases what must be sacrificed to attain it. Where energy and time costs change, a shift of choice occurs in the direction of maximizing the values that can be attained under the new conditions. For example, people who have been using a crop suddenly discover new seeds that yield more energy without requiring any other change to obtain that increase; thus they can do more things or work less hard and long than they previously did to secure what they had formerly expected from their efforts. But we must also note that the norms that distributed the previous yield do not suffice to determine who

[3] Fred Cottrell, *Energy and Society* (New York: McGraw-Hill, 1955).

should receive the increase. And because there are no norms to legitimatize the use of this new power, there will be a struggle to determine who will be able to use the new power source or, alternatively, to destroy it simply because it disturbs the previous power balance. In many societies the latter alternative has resulted.

It is not necessary to point out here the increased rate of energy conversion that has recently characterized the application of science and technology. It is documented in the rising consumption of gas, oil, coal, falling water, and atomic energy. But, as we have already noted, the significance of this increased energy flow in changing the balance of power among claimants on power has not received the kind of careful study as have some of its more immediately visible and acceptable effects. But whether or not the origin of the increased energy flow is understood, a great struggle is going on among various groups of people to claim the potential it has made available. Nations, states, regions, classes, religions, and others, including age cohorts, all claim as legitimately theirs at least part of what is newly available. But legitimacy stems from the past. Most of what any generation regards as being good was learned in childhood. Legitimate power, whether that of the parent, the priest, the teacher, the trader, or the governor, derives for the most part from attitudes learned in the early years. It is difficult enough for those growing up to learn to accept power exercised by an unfamiliar source as legitimate, even when the results seem to be beneficial in terms of already internalized values. It is even more difficult for older people to accept new authority, for they see it as destroying rather than enhancing many of their cherished values.

So we can be certain that where a rapidly increasing flow of energy results from the successful application of science and technology, there will be an endemic power struggle. Whether the increases in power go to one or another group, making use of one or another institution to attain values sought by that group, is affected by a series of factors. It is in part determined by the effectiveness with which new forms of energy can contribute to achievement of the values sought by those who control the new energy. In part it is due to the effectiveness with which those who control various institutions can use these social arrangements to maximize the return which technology and science make possible. In part it is affected by the position of power occupied by those who exercise legitimate control over the society during the time that new energy is being pumped into it. As men gain control over more energy, they increase their ability to modify the behavior of those who have not made such gains. They can use energy to give increased rewards for compliance with those norms, the achievement of those goals, the enhancement of those values which they wish to maintain or advance, whether these be economic, political, religious, military, or whatever. If they wish to do so, they can also use their increased power to seduce and corrupt those who are amenable to various forms of bribery. And they can use increased energy to threaten and coerce those who will not be otherwise moved from their adherence to what they consider to be higher ends and legitimate means of attaining them. What we wish to emphasize here is that increased energy flow makes it possible to exercise many forms of "power"; it is not confined solely to the achievement of material ends or the application of naked force.

In most societies prior to the nineteenth century, and in many until this day, a close relationship existed between human effort and the achievement of human goals. Men learned what they could expect from nature in return for a given kind and amount of effort. The flow of energy was channeled by norms long established in the culture and taught to the growing child. The value system in operation might be such that only a minimum effort, just sufficient to ensure survival, was expected. Or it might decree that men be worked as early as possible and so hard that only a limited population could survive to breed and raise children to the point where they could, in turn, be put to work. Or, the goods and services expected might consist primarily of minimum essentials for survival plus elaborate instruments for warfare or worship. But always those with the legitimate power to direct the energies of men were strictly limited in what they could do by the fact that they depended on manpower for mechanical energy. Close relationship between the values now denominated as economic, political, and religious was ensured by the limited amount of power that existed. The kind of loose relationship between competing sets of values and institutions that now exists in the industrialized part of the world was not possible. Any protracted struggle to secure the dominance of one institution over the others was likely to weaken the ability to achieve what was considered legitimate in each field. Institutions, the values that legitimatize them, and the power they could direct were generally so naturally interdependent that they became mutually supporting. Using Moore's categories, we would say that the particularistic system was very widespread, and the market and the fisc were less used.

The development of extensive trade was dependent on a breakdown of this monolithic system. Trade was encouraged by the fact that goods brought from another place by sailing ships could be laid down at less cost in terms of local values than they could be obtained from the people of the area, who had learned to expect more for their effort. For example, if cotton could be produced by slave labor in Virginia and delivered in London more cheaply than linen or wool from English sources, life chances decreased for the English farmer. He was less able to meet expected norms. This breakdown of the old morality and its replacement by the morality of the trader has been widely documented; its importance to this discussion is that the model for understanding how an old system based on limited energy can be modified to permit the constantly increasing use of new sources of power, without destroying itself, is based primarily on English experience. A great expansion of power through the use of the market was considered legitimate by the contemporary Englishman. Price, as a means of measuring values and allocating returns from the productive system, served the British very well during the years when the primary sources of differential costs were to be found in such ecological factors as differences in soil and climate, the network of plants and animals that had evolved in various parts of the world, and differences in culture that permitted other segments of the population to be exploited for the advantage of those who could profit from trade.

What is generally neglected in accounts of the spread of this system is the fact that increases in energy were not only being channeled into means to promote trade and voluntary acceptance of the new way of life, but were also used to produce naval ships and arms. In turn, through protecting the expansion of trade, these could promote an increasing flow of energy to reward, seduce, corrupt, or coerce those who would not enter into "voluntary" trade. Trade was generally held by British apologists to be sanctioned by the advantages it gave to both buyer and seller. Nevertheless, the groups that resisted the trader were brought under control by the application of all kinds of power. That power was furnished by the new trading system, which could utilize increasing energy from wind and flowing water.

The ideology of classical economics supported the expansion of trade. For centuries philosophers had asked the question, "What is the limit to the legitimacy of the market as a means of channeling power?" The economists asserted the primacy of economic values over all others. They pointed to the necessity of permitting the free market and the price system to determine the flow of power. The state was to interfere only when these economic values might be subordinated to others. Naked power was justified as necessary to preserve opportunity for the trader. If traders were free to compete with each other, the operation of the price system would bring all kinds of values into their proper relationships and all kinds of power into harmony with one another.

Although many critics immediately pointed out the absurdities of this position, it continued to gain credence, for, whatever logic and argument from authority might say, the pricing system did provide greater freedom for the application of science and technology. In turn, new applications increased the flow of energy, and by feedback strengthened the new ideology. Thus, no matter how easy it was to dispose verbally of the pretensions of the trader and his industrialist partner, the ideology has become part of the sacred wisdom, the traditional logic, of our day. It is generally assumed that there are economic values that are quite different from other values. Many of us think that freedom consists in allowing economic values to dominate values that are created and served primarily by other institutions.

It is as difficult, however, to isolate economic goods and services as it is to separate power from the social and technological system in which it functions. Whatever may be the initial definition distinguishing economic goods from other goods, or economic services from other services, the final outcome usually classifies as "economic" those goods that are measured in terms of price. Without this common denominator it is not possible to know what is increasing and at what cost. But this causes problems, too. Even in a "free economy" it may be more profitable to build a military airplane, which is paid for by taxes and justified by a common need for defense, than to build a commercial plane, which derives its sanction from the utility it provides the individual passenger. Does that make an airplane an economic good, regardless of whether it is built for government or for private enterprise? Is everything that is paid for, whether by taxes or not, an economic good? What happens to the idea that economic goods always represent the free choice of the consumer—the argument usually offered to show why economic values will always take precedence over other values? On the other hand, if we shift to a definition that describes economic goods as those that are scarce, we open the door to include almost all valuable goods and services. We would then have to show that the market offers the best means of providing scarce religious, marital, military, and political services, which, of course, is impossible.

The greatest obstacle facing those who attempt to compare scientifically the results of using "political" power with the results of using wealth and money income as the means of allocating goods and services is the large body of existing literature which asserts that the problem has already been finally and authoritatively solved. It is widely held that economic law is a variety of natural law (a natural law being a truth that is self-evident) and that anyone who questions it is an impious fool. "Everybody knows" what we mean by production and why production and distribution are indissolubly linked through economic law. But when the time comes to demonstrate this, all that can be shown is that production means so altering a situation that the goods and services involved will now bring a higher price than they previously did. It is easy then to assert that goods and services not produced for sale are not, in fact, production at all, even if their value has been enhanced or the satisfaction from their use increased.

This makes it possible to assert as unquestionably true that government itself can produce nothing and that anything done by the government must be done at the cost of decreasing economic goods and services. We can thus accept without qualification the idea that although an automobile manufacturer is productive, the government that supplies roads and streets is not. The manufacturer of liquor or tobacco and its sales promoters are productive; public school teachers are not. Insurance salesmen are productive; firemen who reduce loss from fire, policemen who protect against theft, and public health officials who help reduce the morbidity and mortality that insurance is designed to compensate for, are not. The supreme irony is that a woman who stays home and rears children is not productive, but a prostitute who peddles her wares in the marketplace is.

If it were possible to wipe out the myth of the infallibility of the price system, it would be easier to show how the system does operate. But myths are a part of the fact with which we must deal. Groups who set out to claim part of the increasing productivity that our joint efforts have made possible are influenced by their beliefs. Many who could otherwise claim a larger share than they do are barred by their own beliefs from exercising the power to do so. Others who do not themselves believe in the infallibility of the price system are prevented from using other forms of power available to them by restraints put on them by people who believe that it is legitimate to use economic power only to achieve certain goals and claim certain kinds of goods and services.

An academic demonstration that in certain areas only those processes sanctioned by the activities of the free market should be chosen by rational men is not a sufficient means to get men to act as if the marketplace were the final arbiter of their destiny. Even those who use the myth when it suits them, as a means of keeping others in an arena where they are at a disadvantage, often do not hesitate to take advantage of their own influence and power, whether these take religious, political, military, or other forms. Examination of the activities of holders of great power, such as corporate managers, shows that they are extremely pragmatic in their choice of means. They may depend on price in a free market. They may equally well seek to manipulate that market and will be prevented from doing so only by the political power of others. They may seek to use political power to subsidize their own activities and to restrict the activities of others who are willing to offer goods in the market at a lower price than they. A great and growing literature demonstrates this. What we want to point out here is the fact that even the high priests of the Temple of the Goddess Price do not hesitate to use other forms of power to secure more power, wealth, or whatever they currently seek. The struggle to establish the right of functionaries to exercise power for the preservation and enhancement of certain kinds of values is not new. Some institutions, such as the Roman Catholic Church, have been able to preserve the legitimacy of their exercise of power through the life span of a series of economic systems. The recent rapid rise to power of labor organizations such as the AFL-CIO demonstrates that the effort to create new rights continues. Labor has not devoted itself to the exercise of power exclusively in the market or government. It has pragmatically chosen to exercise power wherever it could be used and to attempt to make its power legitimate by utilizing whatever existing values could be made to support its claims.

Apparently, the kind of economic law cited by many ideologists is only a rationalization for the exercise of a particular kind of power, by a particular set of people generally called businessmen. It does not now determine, and has never been the sole determinant of, who gets what and what he must do to get it.

If we use the power struggle as a rough model for understanding what goes on, we should expect that as new sets of people are added to a population or as their relative numbers in a population change, they will be likely to seek a stronger place in the existing power structure and to use their increased power to raise their own values in the hierarchy of values that the system serves.

The aging constitute such a new set of people. It is only recently that the application of science and technology has permitted a large proportion of a population to survive beyond fifty years. As a consequence, legitimate means do not exist to provide commensurately for the rapidly rising needs of these people. We have faced this kind of situation before. For example, when the American people decided that their society could achieve its goals only if all children had the opportunity for free education and were compelled to avail themselves of it, they diverted from the control of the marketplace sufficient goods and services to provide free public schools. The decision was not made on the basis of economic law, but it has mightily affected the flow of goods and services produced since that time. Similarly, a decision that older people now have the right to certain things that were previously not guaranteed will alter the kinds of goods and services produced and the way they are distributed. The decision to make this disposal of our increasing productivity may be said to be moral, religious, political, or economic; but regardless of how it is classified, it will result in many changes in the power structure of our society. Overall production may be increased sufficiently as a result of increased demands that all legitimate claims on the system can be met. On the other hand, we may have to devote less time, energy, and resources in the future to the production of those goods and services that people are made to want by the activities of businessmen who hope to make a profit. Or it may be that when all of the claims that are regarded as being legitimate are summed up, they will exceed the physical and social capacity of the system to produce.

The result may be called "inflation," "disorganization," "demoralization," or some other term. But the struggle to satisfy the rising tide of expectations can utilize only as much power (in the generic sense that we have used it) as the system can generate, and eventually some kind of accommodation between claims must be forthcoming. Again, this may be variously described. It might be called in economics "equilibrium" or the "balance of countervailing forces," in politics "checks and balances," and in international affairs "the balance of power."

A set of people recently created by new circumstances will seek, often blindly and with much resultant waste, institutional means to deal with the situation in which they find themselves. The struggle of the aging for legitimate new claims on increasing sources of power must then be viewed not as something apart from, but as a part of, politics, the means by which various groups wielding various amounts of power in various forms are brought to some necessary accommodation with one another.

The existence of so large a number of older people in the family, church, market, union, or state is a disturbing element to each of these institutions. The particularistic means of distribution becomes inadequate. None of the old institutions has effectively provided roles for so many elders. None has adequately provided the resources they require. There is an effort to preserve the previous balance among contending groups for scarce statuses, services, and goods in each of these institutions; but those in control often expect to continue to allocate to older members only the little that previously was adequate for the few who survived, and at the same time, expect to retain control of the many who now are here and must be served.

One needs only slight familiarity with the American family to know, too, that frequently the needs of the old are neglected in the face of the already accepted claims of the young and middle-aged. Nor does the church have the resources to care for them when the family is inadequate. Of the major institutions that might do the job, the market and the state remain. Each might lose power relative to the other if this new class of people, discontented with the ability of either government or business to satisfy legitimate claims, should exercise their influence to reduce the future power of either business-men or of those operating particular branches of government. But few seem to be aware of this threat.

Neither government nor business has so far made much of a record in recognizing either the needs or the potential power of older people. Business has been increasingly concerned with cul-tivating the tastes and meeting the needs of the young. The income it has allocated to the aging is small. Studies in income distribution cited elsewhere in this volume provide adequate testimony and proof if any is needed. They show clearly that neither the needs nor the desires of older people receive primary consideration. There is little evidence that the means exist within the present power structure of business for older people to change this. The concern of the middle-aged for their children and their lack of concern for their parents carry over to such an extent that they make no coalition with the older generation to limit the insatiable demands of the young. In fact, there are increasingly strong movements to force early retire-ment, to make older men in business relinquish even their present hold on the reins. Too many groups have the ability to make stronger claims on management than older people can. And they are using that power to the disadvantage of the elders. Spengler's figures in Chapter 2 showing the declining proportion of older men in the labor force provide clear-cut evidence. Business is simply not going to take adequate care of most of the aging.

In a few of the professions, older people retain respect and power. In most activities, however, the older man loses his status and power at an ever earlier age. And once that power is gone, the claims of the aging will receive less, not more, attention. In a few situations older blue-collar workers have been able to retain control of certain unions and, using union power, demand from management terms favorable to themselves; but in most cases this power must rapidly decline. It was gained only where the older workers had control over entry to a trade and where there was a declining de-mand for the skill. In these situations, older men slowly became the majority. Such situations are not numerous, however. In new and growing industries, the number of younger workers constantly in-creases relative to that of older ones, and the concerns of the young become the concerns of union leaders. Those leaders who disregard the demands of the young and middle-aged workers are displaced, and the older group loses power.

In the past, some older men were able to protect their power and defend their interests through ownership and management of private businesses. The growth of the corporation has made this a precarious ploy in many areas. The institution of property has been so changed that most old men in business have a far less strategic position than they formerly did. And big corporations, guided by young men taking advantage of advances in science and technology, have endangered the survival of many kinds of small business. Economic law in this case turns out to be the law of the jungle, in which the older owner of the small business is easy prey. Business, then, is not likely to solve the problems of the aging. Because of this, a grudging willingness is developing to accept the idea that even though it might be "immoral" to use political power in government to countervene what business considers to be just, the needs of older people may have to be served regardless of their economic productivity, just as those of another great age category, children, have.

There is very little ideology behind this growing belief. Even in the free part of Europe, the word *socialism* has a very favorable connotation for large sections of the population, and a great deal can be done there by showing that it is required in order to achieve democratic socialism. In the United States, of course, this is not so. Americans see a strong connection between socialism and communism, and both are held to be responsible for many things that have happened abroad which here are hated and feared. Those who adhere to socialism find that the word is an epithet that weakens rather than strengthens their chance of achieving what they want.

No other generally accepted body of doctrine would require political consideration for the aging except the Judeo-Christian religion. And the rise of secularism and sectarianism makes this in many areas a doubtful political asset. Even charity has become a nasty word because its practice may endanger the Protestant ethic that connects salvation with work. Welfare also has invidious connotations, even for a considerable number of older people who need assistance.

Those who set out to provide new means of satisfying the needs and attaining the goals of older people have to be eclectic and pragmatic. They cannot rely upon a general belief that lends itself to mass communication. Where they do depend on a widely accepted value that can be used to evoke a usually favorable response, they often find that others have already preempted its use to support a program not confined to the service of the aging. Health is one such commonly accepted objective. Until quite recently far more attention has been paid to the health of children and to people who suffer from a particular disease, such as tuberculosis or polio, than to any of the diseases confined to older people; and strong organizations exist to protect these interests. The recent increase in the study of mental disease, arthritis, cancer, and heart ailments represents the beginning of a new trend. As the results of these research programs begin to be applied, the servitors of health will reflect more interest in, and attempt to exert control over, funds, organizations, and personnel dealing with geriatric problems. Over time, a new bias will certainly develop, and this will be greatly accentuated by the Medicare program. But for the moment control is firmly in the hands of people other than those primarily interested in the health problems of the aging. There is a similar situation in housing. Despite ideal norms prescribing adequate housing, they are in many ways more honored in the breach than in the performance.

Universal education as something everybody ought to have even if he cannot pay for it has generally come to mean education of the young. Income-maintenance for heads of families with dependent children occupies a strategic claim on the goods and services made available through the general belief that nobody shall starve. Those who hope to use political power for the benefit of the aging as a disadvantaged set of people are competitors with similar groups interested in enlarging support for specific functions. They can look to no set of experiences widely shared by youngsters growing up in this country that would cause them to give preeminence to the needs of the aging. Either they must depend primarily on values and attitudes that develop during the process of growing older, or they must join with others who now use regularly generated attitudes toward specific values applicable to all ages—for instance, the maintenance of at least a minimal income, good health, adequate education, recreation, and housing. They will often find that, as new claimants to a limited amount of power, they are not welcomed by those who already depend on these values and who feel they cannot, even with their present resources, achieve what they have organized to achieve.

Mass communication, appeal to already accepted generalizations, sloganeering, and similar devices do not evoke the response from the powers-that-be that is expected by those who think that public opinion rules. The basic idea is that if you want to gain political power in the agencies of government, you must show politicians where they may win or lose the votes they need to retain their power, and how much they can depend on obtaining these votes. This is not as easy as many amateurs in politics or political science are likely to believe. It is true, and most politicians now know, that there are more than eighteen million people over sixty-five in this country. They know that one out of five who voted in the last presidential election was over sixty. They know that this is potentially a larger minority than any of the many minorities that they now cater to. If those who want government to do something for the aging could mobilize this potential, they would hold immense power. Some are sure that it can be mobilized. People who hold this view generally look upon it with either great hope or complete aversion. On one side are those who expect to organize almost all of the aging and thus achieve a world in which their legitimate aims can be secured. Others fear that this colossus will be used by demagogues to rob the taxpayer, deny children their due, seize from business its just profit, produce inflation, and even bring on communism. In a moment we will look at the probability that the aging can become such a leviathan. But first, as a practical matter, we have to look at the way those now in the seats of power estimate the situation, for this will be the basis of their own response to the movement. The evidence is that most politicians do not believe that the potential political power of the aging can be mobilized except in support of a few limited objectives. Evidence of this is to be found in the political platforms. The pious wishes uttered there are better evidence of priorities to which politicians think they must give lip service than of the zeal and the intention to exercise equal power to support each plank. Few of the objectives generally sought by those interested in improving the lot of the aging are very high on the list of priorities presented by either party at the national, state, or local level. Apparently politicians do not assess the power of the aging in pursuit of many objectives as being very great. And policy emerges out of pol-

itics. Given the resources government can command from the operations of the society, politicians must choose those things that are
possible from among the many things the people want. They know
that to gain anything people must sacrifice something else they
might have had. They try to judge the worth of an objective in terms
of what the voter is willing to sacrifice to achieve it. If they judge
correctly, they can continue to make policy; but if they err too
greatly, policy will be made by others who have organized a more
effective coalition in support of the policies they wish to pursue.

Evolving governmental policy toward the aging must recognize
which of their needs and desires is likely to become the basis of
effective political power and how this is to be done. It will not do
merely to say that there are so many old people or so many older
voters, for it can be presumed that these facts are presently known
by the politicians or will quickly be recognized. Instead, politicians
will have to learn two things. First, they must learn what new needs
or desires develop in the personalities of people as they grow older
to make them change the evaluation they previously assigned to
various kinds of achievements or relationships. Are they likely, for
example, to downgrade the significance of education and reduce
their political support of schools because they no longer have children to be educated? In most cases, the answer is no, because they
do have grandchildren or because they believe that the future of the
nation is dependent on education of the young. Does a banker stop
thinking like a banker, a farmer like a farmer, a woman like a
woman, because he or she has passed the age of fifty, sixty, or sixty-
five? Not on most issues perhaps, but on some. The degree to which
age influences priorities among values is one central fact to be discovered. The other is what part of these new objectives, goals, or
values is likely to be achieved through government, and what part
may be better served through voluntary associations, community
activities, family arrangements, private pensions, insurance schemes,
and so forth. How important are the new values as contrasted with
the old? Will a man change his party identification, ally himself with
new pressure groups, and give time and money to support them?
Will he change his vote and cast it? Or will he only passively wish
he might attain his new goals but refuse to pay the necessary price
for their achievement? These things the successful politician must be
able to learn if he is to espouse the cause of the aging. If he is to

remain in power, he must distinguish between pious platitudes and the ability to deliver the vote.

We have more answers to the first set of questions than to the second. Gerontologists have specialized in examining the needs of the aging. Such activities as those of the Office of Aging and the Special Committee on Aging of the United States Senate have produced sufficient evidence about these needs to convince all but the purposefully blind and deaf of their existence. In broad terms, they include the needs for increased income, medical and hospital services, housing, recreation, education, and protection from fraud. Specific needs in all these areas are spelled out. The misery in which many of our older people live is exposed for the affluent to look at before they turn away to achieve their own satisfaction.

As indicated in some of the other chapters of this book, the evidence is mounting that as people grow older, they lose interest in doing some of the things they previously enjoyed. They abandon roles that they feel are no longer appropriate or rewarding to older people. They do not have the energy to pursue activities in which they once found satisfaction but which now require too much effort for the reward enjoyed. However, because there are fewer possible sources of achievement and satisfaction, these sources loom larger than they previously did. It is from these that new or strengthened social organization for and by the aging might emerge. Those familiar with older people will already know of these emerging sources of organization. Organizers who wish to achieve what must be done to satisfy a new order of urgency can learn both from older people themselves and from those who are closely acquainted with them how their value hierarchy is changing. They can then try to estimate whether it is through government, the market, or some other form of organization that success is most likely to come.

In the past, administrators of aid programs for the aged have tried to get children to assume responsibility toward their parents; they are generally agreed that no amount of power over the family which is likely to be given to government will serve as a sure means of meeting the needs of most older people. Ethel Shanas and others are discovering that children are still assuming a great part of the burden of caring for the aging, but that such aid is often given grudgingly. Those who are pressed by the fear of public condemnation to care for their older relatives often seek to escape the burden.

Those who are recipients of aid grudgingly given reach out for something they can take with dignity and self-respect. We have already shown that the market is not a likely means to that end. To the extent that price governs, business responds to purchasing power. Unless it can be shown to business that older people are likely to come into possession of more money than they now have, they are not likely to be able to satisfy their desires through the market. "You can't mix sentiment with business" may mean only that you cannot respond to those sentiments that are not backed with power. Nevertheless, firms that increase their costs in the attempt to respond to the growing needs of an older set of workers must recoup the costs elsewhere, and other groups who expect to benefit from that business may suffer a decline in their own satisfactions and threaten the "sentimental" manager. Only in a few cases, where a single owner or family has both the power to claim the resources necessary to care for older people and is already devoted to a value system which puts the welfare of the aging high in its concern, is it likely that the new needs will be met by old business organizations. Although some people think that private insurance, profit-sharing plans, encouragement of thrift, and other arrangements sanctioned by the old morality will provide a voluntary base that will supply what is needed, the evidence indicated by J. J. Spengler and Juanita Kreps points the other way.

Another source of help for older people is the great group of private agencies that have evolved over a long period of time. They serve those who suffer from the chronic failure of old institutions to deal effectively with the deviant individual who shows up in every society, as well as those whose needs are dramatic and limited enough to be dealt with more or less successfully from the resources made available through religious or charitable impulse. Many of these private organizations are strong opponents of any interference with the particular arrangements they have worked out to fulfill certain of the needs of older people. They feel that, even when they are giving service not paid for by the client, their activities strengthen the older person, but that if government were to do the same thing, it would weaken the moral fiber and destroy the independence of that client. They resent the intrusion of any agency into a case they are handling, especially when that agency takes into account other categories of family or individual need than the ones they are prepared to handle. Broad concepts of welfare that merge maintenance of income, treatment of disease, provision of particular services (such as housing, financial assistance, education, and counseling) call for a different kind of administration than can be provided by those who are concerned with only one kind of need; this results in conflict. The American Medical Association has made it clear that it regards the medical profession not only as being expert in the prevention and cure of disease but also as being a final authority on who should receive and who should pay for medical service. This is the outstanding case among a variety of similar instances. Thus proponents of the use of government to supply the unmet needs of older people must not only combat the hostility or indifference of those who do not give high priority to the requirements of the aging, but must also be prepared to face objections from others who recognize their priority, but who feel that these needs can be met better by other means than government agencies. Included in these two categories are a considerable number of older people themselves. They reduce the political impact of the fact that there is such a large number of older voters. They make it difficult for a politician who has a real concern for the aging but is not sure whether an attempt to help them through governmental means may not actually reduce the number of votes he will receive from them.

Opposition to Medicare by many of the aging themselves is not the only case in point. Many older persons resent the inclusion of the Office of Aging within the Department of Health, Education, and Welfare because of the connotations that "welfare" has for them. The American Association of Retired Persons has been reluctant to undertake any general move to identify their members with either political party. In the presidential election of 1964, they took no active part in support of the issue of the payment of hospital bills of older people from the social security funds. The foundations engaged in research into some diseases endemic to the aging, such as arthritis and heart disease, have assiduously attempted to avoid a political alliance that would cost them the social and financial support of some of their backers and, incidentally, would endanger their tax exemption. The list could be extended indefinitely. We have, however, indicated the general nature of the politics involved in discovering the special needs of the aging and in deciding which of these it is strategically wise to attempt to satisfy through government. We need to examine particular cases. Prominent among the policies toward the aging that must be adopted are those relating to income maintenance, health, housing, recreation, and education. Perhaps most observers regard them as being politically significant in that order.

The necessity or desirability of some form of government guarantee of income maintenance will probably not again be a political issue. Republicans generally agree with other observers that the fear that their candidate for the presidency in 1964 might induce his party to adopt some form of voluntary program to replace OASDI or reduce its benefits was a major factor in causing a large number of older people to vote for his opponent. This only confirmed evidence already generally accepted by most party leaders in both parties that no one dares decrease OASDI benefits or coverage. Social security is now considered to be a legitimate means of distributing purchasing power to older people even though they are not, in terms of the market, productive. In fact, from the time of its inception, a strong effort has been made to give social security the sanction of sound business practice. Insurance has long been recognized as being legitimate. Thus social security could be regarded as being good, even when it gave money to people who were no longer working, if the money they received was viewed as having been paid by them in the form of insurance (though the premiums were collected as a tax). Social security was set up under a special board. A trust fund was created as is required in private insurance. The amount to be paid from these reserves was related actuarily to the reserves. Those who were unable to live on other resources plus insurance were expected to turn to another program, which was clearly designated as welfare and called Aid for Aged, or old-age assistance. Those over sixty-five who were fortunate enough not to lose their jobs (it was not assumed that retirement was an eagerly sought privilege!) were not to receive these insurance payments. Thus the recipient was able to accept payments from government with self-respect. The preservation of this image is of primary concern to those who know the aversion many people have to anything that smacks of welfare. The destruction of that image is of equal concern to those who look upon all government interference with economic law as anathema and who hope to put the clock back by lumping social security with other forms of aid which they regard as being socialistic.

During the 1964 election campaign, they pointed out that many groups were brought into the system who would contribute to social security a very small amount relative to what they would recover. They claimed that the reserves were thus made inadequate in business terms. Another doubt about soundness was raised because it is not yet known how the disability feature of OASDI will work out when the population is stabilized. Of course, general taxes could be used to guarantee the payments, but that would make it clear that the system was nothing but another device of "tax robbers" to secure for their clients what ought to have gone to those who were truly productive. It is true, of course, that many state and local taxes are more under the control of the voter than the social security tax; thus the effort to give the social security tax the appearance of a voluntary insurance premium is fraught with difficulty.

The inclusion of the Office of Aging within the Division of Welfare in the Department of Health, Education, and Welfare endangers the image. But for the case worker who frequently must use social security payments as one resource and must find for his client additional funds or services in the form of subsidized housing, free hospital, nursing, and medical care, specially designed, government subsidized recreational facilities, and so on, the effort to keep the social security image pristine hardly seems to be worthwhile. It seems to the case worker that increasing the respectability of all forms of welfare should be the objective, rather than preserving a precious self-delusion that this kind of distribution through taxation is good and all others subject to suspicion.

Nevertheless, the prejudice remains an essential part of the mythology. From the politician's point of view, if he can at once take care of old people and retain the support of the middle class by accepting the necessary fictions that surround social security, and if providing equal services to the aging through more easily identifiable government interference with the law of supply and demand loses votes for him, why not do it? Thus there is pressure to increase income to the aging through this respectable form of support. Through increased purchasing power the aging are given wider choice as to the form in which they will obtain what is considered to be their share. But this hinges on another question of choice. Many voters will have to be induced to accept additional taxation if the increased income is to come from the social security tax. There is, of course, a necessary increase attached to Medicare, which is itself a form of compulsory collectivized service avidly sought by many who are at the same time seeking to give the social security recipient free choice in other directions. On the other hand, if this additional income is to come from general taxation, we are back in the realm where the aging must compete with others who seek to use tax money. Since social security was originally passed, a number of costly new services for the aging have developed. These compete not only with income maintenance for dollars that might be spent for the aging, but also with programs such as those dealing with housing and education that might or might not give older people more satisfaction than that derived from having more cash to spend.

The voter, aging or not, has a host of choices that must be expressed at the polling place as well as in the marketplace, and there is no clear evidence that his freedom of choice is always greater in the latter than the former. Good strategy requires that the size of the total amount to be spent for all kinds of services to the aging not be reduced in the effort to obtain a particular part. Those planning the program of legislation developed for the 89th session of Congress have sought a modest increase in money income. This increase can perhaps be justified under the program the voters have already approved. How much larger it could be made without endangering at least part of the support for social security or reducing the likelihood of achieving some other objective is a moot point. There is some evidence that resistance to hospitalization for the aging supported by a social security tax came from those who thought the increase in that tax ought to be used to produce higher incomes; and appropriations for health care could be taken from general revenue instead. A version of that latter plan was presented by a spokesman for the Republican party after the congressional election of 1964. It is clear now that those who want to rely on making hospital care an integral part of social security, supported from the same tax source as the rest, will have their way.

Another movement prefers to maintain income for the aging by finding jobs for them. Considerable effort has gone into governmental programs demonstrating that in many positions older people are more reliable than and as productive as younger ones. The point missed here is that very often an employer is aware that the man he retires is at least as productive as the one he hires to replace him.

Retirement is often not related to productivity; it is made to serve other social purposes, including making way for a younger man, presumably one with a family to support. It is assumed that if the breadwinner of a family is unemployed, it is likely to cast a heavier burden on the tax rolls and result in other, greater costs to society than that incurred by retiring the older man.

Efforts to use older people effectively in jobs that demand far less than their best efforts (and, as a result, make their contribution much less than it previously was and reward them with lower income) have not been successful enough to reduce the stockpile of people retired before their productive capacity has ebbed. A growing number of private firms are discovering that even young men see what lies ahead for them and demand that part of their present income be deferred to their later years. Government taxing policies encourage this, but so do the retirement policies of private firms. Supplementary pension systems not only exist among the salaried but have also been won by many blue-collar workers through collective bargaining. Of course, the result is that a considerable number of voters have no wish to increase payments made through OASDI; instead they expect to arrange for themselves other ways to increase their retirement pay. The evidence is scanty and does not all point in one direction. Some surveys show willingness on the part of workers to pay increased taxes to ensure increased benefits in their later years. Other evidence shows that the wish to have money to spend now on things for immediate consumption, like a car, or for expenditures that may also be involved in the future, like mortgage payments on a house, influences workers to object to diminution in their take-home pay. Such voters are content to keep social security payments at a level not much, if any, above subsistence level. Thus, although a movement to give increased help to all of the aging who receive OASDI payments through increasing money payments to them would theoretically give them greater choices and, presumably, greater satisfaction, the political power to do this is probably lacking. Emphasis on securing particular gains by using the sentiment that supports aid to other categories, such as medical care, housing, education, and recreation, may result in a wider range of services actually available for choice than could come through any conceivable increase in money income from the government. In fact, it is difficult to recommend policy for any kind of aid without considering alternative combinations of ways to secure the maximum gain for the aging.

When we talk about maintaining income through governmental sources, we are dealing with the activities of the national government. Social security deals with the individual in whatever state he lives and with his employer regardless of whether he is an individual or a giant corporation. It was partly because of the growth of the corporation and the ease with which it could escape state taxation that previous efforts to set up pension systems at the state or local level proved to be unsuccessful. Politics dealing with income maintenance must be dealt with primarily in terms of national elections and authorities receiving their directives from Washington.

Health care for the aged, however, is quite another experience. State and local governments have been dealing with health for a long time. There is a host of governmental health agencies at municipal, county, and state levels. A multitude of private agencies, hospitals, clinics, foundations, associations, and so on, provide services for people in a given area, of a given religion, or suffering from a particular disease. Many of them have well-established relationships with politicians at all levels of government. And, of course, the American Medical Association is strongly represented on the staff of practically all of them. To know what is feasible for government to do about health, one must have a thorough understanding of politics in the geographic region where the governmental intervention would take place. This is politics at the grass roots. A growing literature describes the way the power structure of the community is related to local government.[4]

A multiplicity of political lines lead into and from the health complex. These make it certain that almost any policy adopted in Washington will have quite different effects among the various states, upon agencies and associations, and on the treatment given various conditions faced by the aging. The results will produce a variety of political repercussions. So far at least, greater success has come from policies that depend on working with these agencies in the attempt to persuade them to give more attention to the health needs of the aging than from efforts, such as those of the Veteran's Administration, to build a set of facilities to serve the health needs

[4] Ralph B. Kimbrough, *Political Power and Educational Decision-Making* (Chicago: Rand McNally, 1964).

of one set of people, directed from Washington and cut off from many local sources of political power.

Specific federal support for research into the illnesses suffered most commonly by older people has increased the likelihood that local doctors and hospitals will have access to new knowledge in geriatrics and to drugs that otherwise would not have been produced. Demonstration programs concerning new hospital architecture and organizations for the improvement of health, including that of the aging, have shown that there are some things the national government can do. But the vast network of health agencies was not set up to deal primarily with the needs of the aging, is not primarily dependent for political survival on the votes of older people, and hence is not amenable to control in the special interest of the aging. The one great power that the national government has in dealing with the agencies is its ability to provide money for those who follow its recommendations or adopt its policies.

The administration of health care under control of local power networks has been accompanied by increasing costs to the point that few individuals can pay the costs out of their own incomes. Those who have been able to shift or meet these costs through insurance or collective bargaining are numerous, but the burden of caring for the increasing numbers of older people has become so great for many people that its transfer onto governmental shoulders is now generally regarded as being legitimate. There will be governmentally supported medical care for the aging.

The political battle now shifts to the administration of the program of social security support for hospital care. It is likely that the medical profession will have a growing influence here, just as it has come to have power over Blue Cross. The struggle will be intense to protect hospitals previously devoted to the care of other kinds of patients from becoming primarily chronic disease hospitals for the aging who could not previously pay for such care. Efforts to enlarge facilities for the care of patients and for teaching the increased number of doctors, nurses, and other hospital personnel that will be required, as well as efforts to expand the period of time in which those who clearly belong in a hospital can be kept there, will certainly be forthcoming. The groups that are disadvantaged by shortages in hospitals and other medical facilities may press for further expansion of socialized medicine. But they may also object strenuously to increases that are financed from the social security tax. This tax and the income tax are taken out of family income. For many young breadwinners who must try to provide medical care for themselves, their spouses, and their children directly or through private insurance such as Blue Cross, a reduction in take-home pay poses an immediate dilemma. It means that current demands on income are being made to provide for future needs. This is perhaps bearable if it is felt that it is primarily to provide for one's own needs. It is much less appealing if it goes to take care of an older person who has already lived the best years of his life, whose contribution in the past can be judged and minimized, and whose present needs seem not to be so demanding as those of the young, who are clamoring for things now with the threat that if they do not get them, they will withdraw their affections later. It is not easy to see whether these pressures will lead to increased support for enlarged governmental guarantee of medical and hospital bills or withdrawal of some of the support that went to Medicare.

The hospitals, which once joined the doctors in demanding that each patient pay his own bill privately, have since become ardent supporters of collective payment of bills. They have no hesitancy in making demands on government at all levels to pay bills for those who do not have insurance and cannot or will not pay for services which the public feels the hospitals must give to those who need it. It is certain that under Medicare the professional hospital administrators and their lay boards will experience a regular flow of payments from guaranteed sources for patients whom they once would have had to refuse admission or dismiss from the hospital even though their medical needs were apparent. This may encourage them to become supporters of more government guarantees, and thus widen the split between the hospitals and the doctors. Certainly if the hospitals do come to a parting of the ways with the AMA, they have very strong weapons to use in the conflict.

Results from the present measures will probably alter considerably the political lineup. This will affect the probability that there will be another forward surge in the effort to meet completely the health needs of the aging.

The administration of this program will also lead to the creation of a larger governmental bureaucracy. As the bureaucracy operates over the country, it will develop new sources of knowledge and will uncover many previously unnoted power structures as these are brought to bear on the administrators of the program. Probably there will be a lull while the results of the present move are being assessed, both in terms of politics and in terms of the effects it has on the health needs of the aging. It is, of course, altogether possible that the mounting costs of medical care for all age groups will lead to an extension of the tax and insurance principal. In fact, a great deal of the resistance to Medicare came from people who regarded it as the camel's nose under the tent.

Another important result, from the political point of view, is the very great political power of the various agencies that now support, manage, and control health facilities and services. By merging the health needs of the aging with those of other age groups, this power is tapped. Funds available for research into community health, chronic disease, dietary research, and so on, are automatically used in part to benefit the health of older people. Funds made available for the development of training in nursing, medical technology, hospital administration, and many other branches of the medical complex serve old as well as young people. Money for medical schools and the advanced training of specialists flows through the power structure under control of those generally interested in health. To set up competing facilities outside these agencies in order to control power more effectively in the interests of the health of the aging is, even if possible, questionable. The issue is whether or not the aging can receive more from having a low priority in the system controlling great power than from having a high priority in a system competing for and receiving much less.

The relative political strength of the aging acting in their own interests in relation to health has been tested. Certainly it has taken a long time and the fortuitous combination of their power with that of other pressure groups has overcome the opposition of the AMA and its allies to a form of payment for hospital care that they disliked. Now that this objective is presumably achieved, we must assess how that achievement has altered the political alignment that can be expected to support the next objective. It is probably true that many middle-aged voters were attempting, in the support of Medicare, to relieve themselves of the threatening burden of hospital care for their parents and for other older persons in their local community who could exercise a claim on resources available there for medical care for the indigent. Whether they would value another objective designed to improve the health needs of the aging as highly as this one is at least uncertain. The same may be said of some labor organizations and other allies in this battle. In any case, it is fruitless to attempt to develop much more in the way of health policy for the aging until the consequences of this past effort become apparent.

The third great area of need for the aging is housing. Housing has been involved in politics for a long time. It is a prime concern not only of those who will occupy the buildings but also many other people, such as those who build them, those who finance them, those who are influenced by their presence and the use to which they are put, and those who would like to use the space for another purpose. All these interests have some stake in any effort to change housing in the interest of the aging. In most cases, they have long-established places in the local and state power structures, including the political parties as well as the government itself. Any effort to change housing will be assessed in terms of the way the changes affect the present position of these organized agencies.

Bankers have an interest in the way housing is financed. It has long been considered moral, even by those who disapproved of using credit for the purchase of other goods, for a man to engage in deficit spending when buying a house. Various kinds of financing are established, each carrying with it the legitimate right to claim a fee, and many are protected by law as well as custom. The states control the kind of credit that can be extended and set limits on those who enter this area. Efforts to develop new forms of credit that do not respect these rights will be bitterly fought. Those who expect to arrange financing of housing for older people must face the fact that if they reduce or eliminate charges in order to reduce the cost of housing, they cut the normally expected profits of many other people with well-established power positions. Provision of housing for older people involves an unusual situation. Usually a man who is buying or building a house is young enough to undertake a long-term loan with little risk that he will die before he can pay it off, so that risk can be cheaply insured. Older people must ask for and receive a different kind of credit. Most of the pressure to use government credit to supply housing originates not from the aging but from young family heads, who demand the kind of credit that best serves their needs. This is the kind of credit that bankers are set up to administer, in which they have the greatest experience and the most reliable knowledge. Since funds for housing are limited, bankers tend to award loans to the young heads of families. The special kind of service required by older people will be given only if an appropriate premium is to be paid. But among those seeking credit, older people as a set can least afford to pay such premiums. Government guarantee of loans and subsidy to cover potential risk are required. Few state or local governments can undertake to cover these costs, which have thus tended either to go unpaid, with corresponding absence of financing, or to be paid by the national government. The success of the Housing and Home Finance Agency in using this instrument to influence private bankers to extend credit and builders to build housing for older people is certainly an important achievement. But the Agency would be the first to argue that it is small compared to the need. The primary issue is whether the aging can exercise sufficient political power to push new plans that will compete more successfully for scarce housing dollars. This political muscle would not be wasted in the effort to change the credit structure involved in housing. And it is certain that the full realization of many of the dreams of the idealists would require just that.

A second power structure surrounds the construction industry itself; it must also be dealt with by those who want better housing for the aging. The forces that operate here are perhaps as powerful and sometimes more rigid than those involved in financing. The division of labor in construction is protected by codes that have evolved, in some instances, over the centuries. In many cases these codes are basically involved in the personality of those engaged in the industry. They extend from the architect's concept of professional integrity to the jurisdictional specificity of the plumber's or electrician's union rules. They are often protected by legal licensing and builder's codes that can be changed by a politician only at very great risk. It may be possible in Washington to create an impression of political power through lobbying, mass demonstration, and research which shows how great the need is and, therefore, the probable tendency of the aging to vote for change; but at the precinct level, every knowledgeable politician is told in no uncertain terms what the immediate consequence of tampering with established influence will be. Efforts by those who want to provide low-cost housing for the aging by revising what are to them archaic and expensive requirements will frequently run into strong resistance from both the contractors and the construction unions. But in many cases unions are among the sources of support the aging look to when dealing with subjects like social security and Medicare, and the local labor hall in many cities has also long been the bailiwick of the construction unions. Efforts to provide low-cost housing through violation of codes that are of vital interest to some of your supporters is simply not good politics.

It is not often that local realtors and the Chamber of Commerce are strongly identified with general movements to aid the aging. Thus, some considerations that are important in setting policies which might disturb union leaders can be forgotten when changes are sought that are opposed by these local organizations. But examination of municipal and county politics will demonstrate the extremely powerful positions realtors and the Chamber of Commerce hold in relation to zoning, taxation, planning, and many other points where housing is affected by government. Here, again, efforts to generate influence in the state capitals or in Washington are likely to be frustrated by local voices. However, the basis for change may be generated by the appearance of new materials and methods. Those who want to use them provide allies who also have a stake in uprooting the local establishment. This may also be foreordained by shifts in land use initiated by technological and demographic changes, particularly through transportation. To be effective, politicians interested in better housing for the aging must be aware of and make use of political influence growing up locally. As a case in point, there are forces at work behind such widespread programs as urban redevelopment. These changes result from deep-seated alterations in our culture and the deterioration of old structures. Those with power to choose whether or not to remain at the city's center have in many cases already abandoned it. This provides an opportunity to take advantage of these changes, to relocate housing for the aging, and to establish new patterns of central city land use. But to do so effectively involves intimate knowledge of technological and other factors that give rise to change. It also involves knowledge about others who seek to reshape the central city. It is important to know who they are, what they want, and how much power they can exert to obtain it. Policy for the aging will only be effectively implemented when these facts are known and those with objectives similar or complementary to those of the aging have been enlisted as allies at the local level. Obviously this calls for much knowledge about other things than the needs and aims of the aging themselves; organization to deal efficiently with housing for the aging will differ considerably from that which deals with income distributed from Washington.

This applies with even more force as it relates to education and recreation. From the point of view of most Americans, education is a local concern. This is true in spite of the rapid growth of higher education, which necessarily is divorced from most of the power structure of the locality from which the students and the faculty come. Many men of power, prestige, and wealth have felt it necessary to concern themselves with the schools.[5] They have set up boards of education that operate apart from partisan politics, and the result is to narrow the power base required to control them. It is only as these groups can be convinced of the needs of the aging for education that anything significant is going to be done. At the center we can provide research, money for demonstration, fellowships to educate people, especially to teach older people, and perhaps a limited program of direct aid for schools that give special consideration to older people. But all of these things depend for their effectiveness on their ultimate ability to convince a large number of people at points widely scattered across the country, facing an extremely varied set of demands, equipped with few and limited or many and almost unlimited resources, that they should add special courses, teachers, teaching aids, and grant special use to space for the aging. What will be possible in a few places will be impossible in the overwhelming majority of cases. What appears as the objective highest on the priority list in one area will be meaningless in another. What will attract clientele in one place will repel it in another. Almost none of the criteria necessary for policy making exist except at the grass roots. Experimenting, probing, evaluating, reporting—these are perhaps the essential practices that must go on in preparation for the adoption of policy toward education for the aging at any other level.

Of all the needs we have characterized as being major, recreation has had the least attention by government. True, we have had public parks, playgrounds for children, museums, zoological and

[5] Kimbrough, *op. cit.*

botanical gardens, public concerts and plays, celebrations and displays. But the overwhelming portion of leisure time was taken up in endeavors where political provision and control was at a minimum. Leisure time activity is of growing concern, and here again needs are being defined, new activities evaluated, experiments being undertaken. But government's part in this is comparatively small. The overwhelming portion of the power structure controlling recreation is outside government hands, and those who do control it are interested in keeping it that way. Therefore, instead of attempting to enter into and share political power with those already organized to exercise it, those who want to promote recreation for the aging find that they have to create new lines of political power in the face of opposition from those who do not want the government to do anything about recreation and from those who do not want the resources available for the aging to be further diluted by having to be shared with newcomers. In these circumstances, politics provides almost no guide for the adoption of policy.

What we have been demonstrating as we have dealt with particular aspects of government in relation to specific kinds of needs simply shows the basis for the generalizations which were made at the beginning of the chapter. It is likely that some of the needs of the aging will be met by the government in Washington, but it is clear that others cannot be met from there. Many of these needs will be served by local or state government. Certain other widespread needs of the aging can hardly be met at all by the use of government power without great alteration in value hierarchies and shifts in the location of power. Certainly the image of the aging as a great political ogre about to overturn the structure of power politics does not emerge from examination of political events. Instead, evidence indicates that at certain points the aging can effectively threaten the balance among other minorities and force concessions. New structures are emerging through which various segments of the older voting population can be organized. A different image of the aging is emerging which will provide a new locus for power based on mass communication. Perhaps if there is not as much to be hoped for as some wish, there is also much less to be feared, and in the end, efforts to use politics for the attainment of the goals of the aging will become as normal as using politics in the effort to secure the aims of young people.

BIOGRAPHICAL NOTE

FRED COTTRELL was born in Idaho Falls, Idaho, 1903, received his A.B. at Occidental, and M.A. and Ph.D. at Stanford. Mr. Cottrell is Professor of Government and Chairman of the Department of Sociology and Anthropology at Miami University. He is Acting Director of the Scripps Foundation for the Study of Population Problems. He has written in the field of Occupational and Industrial Sociology, International Relations, Economic Development, and Gerontology. His publications include *The Railroader* and *Energy and Society*. His essay "Men Cry Peace" was co-winner with that of Quincy Wright in an international contest conducted by the Institute for Social Research of the University of Oslo. The special area of interest in the field of gerontology is concerned with the effects of technological change on the aging and the political implications of the changing position of the aging. He is past president of the Ohio Valley Sociological Society and former member of the Council of the American Sociological Association.

II

CRITICAL AREAS AND SPECIAL PROBLEMS OF AGING AND SOCIAL POLICY

II

4

Retirement as a Social Event in the United States

George L. Maddox

Modern men in Western societies are bound to a wheel of change. The inexorable turning of this wheel makes much to which particular human beings are attached obsolete and all things obsolescent. Living perpetually on a frontier, in a world that is always in the process of becoming, can be exhilarating to those whose personal and social resources make them competent, autonomous individuals. Even the painful recognition that one does not have the right answers is somewhat neutralized by the expectation that one can, will, and indeed must ask the right questions first. There is some comfort in the thought that never in history have men accumulated more things, assembled more information, and achieved control over more aspects of their environment than at present.

In the face of unparalleled success and aspirations, the condition of many elderly persons in the United States is something of a scandal. An enormous and growing literature calls to our attention their increasing number and their personal troubles, chief among which are the high probability of economic deprivation and an ambiguous position in the social structure. The personal troubles of the elderly in our society are difficult to dismiss. This is true in part because of their social visibility as reflected in the emergence of a new professional field of interest (gerontology) and the reemergence of social services and security for the elderly as a political issue in the nation. The incongruity of their plight amid affluence increases our discomfort. But more than this, the troubles of so many elderly persons are difficult to dismiss precisely because the economic deprivation and personal obsolescence associated with age are recognizable as products in large part of the social environment in which we too live. Thus the current situation of the elderly is not only a commentary on how our social system has operated in the past; it is also a disturbing prophecy about the future of any contemporary man. The high social visibility of being elderly and our own personal and social involvement in this condition have prompted many to view some of the personal troubles of the old as a social problem. Retirement is a case in point.

I

Departure from the world of work, with the implication that the separation is intended to be permanent, is an event of considerable social and personal significance in our society. Historically, work has been a central life task and interest of American males as well as a source of income. Work outside the home has assumed importance as a source of personal and social identity for many American females in recent decades. However, the significance of retirement for the female, as compared with the male, has not been systematically explored and currently remains primarily a matter of conjecture. For this reason, in this brief discussion, attention will be directed to the retirement of males.

For better or worse, retirement is a rite of passage, usually an informal one, between productive maturity and nonproductive old age. For some employees, usually those with long years of service for a particular employer and typically (although not exclusively) those in the middle and upper ranges of status, the transition from the world of work to the world of nonwork is marked by a public ceremony and the presentation of a memento. For most employees, however, this significant transition appears to be unceremonious, perhaps almost intentionally so, as though retirement were an event which one does not wish to mark especially. At any rate, retirement is not ordinarily an event which is noted in the daily newspapers as being of public interest. For some employees, retirement may be unintentional and unmarked, as in discovering that the loss of the last job and subsequent failure to be reemployed constitute their retirement.

Predictably, an event of such personal and social significance

might be expected to generate a substantial descriptive and inter-
pretative literature.[1] In fact, the primary task of this presentation will
be the identification and assessment of the messages about retirement as a social event in the United States suggested by research.
By way of previewing what is to follow, it will be argued that retirement lives up to its advance billing as a troublesome personal
and social problem. But current interpretations of retirement are
seriously marred by the inadequate attention to variations both in
the social context within which retirement takes place and in the
personal biographies of the elderly individuals. Too often retirement
is treated implicitly as a fact with a given meaning, rather than as a
sociological variable to be understood within the social life-space of
an individual. It will be argued (1) that the assumptions about
homogeneity among the elderly and about the meaning of retirement for the elderly male warrant critical review, and (2) that these
assumptions are inadequate points of departure for discussions of public policy with regard to the elderly.

II

Although most retirees in our society depart from the world of
work at about the same point in the life cycle, they do not leave for
identical reasons. Many retirees, perhaps as many as one-half, leave
the work force for reasons of poor health;[2] unless they have special,

[1] For example, Wilma Donahue, Harold L. Orbach, and Otto Pollak in
their article "Retirement: The Emerging Pattern," in Clark Tibbitts (Ed.),
Handbook of Social Gerontology (Chicago: University of Chicago Press, 1960),
present a comprehensive review of this literature.

[2] Data from systematic surveys which would permit firm conclusions about
the relevance of poor health as a factor in retirement are limited. Fred Slavick
and Seymour Wolfbein, "The Evolving Work-Life Pattern," in Tibbitts, *op. cit.*,
summarize research by P. O. Steiner and Ralph Dorfman indicating that 3/5
males not in the labor force had retired because of poor health, and by Margaret
L. Stecker indicating that 2/5 of the male social security beneficiaries of this
category were unable to work. Stecker's report, "Why Do Beneficiaries Retire?
Who Among Them Return to Work?" *Social Security Bulletin*, 18 (May, 1955),
3-12, indicates the experience of OASDI beneficiaries as of 1951 and may be
compared with a more recent but similar report by Erdman Palmore, "Retirement Patterns Among Men: Findings of the 1963 Survey of the Aged," *Social
Security Bulletin*, 27 (August, 1964), 3-10. In both instances about 40 percent
of the male retirees indicated that poor health was the principal explanation of
their retirement.

scarce skills, most of the remainder are removed from the world of work more or less willingly by the inexorable operation of established retirement procedures. One still encounters arguments about whether individuals whose health does not disqualify them from working can perform adequately in the modern industrial environment; the cumulative evidence indicates that the elderly worker's potential is, in fact, rather consistently underrated.[3]

As it turns out, the argument is largely irrelevant because, given a labor market characterized by a sustained high level of unemployment and little immediate prospect that this situation will change, there is little bidding for the services of elderly workers.[4] The contemporary economic situation is one characterized by a surplus of manpower which reflects the combination of spectacular technological innovations in the work place and increasing life expectancy. Currently there is no certainty even that available manpower under sixty-five years of age can be utilized in conventional productive positions in the labor force. Consequently, arguments that assume continuing full employment have a somewhat academic sound. Arguments about strategies for keeping the young off the labor market longer, for making early retirement less painful, or for spreading the work through shorter workweeks or more holidays seem more to the point, at least for the current generation of older workers. Although discussion of what constitutes an equitable distribution of work among persons of various ages continues, current strategies do not favor the older worker.

[3] Professor Spengler, in a paper in this volume, takes note of this issue and agrees with the majority that, with some understanding on the part of supervisors, many workers beyond the usual retirement age can and, when permitted, do perform adequately. On this point, see also the detailed discussion of Alan T. Welford, "Social-Psychological and Physiological Gerontology—An Experimental Psychologist's Approach," in Richard H. Williams, Clark Tibbitts, and Wilma Donahue (Eds.), *Processes of Aging*, I (Boston: Atherton, 1963).

[4] A. J. Jaffe, "Population, Needs, Production, and Older Manpower Requirements," in H. L. Orbach and Clark Tibbitts (Eds.), *Aging and the Economy* (Ann Arbor: University of Michigan Press, 1963), speaks for the apparent majority when he argues that all persons over sixty-five could be withdrawn without affecting per capita production of goods. Whether this situation would be effectively or satisfactorily changed by an increase in the total output of goods and services or by manipulations of the work force to distribute income differently among workers of various ages or over the worklife of an individual is discussed by Professors Spengler and Kreps in this volume. In the balance, there seems to be little reason for optimism about a significant increase in employment opportunities for the elderly worker in the foreseeable future.

The most immediate consequence of retirement for the worker and his household is economic. Whatever the standards of adequate income employed, there is common agreement that the substantial number of elderly individuals who have inadequate incomes reflects in part the loss of wages which typically accompanies the retirement of the head of household from the labor force.[5] Inadequate incomes for the retired elderly are not simply a matter of wage loss, however. For many of them the economic impoverishment associated with retirement of the head of household is only an intensification of a lifelong problem. In one of the few studies in which lifetime earning patterns have been investigated, 31 percent of a probability sample of elderly heads of household had never earned an annual income of more than $2,000, and an additional 18 percent had never earned more than $3,000 in any year. Among these same persons, 66 percent reported savings of less than $500 over the previous five years, 50 percent were not homeowners, and 74 percent were not covered by hospital insurance.[6]

For purposes of understanding the economic problems of retired individuals, it is important to distinguish between the permanent impoverishment of a substantial minority for whom retirement is just one more economic insult and the relative economic deprivation of a presumed majority of retirees. In the case of the former, satisfactory resolution of their economic situation is clearly not a matter of manipulation of the retirement age, of more permissive retirement policies, or of improved social security benefits. A frontal attack on the social factors associated with perpetuation of a cycle of poverty is called for in the long run. In the short run, the hard core of permanently impoverished elderly persons must be optimistically viewed as a temporary problem necessitating a humane program of economic relief as a matter of social justice.[7]

In the long run, there are many indications that a social philosophy appropriate for an affluent society with a humane tradition will

[5] See Chapter 5 of this volume by Professor Kreps; see also C. A. Leninger, "Some Aspects of the Economic Situation of the Aged: Recent Survey Findings," in Orbach and Tibbitts, *op. cit.*, which reports aspects of the excellent work by James Morgan, Martin David, Wilbur Cohen, and Harvey Brazer, *Income and Welfare in the United States* (New York: McGraw-Hill, 1962).

[6] Morgan et al., *op. cit.*, pp. 199 ff.

[7] A similar conclusion is reached by Professor Spengler in Chapter 2 of this volume.

continue to develop. In all probability, appropriate mechanisms for guaranteeing minimum access to social facilities and resources will also continue to emerge. For the elderly these guarantees will include improved social security benefits, greater and more widespread access to health and educational facilities, and for a substantial percentage of aging workers, the prospect of a guaranteed annual wage.[8] Our economic resources are sufficiently great and the shared ethic which informs our public policy sufficiently humanitarian to provide a reasonable guarantee of continuing and increasing access of the retired individual to the fruits of our economic productivity. What proportion of our resources is to be committed to the achievement of minimum economic security for all elderly persons, and how and with what effect, will continue to be discussed, sometimes debated. Nevertheless, the prospect is encouraging that, in the future, retirement will not in itself mean severe economic deprivation for the elderly individuals in most households. This fact alone makes and will continue to make the idea of retirement less forbidding than it has been in the past.[9]

III

Retirement from the world of work is more than a matter of economics, important as economics may be in creating personal troubles for older males who are separated from the work force. Retirement is a social as well as an economic event. Consequently, improvement in economic security for retirees will tend to reduce the negative effect associated with departure from the work force, but by how

[8] For a popular but concise summary of the evidence which suggests the probability of reducing the uncertainty that has plagued the working man, particularly the older worker, see A. H. Raskin, "Automation: Road to Lifetime Jobs?" *Saturday Review* (November 28, 1964), pp. 14 ff. ·

[9] For example, Morgan et al., *op. cit.*, p. 440, in their report of a survey of the general retirement outlook among heads of households thirty years of age and older, illustrate the positive relationship between economic resources and optimism about retirement. Among respondents, 22 percent of those with neither pensions nor social security expected that "things will be all right" in retirement; among those with social security only, 66 percent were optimistic; and among those with both social security and private pensions, 76 percent were optimistic. Moreover, in the comparison of reasons for retirement among male OASDI beneficiaries made possible by the reports of Stecker, *op. cit.*, and Palmore, *op. cit.*, the number of individuals in good health who reported retiring voluntarily increased from 3.8 percent in 1951 to 19 percent in 1963.

much is not obvious. The contemporary American worker approaching retirement has been socialized in a milieu which has defined work as a central life task and interest for the male. In addition to his source of income, a man's job means a point of personal and social anchorage with considerable significance, both for the emergence and maintenance of a satisfactory self-identity and for the experience of adequate social intercourse with his family and peers.[10]

Thus the argument has followed—and with considerable justification—that any tampering with the work role, the great balancing factor of life, runs the risk of creating a profound alienation and disequilibrium among the affected individuals.[11] In an environment characterized by a religious devotion to work[12] and peopled by individuals dedicated to conspicuous production as an important means of self-identification and self-justification, retirement would be expected to have social as well as economic significance. There are continuing expressions of concern with ways to keep elderly males in the work force in spite of the fact that their productive capacity is not bid for and with multiplying activities for the elderly which have the form and appearance of productive work.[13] This concern not only motivates attempts to increase income among retirees but also illustrates residues of a cultured heritage in which work is a central life task and interest.

This characterization of the contemporary social milieu would lead one to expect retirement to be a troublesome challenge to the retired individual's conception of himself as an adequate, worthwhile individual, even if his income were reasonably adequate. Whereas the characterization is correct historically and in its general emphasis, especially when applied to the contemporary generation of workers in or approaching retirement, it is deficient in specific

[10] The centrality of the work role for males in our society is an assumption well grounded theoretically and empirically. See, for example, Sigmund Nosow and William H. Form, *Man, Work, and Society* (New York: Basic Books, 1962), Chapters I and II.

[11] A particularly cogent statement of this argument is found in Georges Friedmann, *The Anatomy of Work* (New York: Free Press, 1961). Friedmann's indebtedness to Freud is acknowledged.

[12] For a historical review of the emergence of the contemporary work ethic, see Adriano Tilgher, "Work Through the Ages," in Nosow and Form, *op. cit.*

[13] See, for example, Wilma Donahue (Ed.), *Earning Opportunities for Older Workers* (Ann Arbor: Division of Gerontology, University of Michigan, 1955).

detail. Job-related work as a central life task and interest to be valued per se is, after all, a culture-specific phenomenon whose historical emergence can be traced to Protestant theology in the Reformation period in general and to Calvinism in particular.[14] If the phenomenon is culture-specific rather than a culture-universal reflecting some sort of instinct for workmanship, then one may entertain the possibility that, since the conditions which brought the notion into existence no longer pertain, emphasis on work as the primary source of meaning and satisfaction may no longer have its original significance. Evidence is accumulating that just such a reappraisal may have been taking place in recent decades.

Robert Dubin presents evidence indicating that among selected industrial workers work is not the central life interest and the work place is not the locus of the most rewarding social experiences for the worker.[15] Remunerative work may be required by society, he contends, but this no longer guarantees that it will be viewed as valuable by workers. Specifically, Dubin found that only one in ten industrial workers in his survey sample perceived their important primary social relationship to be located in the work place; instead, the job was endured as a necessary condition to secure satisfaction elsewhere. It is important to note that Dubin was describing not the elderly worker but the industrial worker without regard to age. A generalization of this suggests the possibility that increasingly the greatest sense of loss associated with retirement will be economic, as subsequent generations of workers, exposed to a cultural tradition in which work as the central life interest has weakened, approach a permanent separation from the world of work.[16] Mounting evidence

[14] Tilgher, *op. cit.*

[15] "Industrial Workers' Worlds," *Social Problems*, 3 (January, 1956), 131-142; for similar evidence, see David Riesman and Warner Bloomberg, Jr., "Work and Leisure: Fusion or Polarity?" in Nosow and Form, *op. cit.;* and E. A. Friedmann and R. J. Havighurst, *The Meaning of Work and Retirement* (Chicago: University of Chicago Press, 1954).

[16] For example, Friedmann and Havighurst, *op. cit.;* and Riesman and Bloomberg, *op. cit.* Margaret Gordon, "Work and Patterns of Retirement," in R. W. Kleemeier (Ed.), *Aging and Leisure* (New York: Oxford University Press, 1961), describes a firm with a flexible retirement policy and a generous private pension plan in which only a third of the employees who reached the age of sixty-five elected to continue working. Moreover, Donahue, Orbach, and Pollak, in Tibbitts, *op. cit.*, p. 368, report studies in which from one-fourth to one-third of selected groups of older employees elected early retirement; in the case of certain governmental civil service employees as many as 59 percent elected early retirement.

suggests that already to some extent, and probably to a greater tent in the future, the economic aspects of retirement among l collar workers may overshadow the negative social reactions to retirement. At the present time such a conclusion does not, however, seem warranted with regard to the minority middle and upper status white-collar workers in the labor force. Although the relevant evidence is sketchy, the very individuals who, half a century ago, were considered to be candidates for a leisure class characterized by conspicuous leisure may now be the unexpected candidates for a "working" class characterized by conspicuous occupational involvement.

Contemporary discussions of the changing meaning of work emphasize that the emerging crisis about work as a life task and interest has ceased to be peculiarly a problem of the old in the modern industrial era. Technology has served man notice that he must find a home, a new anchorage point for himself, outside the world of work, certainly by the time of retirement if not before then. But what that home will be remains to be seen. Georges Friedmann[17] toys with the notion that increasing free time makes possible self-expression through political action, a possibility which has concerned some who observe the elderly as frustrated and alienated participants in political activity in the United States. To date, however, these observers do not feel that an effective political bloc of elderly persons is likely to appear or could be sustained even if such appeared.[18] Others have expressed some hope that the free time increasingly at the disposal of all adults in our society might be something more than free-from-work or recreation time against the prospect of returning to work. As a case in point, Sebastian de Grazia is quite pessimistic about the possibility of free time's becoming discretionary time, the use of which would result in substantial self-fulfillment and, hence, satisfaction for the contemporary individual who has much free time to spend and the prospect of even more. The reasons for this pessimism are three: (1) the absence of a strong cultural tradition of leisure; (2) a preoccupation with the accumulation of "things," and with wanting "things" which cost money, work, and

[17] Tibbitts, *op. cit.*, Chapter VIII.

[18] See, for example, Frank A. Pinner, Paul Jacobs, and Philip Selznick, *Old Age and Political Behavior* (Berkeley: University of California Press, 1959). Also Angus Campbell, "Social and Psychological Determinants of Voting Behavior," in Wilma Donahue and Clark Tibbitts (Eds.), *Politics of Age* (Ann Arbor: Division of Gerontology, University of Michigan, 1962).

time and hence lead to moonlighting, overtime, and a working wife rather than to the development of a tradition of leisure; and (3) the suspicion that leisure, that is, discretionary time utilized for self-fulfillment as distinct from off-work time, may be beyond the capacity of most people.[19]

A key point in the pessimistic argument of de Grazia, Riesman, G. Friedmann, and other observers of work and leisure in the United States is that a great fracture has appeared in the ethos which historically made work a major anchorage for the male. Off-work time, condemned in the nineteenth century as idleness, has achieved an increasingly respectable status. And work, which is still an important stabilizing force in contemporary life, has an uncertain future. The situation is further complicated by an unequal distribution of work and leisure, and hence income, over the work life of an individual, and by an inverse relationship between income and the amount of leisure preferred. Leisure per se is not perceived in the typical instance as an attractive form of income, although various mechanisms, such as the guaranteed annual wage, contribute to a change in this direction, at least among blue-collar workers. It is important here to note again that the issue of how to make life socially and economically bearable, if not interesting, when one is not working is visibly a current problem of the elderly. But it is not their problem alone, and this fact will become more evident as off-work time increasingly accumulates for individuals at every age level.

IV

The apparent failure of many industrial workers to find their work a stable and satisfying anchorage point has understandably led to discussions about constructive uses of free (or discretionary) time that might supply the meaning in life which work does not. The prospect that a satisfactory separation is possible, at least in the short run, is not very bright. Wilbert E. Moore has succinctly suggested why this is so.[20] His argument focuses attention on the difficulty, if not the impossibility, of arbitrarily separating a social role from the social life-space available to an individual.

[19] *Of Time, Work, and Leisure* (New York: Twentieth Century Fund, 1962), pp. 300 f., 369 f.
[20] *Man, Time, and Society* (New York: Wiley, 1963), pp. 37 ff.

Moore argues that the use of discretionary time is a problem when work is a problem. An individual's interests are most likely to be sustained and his aspirations realized when his important social roles have been extensively meshed in a network of satisfying social relationships. In fact, he continues, one index of social participation and integration of an individual might be a "perceived scarcity of time scale," with perception of scarcity positively associated with both social participation and integration. In his discussion of "the orderly career," Wilensky provides additional insight into the importance of focusing on the work role within, not apart from, its total social context—that is, work experience in which some meaningful positioning of self in relation to others and reasonable advancement are both probable and predictable.[21]

An orderly career is experienced by approximately half the individuals currently in the labor force. Predictably, the individuals most likely to experience an orderly career hold prestigious and economically rewarding positions, whether white-collar or blue-collar. Predictably also, one of the characteristics of such individuals is an above-average exposure to education. Prestige, money, and education are, in turn, important social resources known to be positively correlated with participation in voluntary organizations, general involvement in community activity, and access to power structures.[22] For some men, work becomes the opportunity for participation in a network of social relationships which extend beyond the work place but which are not initially independent of it. Moreover, prestige, money, and education are personal as well as social resources in that they enhance the probability of ego gratification, of a sense of control over the environment, and of a variety of satisfying skills that do not necessarily require interaction with other individuals (e.g., reading and hobbies). In sum, these resources maximize the probability that an individual will develop a satisfying self-image and that he will be able to maintain a satisfying conception of himself even in the event of change.

[21] "Orderly Careers and Social Participation: The Impact of Work History on Social Integration in the Middle Mass," *American Sociological Review*, 26 (August, 1961), 521-539.

[22] Prestige, money, and power are essential ingredients in the determination of the shorthand designations used to position individuals in a stratification system by social class. While both Wilensky and Moore correctly resist the simple equation of orderly career and a superordinate social class position, the probability of their positive correlation is high.

society in which the work role is increasingly irrelevant as
of satisfaction for many workers and in which the prospect
rderly career remains a common fate, a pessimistic forecast
about the personal and social consequences of retirement seems
quite realistic. Such pessimism would seem warranted even if adequate provision were made for retirement income by one or another
mechanism. But it is equally important to note that this forecast
applies not to workers in general but to specific workers, particularly
those whose work experiences have not served to integrate them in
a network of satisfying social relationships in the preretirement
years. It is necessary, therefore, to discuss not only the differential
meaning of work with occupation controlled but also the differential
social participation and integration likely to be correlated with this
placement. The need of this kind of specification and differentiation
in discussions of retirement as a social event may seem painfully obvious. Yet it is equally obvious that discussions of the social aspects
of retirement typically treat this social event as though it had the
same, or at least a similar meaning for all workers.[23]

Neither Moore nor Wilensky extrapolates his argument to include the elderly person. If this were done, one would expect that
an individual's being elderly, or retired, or both, would not in itself
be a sufficient determinant of the probable degree of social participation and integration or of a positive self-concept. Rather, one would
expect that the presence or absence of an orderly career in the life
experience, together with its implied correlates, would constitute a
crucial antecedent variable.[24]

 Failure to conceptualize reaction to retirement as a variable
(rather than as a social event with a single meaning) related to the
particular configuration of experiences which constitute an individual's biography has been a crucial flaw in many studies of retirement.
Another flaw of equal importance has been the frequent failure to
introduce as an intervening variable the opportunities and constraints in the specific social milieu into which an individual retires.
Current critical discussions generated by the proposal to interpret

[23] A notable exception is, of course, the work of Friedmann and Havighurst,
op. cit.

[24] This is in fact essentially the argument developed in the work of John Mc-
Kinney, Ida Harper Simpson, and Kurt Back. Their study of work and retire-
ment, which was supported by the Ford Foundation, appears as Chapters 2-6 in
Social Aspects of Aging (Durham, N. C.: Duke University Press, 1966).

growing old as a process of disengagement have highlighted the unfortunate consequences for adequate understanding of the aging process which follow from these flaws in interpretation.

V

The concept of disengagement has been introduced to identify the modal process of mutual withdrawal of aging individuals and society and to describe the state of affairs most likely to produce mutual satisfaction. Retirement is one of the components of the disengaged process and state as initially described by Cumming and Henry, the original proponents of the concept; the positive contribution to the maintenance of morale among elderly males which they implicitly attribute to retirement is of special interest here.[25]

Cumming and Henry argue that the implicit theory of aging most often found in the gerontological literature is the antithesis of their position. That is, theories of development have typically emphasized the importance of continued growth, of the expansion of life goals, and of social interaction for the maintenance of self-esteem through the middle years. By implication, they believe, this model has been applied to the final phase of the development process, an extrapolation which has led to the popular expectation that happy old people have to be active (engaged) old people. The notion that satisfied old people could be disengaged has not been the preferred mode of characterizing the aging process. The expectation, based on disengagement theory, that retirement contributes to the probability of achieving life satisfaction among elderly males has generally seemed improbable.

Cumming and Henry have challenged the preferred formulation. They have noted "the common reduction in life activities and in ego energy found in most but not all older persons." Moreover, they have proposed that this process of social and psychic withdrawal is to be explained as much, if not more, by psychological events indigenous to the individual as by societal reactions involving the inclusion of the older person from social interaction within the society. Disengagement is intrinsic, hence inevitable. Consequently this proc-

---

[25] *Growing Old: The Process of Disengagement* (New York: Basic Books, 1961), Chapters VII and VIII, especially pp. 149 ff.

ess, of which retirement is an integral part, is not only said to be a correlate of successful aging; it is also purportedly a condition of successful aging. While retirement may lower morale temporarily, they argue, this event is not a problem for most men in the long run *if* health care and economic independence are guaranteed and *if* there is satisfactory integration into an appropriate network of social relationships.

The adequacy of the disengagement interpretation of the aging process as initially described by Cumming and Henry is currently under critical review by them (both of them have had further thoughts)[26] and their colleagues,[27] as well as by others.[28] The empirical evidence advanced in support of disengagement as modal, intrinsic, and inevitable in the process of aging has not convinced even its advocates. However, lack of proof is not a crucial indictment of a theoretical orientation's potential utility, certainly not in the initial stages of its formulation and application. The more serious immediate objections to hypotheses generated by disengagement theory have been theoretical. A quite basic objection to the initial disengagement formulation, for example, is its tendency to treat as relatively insignificant those variations in the constraints of social environment and in the cumulative patterns of experiences which constitute the biographies of individuals. The potential significance of factors that might modify the disengagement process is recognized, and as in the case of retirement, variation in some relevant factors is noted. But the emphasis on the modal, intrinsic, and inevitable qualities of the process tend to be overriding in the analysis and interpretation of data.

[26] See, for example, W. E. Henry, "The Theory of Intrinsic Disengagement," unpublished paper read at the International Gerontological Research Seminar, Markaryd, Sweden, 1963; and Elaine Burgess, "Further Thoughts on the Theory of Disengagement," *International Social Science Journal,* 15 (1963), 377-393. In fairness to these authors, it should be pointed out that one chapter (XII) in their monograph suggests some conditions under which the course of disengagement would be modified. The main thrust of their original argument, however, is essentially reductionistic; disengagement is said to be inevitable because it is intrinsic.

[27] R. J. Havighurst, Bernice L. Neugarten, and S. S. Tobin, "Disengagement and Patterns of Aging," unpublished paper read at the International Gerontological Research Seminar, Markaryd, Sweden, 1963.

[28] A. M. Rose, "A Current Theoretical Issue in Social Gerontology," *The Gerontologist,* 4 (March, 1964), 46-50; and G. L. Maddox, "Disengagement Theory: A Critical Evaluation," *The Gerontologist,* 4 (June, 1964), 80-83.

The possibility has not yet been adequately explored that an individual's life style—reflecting, for example, an orderly career and its correlates—developed during his mature years might be an important variable intervening between his response to retirement and the hypothesized intrapsychic processes of withdrawal. Evidence suggests that retirement for a middle-class male with a college education and the experience of an orderly career is not likely to have the same meaning as it does for a lower-class male with minimum education and the experience of a disorderly career.[29] Cumming and Henry appear to concede this much in arguing that response to retirement is conditioned in important ways by health, economic status, and social integration. However, this concession does not lead them to modify their claim that the disengagement process, which involves retirement for the male, is intrinsic and hence inevitable. Such an interpretation places inadequate theoretical emphasis on situational and experiential factors. Whereas the individual who has experienced a disorderly career may indicate a more favorable preretirement attitude toward his departure from the work force, especially if there is a reasonable prospect for economic security, the individual who has experienced an orderly career brings to this change of status substantially superior personal and social resources, and hence a substantially superior capacity to explore alternatives and, if appropriate, to make compensatory adjustments. With advancing age, which implies a relative decrease in physical resources, the capacity for changing one's "main bets" and for rearranging the "side bets" diminishes in the typical case.[30] However, neither theory nor such evidence as is available encourages one to treat the experience of retirement either as though it had a common, nonsocial explanation or as though it had common meaning and import for individuals with substantially different personal and social resources.

A second objection to the interpretation of the aging process suggested by disengagement theory is the inadequate attention given

[29] The Duke University Work and Retirement Study, *op. cit.*, and research reported by A. C. Kerckhoff, "Husband-Wife Expectations and Reactions to Retirement," *Journal of Gerontology*, 19 (October, 1964), 510-516, lend empirical support to this expectation. See also Friedmann and Havighurst, *op. cit.*

[30] See, for example, Howard S. Becker, "Personal Change in Adult Life," *Sociometry*, 27 (March, 1964), 40-53. Becker conceptualizes the differential capacities for change in terms of the existing commitments and resources of individuals which make the "side bets" more or less possible and probable.

ons in situational constraints. In a discussion of adult so-
, Howard Becker[31] has noted an unfortunate tendency to
at the behavior of individuals in a particular social setting
accurately reflects the cumulative social and personal commitments
they have made through time. Their apparent situational adjustment
encourages the assumption that, even if the social constraints of that
particular situation were otherwise, the observed individual's behavior would not, in fact could not, be very different. While Becker has
nothing to say about disengagement theory, the orientation to understanding behavior which he criticizes is illustrated by the initial formulation of disengagement process. Arnold Rose focuses on this same
fault as his major criticism of the disengagement formulation.[32]
Becker and Rose agree in the argument that developmental theorists
of various persuasions are far too prone to equate observed situational adjustments of individuals with the behavior which would be
observed even if the constraints were different. Neither author thinks
that the evidence warrants such a conclusion. Rose believes that, particularly in the case of the elderly, "it is a matter mainly of social
fact, not so much of natural inevitability, that the American reaching
the age of 65 shifts into a social role of disengagement."

In sum, despite an extensive literature on retirement which provides many impressions, explanation of the observed variations in
the social consequences of retirement in our society remains to be
explored systematically. The available research has been hampered
by substantial methodological problems and, too often, by a simplistic

perspective which has not given adequate attention to variations
either in personal biography or in situational constraints. One conclusion seems clear, however: to continue to speak of retirement as
though it were a single experience with a predictable consequence
serves no useful purpose.

VI

In our society a substantial number of highly visible elderly
persons are economically and socially impoverished. Action is needed
to relieve these conditions as much as possible. Appropriate action

---

[31] *Ibid.*
[32] Rose, *op. cit.* See also Zena Blau, "Structural Constraints on Friendship
in Old Age," *American Sociological Review,* 26 (June, 1961), 429-439.

is apparently being taken, is under serious discussion currently, or is amenable to discussion. That much remains to be done is granted. But it is reasonably clear that no general conspiracy currently exists to deprive the impoverished elderly in this country of their right to live decently. However, preoccupation with this highly visible minority, substantial as it may be, should not obscure the heterogeneity of any given generation of elderly persons or the importance of distinguishing between current and future generations of the elderly.

Reference to the contemporary elderly, who are retired or retiring, as though they are essentially alike is seductive since it accommodates our need to simplify complex phenomena. We may think of the retired elderly of this generation as forecasting the situation of their counterparts in the next generation. However, policy with regard to retirement based on either of these assumptions is made at the risk both of disregarding the needs and the situation of particular individuals and also of fighting the wrong battle in the wrong place. At the moment we are probably correct in focusing our resources on the economically and socially impoverished individual. The personal consequences that follow from the syndrome of inadequate health care, limited education, economic deprivation, minimal social integration, and status anxieties associated with a disorderly work career cannot be undone easily. However, they may be ameliorated by financial assistance and social mechanisms (e.g., public housing, social casework, planned group activity) which maximize inclusion of these individuals into the ongoing social life of the community, limited as it may be.

Increased economic security is a reasonable prospect for the majority of the elderly approaching retirement. With increased economic security, the negative effect commonly associated with permanent departure from the world of work may be reduced, although probably not eliminated. For many elderly workers, retirement clearly marks their increasing obsolescence and is not a welcome rite of passage. The concern of social policy makers to minimize this sense of obsolescence may reflect a sentimental bias—which on occasion critics have labeled humanitarian stupefaction—toward a society in which everyone is happy. But this is not necessarily either the origin or the justification of concern about social policy designed to reduce needless social isolation among retired elderly persons and to increase their social participation and integration. Whatever the origin and justification of concern about the social status of the elderly, consequential efforts at improvement lie not so much with what is done with the current generation of retirees as with what is planned for those who constitute future generations. The matter of education is a case in point.

In discussions of the relevance of education for the problems associated with retirement, manipulation of exposure to formal instruction is commonly mentioned as one strategy for delaying the entrance of the young into the labor force and, hence, for reducing the pressure for removal of the elderly. Such a strategy might be dismissed both as being unlikely to produce the desired effect on the availability of jobs in a shrinking job market and as being very likely to produce equally undesirable effects among the young who wish, for whatever reason, to begin working. There are two, more adequate reasons for focusing our attention on education in terms of increasing the average years of school completed and of improving its quality —specifically, the improvement and increased flexibility of work-related skills which will maximize the opportunity for employment, and the development of personal resources which enhance the capacity for satisfying discretionary-time activities.

Our educational problems are complex. Focusing attention on education as one mechanism for dealing with some problems associated with retirement is intended to emphasize the developmental nature of behavior, not the simplicity of educational problems as compared with those of retirement. A new and independent status for the retired elderly will simply be more likely if the personal and social resources appropriate to this status are developed in the younger years.

The educational issues relevant to our discussion include, in addition to the obvious use of financing and staffing, (1) expanded educational facilities, (2) the necessity of remedial education for the culturally deprived, and (3) the possibility that what has heretofore been considered free-from-school time might need to be programmed in the interest of developing skills, interests, and habits appropriate for the creative use of discretionary time and in the interest of redefining leisure as a good to be sought rather than tolerated.[33]

Reduction of the number of individuals with grossly inadequate

[33] In the Soviet Union, for example, mandatory use of work-free or school-free time is carefully controlled. Although ostensibly this control is in the interest of developing technological proficiency, the arts and the development of social skills are not neglected. See, for example, Moore, *op. cit.*, p. 35.

exposure to the educational system may be expected to increase the number of those with the knowledge, skills, and attitudes which either make them fit the needs of the current labor market or, more important, provide them with the resources to adapt with minimum effort to the changing needs of that market. Moreover, in a world in which the ratio of hours spent in the nonwork and work roles is changing dramatically in the direction of nonwork, the necessity of having the educational system address itself to the development of personal and social skills which are relevant for living as well as for make a living is increasingly clear.

For all this, there is no assurance that in the immediate future the ambiguity which has characterized the social role of the retired person in our society will be relieved. Talcott Parsons has suggested that "we need a reconstituted institutionalized reward system as offered by the society, which makes it unmistakable, that for most it is good to be old."[34] One might well settle for a modification of the last phrase to read, "that for most it is *not bad* to be old." But whatever the preference for phrasing, one point is clear. Attempts to provide a meaningful place for the retired individual must involve more than slogans. If social life for the elderly is to be meaningful and satisfying, there is no substitute for the continuing experience of social integration in community life, not only in the later years but also during a substantial portion of the years which precede them.

BIOGRAPHICAL NOTE

GEORGE L. MADDOX was born in McComb, Mississippi, in 1925 and was educated at Millsaps College, Boston University, and Michigan State University (Ph.D.). Now Professor of Sociology and Medical Sociology, Departments of Sociology and Psychiatry, at Duke University, Mr. Maddox has published a number of articles, particularly on drinking behavior among adolescents and on social aspects of human aging. He is the coauthor of *Drinking Among Teenagers: A Sociological Interpretation*. Professor Maddox is a member of the Kent Fellowship Advisory Committee, Danforth Foundation, and of the Research Utilization Advisory Committee, National Institute of Mental Health.

[34] "Viewpoint: Old Age as Consummatory Phase," *The Gerontologist*, 3 (June, 1963), 53-54.

5

Employment Policy and Income Maintenance for the Aged

Juanita M. Kreps

The secular decline in the labor force participation of older men, interrupted only by the sharp rise in demand for labor during World War II, suggests that increasing attention will need to be given to the maintenance of retirement income in the decades ahead. Moreover, the economic plight of today's aged is intensified by the shrinking number of job opportunities for workers in their late fifties and early sixties and by the pressure for early retirement. Attempts to formulate policy dealing with the position of the aged must therefore take into account both the immediate pattern of economy-wide unemployment, which penalizes the older worker and threatens the adequacy of his future retirement benefits, and the secular trend toward earlier retirement, which makes it necessary to spread work-life earnings over a longer nonworking period.

Progress in solving both the short-run and the long-run problems has first been impeded by failure to distinguish between the two. Under pressure to improve the low-income status of today's aged—a status conferred on them by past events—we are constantly in the position of preparing for the last war, as Professor Spengler notes earlier in this volume. In concentrating on these tactics, we may fail to set in motion a course of events that will insure adequate income and employment opportunities for future aged, whose lot we clearly can control. The second deterrent to a solution to the aged's problems arises from the fact that retirement practice has come to be used as a measure for reducing labor-force size, and hence lowering the number counted as unemployed. What we have tended to view as a problem of the aged—lack of job opportunities—has in reality been a problem of the age. Since the difficulty arises from circumstances not related to the age of the individual but rather to the state of the economy, policy of necessity pertains to economy-wide measures. Finally, progress has been slowed because of society's failure to agree on the goals of policy for the aged. Since the goals implicity embedded in present programs are only vaguely defined, it is difficult to analyze the feasibility of these aims within the constraints placed by total national product and the competing claims of other age groups.

In the ensuing analysis, four major questions are raised: (1) What are the *origins* of the income problems of this particular age group? (2) What *timing* is involved both in the appearance of the problems and in the introduction of programs? (3) What *goals* are to be sought for the aged? In particular, what is to be their income position vis-à-vis that of other age groups in the society? (4) Within what areas and subject to what *constraints* are these goals to be pursued?

I: Origins of Need for Social Policy

Broadly summarized, the economic dilemma of today's aged originated in the demographic and technological changes of the twentieth century. Greater life expectancy has affected the individual person's view of his survival possibilities, and hence his appraisal of his needs in old age. Concern on the part of the middle-aged person with his post-sixty economic status would have been a bit far-fetched in the early nineteenth century. Expectation of life at birth was thirty to thirty-five, with only 60-66 of 100 newly-born reaching the age of ten, and perhaps a dozen of these reaching age seventy. By contrast, 98 out of 100 of today's newly born persons will live to age ten, and three-fourths of the 98 will live to the age of seventy.

But neither the view that the individual has of his greater life expectancy nor the increase in the relative number of older persons in the population evokes a need for change in economic policy unless these demographic trends are accompanied by some change in the patterns of work and income distribution. Since the health of older persons is gradually improving, their work capacities could be expected to extend to later ages. Their earnings could thus sustain them during the longer work-life span; or, viewed in lifetime perspective, each man's total output would be sufficiently increased to provide for his needs during a longer life-span. Under such arrangements lifetime income not only reflects the individual's productivity, the income is also apportioned relatively evenly over most of his adult life, so that he receives wage income in the later years as well as in the years up to the age of sixty-five.

The need for a new economic policy, dramatized and given voice by the collective aging of the population and by the individual's perception of his own future, must in fact be explained by a currently changing industrial framework within which jobs and earnings are beginning to be concentrated within the years of twenty to sixty. And although total life earnings from work—now compressed within a shortened portion of adult life—are increasing, their temporal distribution is nevertheless changing. The problem of evening out one's total income through the life-span, rather than receiving all of it during working years, becomes more acute as the industrial setting further telescopes man's work-life span.[1]

Reduction in the portion of man's adult years spent in working is largely attributable to the forces of technology. In fact, technology can be credited to a great degree both with making reduced work life necessary (by raising productivity and thus lowering the amount of labor required for any given volume of output), and with making it possible (by producing enough goods to sustain both the working and nonworking members of society). Moreover, technological developments also affect decisions as to the age composition of the employed labor force. The pace of automation in the 1950's and 1960's has created demands primarily for workers with education and up-to-date skills, and these demands are increasingly met by younger, more recently schooled workers.

A period of rapid technological advance, which at least in the short run disemploys large numbers of persons, is of necessity a period in which a society by implication decides how jobs and earned income will be allocated and, as a corollary, how nonworking groups are to be supported. Thus, when the supply of labor exceeds the manpower needs of the economy, critical questions are posed:

---

[1] Seymour L. Wolfbein, *Changing Patterns of Working Life* (Washington: U. S. Department of Labor, 1963).

(1) Who will comprise the labor force (and what mechanisms will bring about this allocation of jobs), and (2) What portion of the total product is to be available for the nonworking groups (and again, what mechanisms will bring about this distribution of the product)?

In a decentralized economy, decisions as to the allocation of jobs and factor income are not necessarily made on the basis of age. However, the individual firm's hiring and retirement policies have in recent years reflected the gradual rise in unemployment and the consequent pressure to find jobs for younger men. In the mid-1960's retirement is being used as a device for drawing workers out of the labor force and helping to restore the balance between labor supply and what many believe to be restricted labor-force requirements. The current movement toward early retirement, evidenced by labor-union action and by the lowering of eligibility age for OASDI benefits, suggests that the decision is being made to allocate the available jobs to young and middle-aged workers.

Retirement policies designed to reduce labor-force size seem defeatist and unimaginative in comparison with policies aimed at increasing the rate of economic growth and hence providing more jobs. In a full-employment economy the availability of jobs solves many of the economic problems of the aged, first by providing continued employment during their youth and middle age, thereby permitting the accumulation of privately held equities and pension claims, and second, by providing full- or part-time jobs after age sixty-five. Efforts to stimulate aggregate demand, most recently made by a tax reduction, are therefore extremely significant.

The extent to which a given increase in demand induces an increase in employment depends primarily on the *composition* of the demand increase. In certain sectors of the economy, increased output can be produced with very little increase in the work force employed;[2] existing capital facilities are simply utilized more fully. By contrast, a given increase in the demand for services furnishes a greater increase in employment. The substantially larger demand for labor accompanying an increase in the output of services is as-

[2] For a summary of postwar trends in output per man-hour, by industrial sector, and a projection of these trends to 1970 and 1975, see Juanita M. Kreps, C. E. Ferguson, and James M. Folsom, "Labor Force Requirements and Labor Supply," in Kreps (Ed.), *Employment, Income, and Retirement Problems of the Aged* (Durham, N.C.: Duke University Press, 1963).

sociated with productivity differentials; real output per man rose about three and one-half times as fast in the goods sector as in the service sector in the period 1929-1961.[3] Thus, the labor required per unit of output in services will be higher, and a shift in the composition of demand toward services will tend to raise the labor input requirements of aggregate product. As the composition of demand shifts away from goods and toward services, demand-stimulation policies may become more effective in creating jobs. But at present the rate of mechanization, particularly in manufacturing, permits great increases in output with no substantial increases in the manpower required.

Concomitant with this mechanization, certain structural problems have acted to worsen unemployment. Resources made idle by automation in one industry or location do not move easily and swiftly into other uses. Lack of geographical mobility, lack of education and training, insufficient knowledge of job opportunities—all militate against the goal of full employment in the present era. Governmental policy now encompasses programs for retraining and relocating workers. Although most of these programs have not been able to deal to any great extent with the particular employment problems of older workers, there have been some successful ventures on behalf of the older group.[4]

The combination of increasing output per man-hour, which reduces the effectiveness of increased aggregate demand as a means of stimulating employment, and the structural problems involved in transferring workers from one job to another has inevitably led policy makers back to a consideration of measures designed to reduce the labor supply. Obviously, labor supply could be limited by means other than early or compulsory retirement. Further postponement of

[3] An analysis of shifting demand composition and its effect on the demand for labor is made in Joseph J. Spengler, "Today's Circumstances and Yesterday's Theories; Malthus on 'Services'," *Kyklos,* XVIII, 1965, pp. 601-613.

[4] For a discussion of the limited extent to which retraining programs have included older men, see Gerald G. Somers, "Training the Unemployed," to be published in Joseph Becker, S.J., *In Aid of the Unemployed.* A summary of some of the retraining programs which have dealt more successfully with older workers' problems is given in *Increasing Employment Opportunities for the Elderly,* Hearings before the Subcommittee on Employment and Retirement Incomes of the Special Committee on Aging, U. S. Senate, 88th Congress, 1963, statement by Donald P. Kent, pp. 28-30.

entry into the labor force would reduce the number of job applicants; policies which keep young adults in school longer are therefore desirable, not only as a means of restoring the labor demand-labor supply balance but, more importantly, as a means of providing a qualitatively improved labor force for the future. Unfortunately, little attention is being given to the kinds of continued education that are appropriate for today's noncollege youth, although high levels of unemployment, particularly among young men, and acute shortages of certain fairly low-level skills (automobile mechanics, TV repairmen, etc.) have coexisted throughout most of the postwar period. Until more educational resources are devoted to vocational and technical training, qualitative improvements in the labor force might be negligible, even if age of entry were postponed. Finally, a reduction in the workweek or some variation on this idea (such as the "sabbatical" plan negotiated by the United Steelworkers Union) is constantly under discussion.

Regardless of what decisions are made on the allocation of jobs, the corollary question of providing nonfactor income to the retiree, the unemployed, and the young adult in school must be resolved. In the case of earlier retirement it should be noted that, except for private pension plans,[5] no retirement income is now available to workers at age sixty and OASDI benefits, when taken at age sixty-two, are reduced. If early retirement is to be used effectively as a means of reducing the number of job seekers, it will clearly be necessary to provide a stronger (income) incentive to retire.[6]

In summary, the economic problems of the aged in this era are attributable to the demographic and technological nexus which has produced on one hand a rapidly expanded labor force and on the other a pace of mechanization that acts to slow the aggregate demand for labor and to change its composition. Used as an instrument of overall employment policy, current retirement practice therefore reflects the pressure of postwar unemployment. Policies designed to reduce unemployment through the media of increasing aggregate

[5] Joseph Krislov, "Employee-Benefit Plans, 1954-62," *Social Security Bulletin*, 27 (April, 1964), 4-21.

[6] For an analysis of the relation between retirement benefits and willingness to retire, see Margaret Gordon, "Income Security Programs and the Propensity to Retire," in Richard A. Williams, Clark Tibbitts, and Wilma Donahue, *Processes of Aging* (Englewood Cliffs, N.J.: Prentice-Hall, 1963), pp. 436-458.

demand and improving labor-force quality have thus been accompanied by measures designed to lower retirement age and thereby
reduce labor-force size.

II: The Goals and Timing of Social Policy

If persistent unemployment means that retirement age is to be
lowered, or even that most workers must retire at age sixty-five, certain questions arise. First of all, what are the related programs that
need to accompany attempts to induce retirement if these attempts
are to be effective and if the retirees are to share in the national
product? This question poses the paradox of providing incentives
not to work, when throughout most of our history society has been
concerned with providing incentives to work. There are parallels
however, the most obvious one being that of restrictions placed on
farm output. This first question is one of goals. In what measure is
the national product to be shared with nonworking groups, the retirees in particular? A second question has to do with timing. Given
a long period, what social changes may occur that will dictate different policies for the aged? The circumstances of the man who
retires ten years hence may have changed significantly both by
reason of a markedly different economic environment and because
of the changes in his own needs and capacities.

The Goals of Social Policy

Although the overall economic goals of a predominantly
free-enterprise system may be quite clear, policy commitments to
any one group of persons may be only vaguely defined. In this decade and the one past, the primary economic objective has allegedly
been economic growth; price stability and full employment were
also major goals. Emphasis on making the *size* of the national product ever larger, however, has not been paralleled by concern with
the *composition* of this output or with its *distribution*. In one sense
it may be argued that governmental attempts to influence the composition (except, for instance, in wartime) or the distribution of
output conflict with the operation of a free price system. Whatever
the explanation, our growth objective has been justified not on the

basis of providing any particular goods for any particular group of persons, but on the basis that growth raises the standards of living of all.

The fruits of this growth would be shared by all consumers if the increased output resulted in gradually falling prices based on the lowered cost of output. But the downward trend of prices which characterized much of the nineteenth century no longer holds. During the twentieth century productivity gains have been taken mainly in the form of rising money incomes. Under these arrangements, the increased output accrues to the worker and the owner of capital who bring about the increase, but not to the person who is not actively engaged in production. Hence, the economic position of retirees on fixed incomes gradually worsens relative to that of the active population. The wage guidelines indicated by the Council of Economic Advisers, incidentally, endorse the practice of wage increases commensurate with the overall rise in productivity.

This worsening occurs even if price stability is maintained. In fact, the emphasis on increasing the money incomes of the aged commensurately with price rises has only helped to obscure the basic consideration of whether retirees are sharing in the nation's growth in output. A policy of tying social security benefits to the price level, while guaranteeing a fixed real income from this source, permits most of the aged no participation in economic progress and may even discourage broader attempts to liberalize benefits. Only by tying retirement income to the growth in output, rather than to prices, will their relative deterioration in income be prevented.[7]

The goal of extending the gains of growth to retired persons may become merely one part of an economy-wide movement to spread technology's expanding output to nonworking members of society. Just as rising productivity per man-hour speeds up the rate of movement out of the labor force and increases the amount of leisure time, so too this rising productivity increases the quantity of goods and services that must be purchased. As the number and proportion of nonworking adults increase, the problem of distributing the national product becomes more acute. To the extent that insufficient demand (rather than resource constraints) limits total output, failure to apportion money claims to the aged and the unemployed results in

[7] Joseph J. Spengler and Juanita M. Kreps, "Social Credit for the Aged," in Kreps, *op. cit.*

lower levels of output than need be the case. Again, the curious inversion seems to have occurred. In the past it has often been argued that distributing income to persons not at work would reduce economic incentives and lower output. Now there seem to be some grounds for fearing that failure to apportion income to nonworking persons will limit demand and thus lower output.

The difference lies, of course, in the decline in need for certain types of human labor. This decline renders unemployable many of today's workers, and because of their inferior educational and skill levels a large proportion of these are workers approaching retirement age. It is therefore important to consider policies dealing with today's retiree in this particular context of diminished job opportunities and to analyze separately the position of the retiree of a decade hence.

The Timing of Social Policy

It is obvious that the present generation of retired persons has scant opportunity to work, and that in the absence of some shift in policy, the age group sixty to sixty-five will be under pressure to retire altogether at age sixty-five or in many cases to retire earlier. This confusion of retirement policy and unemployment policy encourages today's worker aged sixty-two or over to dilute his social security benefits and accept a reduced private pension, if any. Once he has decided to do so, he is thereafter classified as retired, rather than unemployed, although often he would prefer to continue working.

Two types of policies are suggested for this immediate situation. First, it would be possible to adopt measures which would spread the work differently and in so doing apportion nonworking time among all age groups. By reducing the workweek, for example, or by major efforts aimed at educating and training young persons, it might be possible to reduce the pressure for early or compulsory retirement. Such measures could be viewed either as a means of creating part-time unemployment for a much larger group as opposed to full-time unemployment for older persons or as a mechanism through which all of society is permitted to share in increased leisure. The view one holds of this process depends on whether he prefers goods to leisure or vice versa.

Not only is the question of goods versus leisure at stake, however; with increased productivity some increase in leisure is inevitable. The use of the word *inevitable,* incidentally, belies our reluctance to embrace this non-Calvinistic use of time. At issue also is the question of the temporal distribution of leisure discussed earlier by Professor Spengler. He suggests that a reduction in the number of workweeks per year is preferable to a shortened workweek or workday, and this distribution of leisure would seem to be preferable also to the shortening of work life via early retirement. For one thing, an increase in the length of the annual vacation would surely have great utility to the man who has fifty weeks of work and only two of leisure. It seems likely, also, that the shorter work year would increase the taste for and consumption of various goods and services. Spreading leisure in this manner would then have the effect of raising the demand for labor along with the increase in leisure. Even more important, perhaps, earnings are not interrupted by lengthened vacation, whereas retirement usually brings sudden and sharp curtailment in living standards. Spreading the leisure among the employed members of society has the advantage of lengthening work life (as compared with conferring an ever lengthening period of leisure on the retiree), and hence spreading earnings over a longer portion of life. Since one of the major problems created by the increase in the number of nonworking years is the apportionment of income during these years, measures to prevent further enlargement of the retirement period are appropriate.

In practical terms, however, there may be little hope of staying the pressure for early retirement of workers in the present sixty to sixty-four age group. A long-term reduction in the number of workweeks will not solve today's problem; in fact, in the case of the lengthened vacation period provided for steelworkers, early reports have indicated that very few new jobs have been created. Even a reduced workweek might affect the demand for older workers' services only moderately, given the present level of unemployed younger persons and the likelihood that industry would economize further in the use of labor if labor costs rose.

In this period of unemployment, it would seem important to deal with the unemployed older worker on the same basis we deal with the unemployed of any age group, that is, through unemployment insurance, and to retain retirement benefits for actual retirement which would ideally not occur before age sixty-five, and certainly not before age sixty-two. In so doing it will clearly be necessary to make increased unemployment benefits available for longer periods. Since many states are now reluctant or unable to make any substantial increases in benefits, but instead are attempting to reduce outlays because of diminished reserves, some form of federal supplementary unemployment benefits is needed. Within the framework of unemployment compensation, special attention should be given to the older workers, who suffer long-run unemployment more frequently than younger workers. It may even be necessary to provide something close to permanent benefits to those older workers who have been displaced by technology and who possess low levels of education and skill.

This second type of policy—of "pensioning off" many of the workers in their preretirement decade, through special unemployment insurance arrangements—has the advantage of being a short-run device for meeting what we hope will be a short-run problem. In the longer run, the problem may be eased somewhat whether or not we achieve full employment, as a result of broad social changes and as a result of improvement in the position of the older worker and retiree. Society's gradual acceptance of (and even demand for increases in) the amount of leisure may result from changes now taking place in the composition of the labor force.[8] As Professor Spengler indicates, this tendency will hold only if income is maintained in the retirement period. Moreover, the long-run pressure for early retirement will diminish if the temporal distribution of leisure and the accompanying temporal distribution of income shift in the direction he proposes.

The economic position of the older person, although always likely to be relatively disadvantaged, will surely improve somewhat in time if his retirement claims are not thinned out by financing unemployment during his later working years. Improvement in educational levels should bring improvements in earning capacity and employment stability. Private pension benefits can be expected to grow for certain groups of workers. The increasing use of part-time work-

---

[8] H. L. Wilensky, "Life Cycle, Work Situation, and Participation," in Robert Kleemeier (Ed.), *Aging and Leisure: Research Perspectives on the Meaningful Use of Time* (New York: Oxford University Press, 1961), Chapter 8. See also his "The Uneven Distribution of Leisure," *Social Problems*, 9 (Summer, 1961), 32-56.

ers indicates some willingness on the part of industry to create arrangements whereby older workers as well as other adults can achieve a more nearly optimal distribution of their time between work and leisure. In addition to these sources of long-run improvement, policies designed to spread lifetime earnings more evenly between working and nonworking years, discussed below, would seem appropriate.

III: Policy Constraints and Mechanisms

The problems inherent in providing economic support for the aged are thus in part short-run, even temporary, and in part long-run and permanent. At present the inferior economic status of the aged can be improved only by creating for them better job opportunities or by transferring to them an increased share in the national product. The former requires a solution to the problem of unemployment, and such a solution will not be found immediately. On the contrary, continued unemployment among workers of all ages will surely lend support to the move for early retirement. The latter alternative involves both an increase in the level of social security benefits and provision for supplementary unemployment benefits to those workers who cannot find jobs during, for example, their ten preretirement years.

Early Retirement and Income Maintenance

In the long run the male's full-time participation in the labor force will tend to become more and more concentrated within the middle years, making necessary a gradual increase in the amount of income transferred to nonworking adults (both young and old) and their families. This trend can be slowed, however, by distributing leisure throughout working life rather than lowering retirement age. Union-management contracts providing for longer vacations would serve this purpose, as opposed to current moves to provide earlier pensions. Moreover, governmental provision for unemployment compensation and job training for the older displaced worker would slow the downward pressure on retirement age, which, in the absence of such provision, will come to be sixty rather than sixty-five.

Permitting retirement at, say, age sixty by offering reduced benefits at that age would seem to allow the maximum freedom of individual choice as between goods and leisure. This freedom is illusory, however, if retirement benefits are merely subsistence level and if the worker is *expected* to retire more or less automatically as soon as his pension is available. There is some considerable danger that optional retirement may soon become compulsory retirement in a period of unemployment, and that in concentrating on reducing the labor-force size, the income needs of persons forced into early retirement may not be given adequate consideration. Under the present social security arrangements, the man who retires at age sixty-two with a wife the same age receives a maximum monthly benefit of about $150, as compared with a benefit of $190 if he retires when he and his wife are age sixty-five. He therefore enjoys a benefit increase of more than one-fourth by waiting till age sixty-five to retire.

Given the income levels of today's aged, it seems unlikely that such a reduction in benefits would be elected voluntarily. Extension of reduced benefits to the group aged sixty-two to sixty-four was designed, in fact, for those persons who for reasons other than disability were unable to find substantial employment. The work experience of OASDI beneficiaries indicates that of the beneficiaries aged sixty-two to sixty-four, a smaller proportion work full time than is the case of the beneficiaries aged sixty-five and over. The composition of the younger beneficiary group further reveals characteristics that adversely affect employment opportunities. Nonwhites are about twice and persons in hospitals and nursing homes about four times as prevalent among the sixty-two to sixty-four age male beneficiaries as among the older beneficiary group. Average earnings in the younger group were only $700 in 1962.[9]

Optional early retirement which merely serves the function of providing income to the present group of older workers who cannot find jobs would be acceptable if this policy did not also have the effect of reducing benefits to the group whose retirement income will be extremely low even without such a reduction. If, in addition, industry, unions, and the public adopt the attitude that workers who can claim a reduced OASDI benefit should do so in order to make their jobs available for younger workers, a hardening of the lower

[9] Lenore A. Epstein, *Report No. 2: Work Experience and Earnings of the Aged in 1962* (Washington: Social Security Administration, 1964).

retirement age is likely to ensue. Such a development is undesirable unless it is accompanied by a significant upward revision in benefits.

The Constraints on Income

The short-run costs of providing adequate income for older workers now being squeezed out of the labor force and the long-run costs of raising the benefits paid to retirees (and paying these benefits for a lengthened retirement period) need to be considered with reference to the economic changes now taking place. In particular, the kind of income maintenance program a society can afford for its aged is a function of its level of output and the competing demands of other age groups. If, given the state of technology, businesses do not employ a large proportion of the older people who wish to work, and if social policy is such that these persons are not being encouraged to work, the argument that maintaining too high a retirement income discourages incentives to stay in the labor force is not applicable. Or, to the extent that it is applicable the higher income accomplishes the now desired end of inducing people not to work. Then the only constraints on the income provided the retiree are the constraints placed by aggregate output and the claims of younger members of the society.

In the decade of the fifties the output of goods and services rose from a dollar value of $285 billion in 1950 to an aggregate of $503 billion in 1960. At the beginning of 1965 gross national product was running at a rate of roughly $625 billion. This growth in the nation's output raised the median income of families from $3,319 in 1950 to $5,620 in 1960. In constant (1960) dollars, the median family income rose about 40 percent in the period 1947-1960; this was a rate of growth of about 2½ percent per year. The median income of unrelated individuals rose from $980 in 1947 to $1,720 in 1960. In 1960 the median income for families headed by persons aged sixty-five and over was $2,900, or about half the $5,900 received by families with younger heads. The median for unrelated individuals aged sixty-five and over was $1,100, or about 40 percent of the $2,600 median for younger persons.[10] Later data from the 1963 survey of the aged

[10] U. S. Bureau of the Census, *Current Population Reports, Consumer Income,* "Income of Families and Persons in the United States: 1960," Series P-60, No. 37.

indicate 1962 median incomes of $2,875 for aged couples and $1,130 for aged individuals.[11]

By what order of magnitude might the income of the aged be raised during the present decade, on the assumption that these trends in total output and in median family income continue? Assume, for example, that median real income for all families rises another 45 percent between 1962 and 1975. If the aged are to share in this rise, on the basis of present incomes their median family income would increase to $4,169 and the aged person's median to $1,639 in 1975. Money incomes would have to increase faster to the extent that prices rose. A 45 percent increase in real income during this period would not reduce the disparity in incomes now existing; in fact, since the aged's income base is so much lower, the absolute rise would still allow the young to gain relative to the elderly.

Given the constraint of the assumed growth in real income, the aged's economic position can be further improved only by some re-distribution of the output. This second constraint—the competing demand of younger age groups for the nation's product—is particularly evident at present, as efforts to train and create jobs for youth, to reduce poverty, especially in certain geographical areas, and to raise wage incomes gain momentum. Such programs are of obvious long-run importance to the aged; success in upgrading the skills and earning capacity of today's worker improves his chances of an adequate retirement income. The question of the aged's proper share in the national product nevertheless continues to go unanswered. In the growing volume of literature on the deprived position of the aged vis-à-vis the rest of the population, questions of *how much* of a shift in income is appropriate, or on what basis the income *ought* to be apportioned, are seldom raised.[12]

Proposals for redistributing income are generally viewed with alarm and this opposition persists even when the proposed redistribution is from son (who works and pays OASDI taxes) to father (who is retired). The impersonal tax arrangements by which the

[11] Lenore A. Epstein, "Income of the Aged in 1962: First Findings of the 1963 Survey of the Aged," *Social Security Bulletin*, 27 (March, 1964), 3-35.

[12] The question of income standards is discussed in Lenore A. Epstein, "Income Security Standards in Old Age," a paper presented at the International Gerontological Research Seminar, Markaryd, Sweden, August 6-9, 1963. The issue of public versus private programs for financing income in old age is discussed in Eveline M. Burns, "Public and Private Provision for Income Security in Old Age," a paper presented at the same meeting.

working generation now transfers income to retirees tends to obscure the true nature of intergenerational support. An increase in payroll taxes may be resisted by the worker, although alternatively he may have to supplement his parents' income directly. In either case, a redistribution of income occurs. But the manner of redistribution markedly affects family relationships, particularly living arrangements. Moreover, the aggregate demand for goods is likely to be influenced significantly, intrafamily support, being less predictable, providing a much less stable demand for goods on the part of the aged.

Opposition on the part of middle-aged and younger persons to a higher payroll tax might be reduced if the relation between taxes and benefits were more clearly understood, and if it were further understood that higher benefits would also be available to the present taxpayer when he retires. But even the promise of a higher retirement income would probably fail to convince a majority of persons of the merits of shifting income via taxes, for vast numbers of Americans have traditionally exhibited very high rates of time preference. Usually, the family's demand for goods and service rises faster than income, with the result that personal debt, rather than saving, ensues. Relatively high income families, along with those of moderate means, often overspend their incomes. They are therefore under pressure to collect as much of their income as possible for current consumption. Failure to spread the family's income more evenly over the life-span through private saving and annuity plans indicates the extent of our unwillingness to postpone consumption. It indicates also the wisdom of relying on some form of forced saving (as in a pension plan) or public transfer to provide income for old age.

Consideration of the question of the aged's proper share of the total income may be one indirect result of the attacks now being made on low income groups in general. The Administration's position that incomes below a certain level should not be permitted implies a willingness to take the action necessary to raise these incomes. Capacity to raise incomes is dependent partly on growth of output, but partly also on the willingness to redistribute what is produced. If the public accepts the notion that a family income of less than $3,000 is "too low," it accepts a definition of the minimum extent to which any family shares in a given output. Although the target group includes all families whose incomes are below a certain level, the dis-

152

proportionately large number of older families who are below this level calls attention to this particular group. Families headed by persons age sixty-five and over comprise 34 percent of the families with incomes under $3,000, but only 14 percent of all families.

Until such time as the concept of a minimum income is actually established, or until some other bench marks are drawn indicating the extent to which the aged are to participate in present and future national product, the goal of economic policy for the aged and hence the constraints on this policy remain undefined. Broadly conceived, the goal might be set, as indicated above, in such a way as to insure that the aged share proportionately in future growth of national income, thus making the rate of such growth the only constraint, no redistribution of present incomes being involved. Alternatively, the goal might be the maintenance of some minimum level of real income for all aged persons, with incomes in excess of this minimum being determined by past savings, wage-related benefits, private pension claims, and so on. Setting such minima would involve some redistribution, presumably through general tax revenues, and the establishment of mechanisms through which these minimum incomes would be maintained in the future.

Policy Mechanisms

The media for publicly transferring income to the aged are already established, and there is growing use of private transfers through the medium of pension funds. The expectation that a decade hence only about 25 to 30 percent of the aged population will be receiving private pensions underscores the continued need for reliance on social security benefits, which by 1975 will extend to nine out of ten persons aged sixty-five and over.

In order for the aged to achieve the minimum incomes currently set as the poverty levels, more than 50 percent of the families and about 60 percent of the nonmarried persons would need increases in income. Alternatively, money incomes somewhat lower than the $3,000 per family and $2,000 per individual have been suggested, in part to take account of the fact that an elderly couple has a lower cost of living than a younger family. For an elderly couple, figures of $2,800 and $2,500 have been discussed. If $2,500 for an older couple and $1,800 for a single person are taken as the poverty lines[13]

[13] See Margaret S. Strotz, "The BLS Interim Budget for a Retired Couple," *Monthly Labor Review*, 83 (November, 1960), 1141-1157; Mollie Orshansky,

(which are the approximate amounts required for the Department of Agriculture's *low-cost food* plan, assuming that the elderly couple spends 27 percent of its income for food), a large proportion of the aged would still fall below these incomes. In 1962, two-fifths of the older couples and three-fourths of the single persons would not have sufficient incomes to meet the low-cost standard. Even the Department of Agriculture's *economy plan*, which has been priced at $1,800 for an older couple and $1,300 for an individual, is out of reach of more than one-fourth of the couples and about three-fifths of the older single persons.[14]

"Budget for an Elderly Couple: Interim Revision for the Bureau of Labor Statistics," *Social Security Bulletin*, 23 (December, 1960), 26-36; *idem.*, "Counting the Poor: Another Look at the Poverty Profile," *Social Security Bulletin*, 28 (January, 1965), 3-29; *idem.*, "Technical Note: Estimating Equivalent Incomes or Budget Costs by Family Type," *Monthly Labor Review*, 83 (November, 1960), 1197-1200; Lenore A. Epstein, *Retirement Income and Measures of Need* (Washington: Division of Program Analysis, Social Security Administration, February, 1964).

[14] These figures are based on the aged's income levels according to the 1963 Survey of the Aged, and reported by Lenore A. Epstein in the table below:

SIZE OF MONEY INCOME FOR UNITS AGED 65 AND OVER: PERCENTAGE DISTRIBUTION BY INCOME INTERVAL, 1962

Total Money Income	MARRIED* COUPLES	NONMARRIED PERSONS		
		Total	Men	Women
Number (in thousands):				
Total	5,445	8,731	2,402	6,329
Reporting on income	4,719	7,709	2,173	5,536
Total percent	100	100	100	100
Less than $1,000	5	44	32	49
1,000 - 1,499	10	22	25	21
1,500 - 1,999	14	13	12	13
2,000 - 2,499	13	8	11	7
2,500 - 2,999	12	4	5	3
3,000 - 3,999	16	4	6	3
4,000 - 4,999	11	2	3	1
5,000 - 9,999	15	4	6	3
10,000 and over	5	†	1	†
Median income	$2,875	$1,130	$1,365	$1,015

Source: Social Security Bulletin, 27 (March, 1964), 8.

*With at least 1 member aged 65 or over.

†Less than 0.5 percent.

If a minimum income is to be guaranteed to the aged, the minimum should be set with reference to the acceptable minimum for all families. However, some of the measures by which the minimum might be achieved for younger families would not affect the aged's income. An increase in the minimum wage, for example, would not improve the position of lowest-income elderly, since most of them do not work. Increases in social security benefits and in old-age assistance payments are essential if the extremely low incomes are to be affected. However, the cost of financing such improvements in income should probably be spread broadly, rather than being limited to payroll taxes.

A very rough estimate indicates that the cost of raising the incomes of aged families and individuals to the level necessary for the economy food plan ($1,800 and $1,300) would be about three and one-half billion dollars.[15] The cost of raising the incomes to the low-cost food plan, $2,500 and $1,800, would be something over seven and one-half billion dollars. Approximately three-fifths of the costs involved would arise from payments made to nonbeneficiaries; reliance on an increase in the OASDI tax to carry the cost does not seem necessary. Rather, the cost could be borne in the same way the overall poverty program is financed, that is, from general tax revenues. Or some combination of general revenues and payroll taxes could be utilized.[16]

Once the aged have been guaranteed certain minimum incomes, the problem of providing them some share in the growth of the national product can be met most easily through increases in OASDI

[15] This estimate was made earlier and reported in Kreps, "The Aged Poor," in *Poverty: The Sick, Disabled, and Aged*, published by the U. S. Chamber of Commerce Task Force on Economic Growth and Opportunity, 1965.

[16] A popular technique for making any desired outlay appear feasible is to compare it with the national defense budget. Hence, it can be argued that raising the aged's incomes to the "economy" level would require an expenditure equal to about 6 percent, and raising these incomes to the "low-cost" budget level an expenditure of approximately 14 percent, of the current defense cost. By the same reasoning, the cost of raising the incomes of all families and persons to the $3,000 and $1,500 levels has been estimated at $11 billion, or one-fifth of the defense budget. Perhaps a more meaningful comparison might be made between the cost of a particular program designed to alleviate poverty at home and the cost of foreign aid, which in a general way is aimed at the same goal for underdeveloped countries. If foreign aid expenditures were diverted to expenditures for the aged in this country, most of the cost of raising incomes to the "economy" level would be covered.

benefits which reflect this growth. Since wages rise in rough proportion to productivity growth, the source of some of the revenue for benefits would logically be some proportion of this wage increase. The possibility of financing improved retirement benefits on a tripartite basis, with employers, employees, and public revenues sharing the cost, should be considered.

IV: Summary and Conclusions

Employment opportunities for most persons past the age of sixty-five are scant, and it seems unlikely that these prospects will improve in the near future. Instead, the persistence of long-term unemployment among older workers and current attempts to draw men in their early sixties out of the labor market threaten both the earnings of workers in their preretirement years and the adequacy of benefits received during retirement. The availability of part-time employment for persons in retirement may offer some supplementary income, but the secular decline in labor-force participation of older men is expected to continue. The position of today's aged is particularly disadvantaged because of their relatively poor earnings in the past, resulting in low retirement benefits, because of their low educational levels, resulting in low job aptitudes, and because of the current level of unemployment, which reduces job opportunities for all persons, but particularly the elderly.

Movements toward earlier retirement age, being attempts to alleviate the *present* problem of unemployment, are in reality attempts to reclassify the older unemployed worker as retired, whether or not an adequate retirement income is available. There is some danger that in this attempt a new class of *future* aged poor will be created. These early retirees will not only have meager private resources, they will also suffer reduced monthly benefits which then must sustain them during longer periods of retirement. Alternatively, it would be possible to provide unemployment benefits or some other form of transfer to these marginal workers until they can qualify for retirement benefits at age sixty-five, and thereby maintain for them their maximum income during actual retirement. These temporary measures would ease the aged's present difficulties but would not create future problems.

Decision as to the appropriate retirement age is but one aspect of the larger question raised by Professor Spengler: what is the best temporal distribution of leisure? Increased leisure, made possible by the growth in productivity, can be apportioned over the work life rather than being concentrated in a longer retirement period. The advantages of such an apportionment are at least twofold: (1) leisure in the form of longer vacations is likely to have a greater utility than leisure in the form of extended retirement (and may well raise the level of demand for goods and services), and (2) earnings are distributed more evenly over the life span.

Even if the present problem of unemployment is treated as unemployment and early retirement is resisted, the future incomes of persons aged sixty-five and over will be maintained at an adequate level only after certain fundamental decisions are made regarding (1) the minimum income, if any, which society intends for all its members, including the aged, and (2) the extent to which nonworking groups are to share in the fruits of economic growth. The first of these questions is far from being resolved, but past measures such as the minimum wage laws, and current discussions, particularly those surrounding the poverty program, reflect a view that incomes below certain minima are unacceptable. The second question has received very little attention, although the economic future of the aged rests in its resolution.

The primary constraint placed on income maintenance programs is of course the size of the national product; to date, no method has been discovered that would enable an economy to confer on its members more goods and services than it produces. However, if the income in question is that of a particular group in the economy, obviously the further constraint of the needs of other groups also applies. Since there are competing needs, defense of higher transfers of income to the aged rests upon the present disparities between the incomes of the aged and those of younger persons, and on the inability of the aged, in most cases, to find jobs.

If the gains from technological progress are to be taken partly in the form of increased leisure, and if a good bit of this leisure is to accrue to mankind during his later years, it is necessary to spread man's ever-growing income over a longer life-span, which includes an increasing number of nonworking years. Allotting the aged person an increased span of leisure without also allotting him adequate income converts leisure from a utility to a disutility and makes retirement synonymous with unemployment. Within the overall constraints of total income and total needs, the temporal distribution of both leisure and income needs to be reappraised.

BIOGRAPHICAL NOTE

JUANITA M. KREPS was educated at Berea College and Duke University (M.A. and Ph.D.). Mrs. Kreps has taught at Denison University, Hofstra College, Queens College in New York, and was a Bryan Lecturer in Economics at the University of North Carolina at Greensboro. She is currently an Associate Professor of Economics at Duke University; a member of the Board of Directors and vice-chairman of the Committee on Employment and Retirement, the National Council on the Aging; consultant and member of the Special Task Force on Older Workers of the Office of Economic Opportunity. Mrs. Kreps coauthored *Principles of Economics;* edited and contributed to *Employment, Income, and Retirement Problems of the Aged;* wrote "The Economics of Intergenerational Relationships," in *Social Structure and the Family: Generational Relations;* and (with Joseph J. Spengler) wrote "The Leisure Component of Economic Growth" for the President's Commission on Technology, Automation, and Economic Progress.

6

Federal and State Programming

John G. Turnbull

I

We start with the oft-used statement, "The economically insecure aged constitute an overhead cost to society." By this we mean
simply that if these aged are unable to maintain themselves, society
must; we have no magic elixir for making them or their problems disappear.

Who are these aged? From what groups are they constituted?
In an abstract sense they can be viewed as all those not able to
maintain themselves from their current labor-market earnings (since
in the absence of such earnings alternative forms of maintenance
must be found), or as those who do not have sufficient alternative
incomes. In the institutional sense they might be described as those
sixty-five and over (or increasingly sixty-two or sixty and over). This
classification by age may appear to be artificial, but it is convenient,
as well as "realistic," since nearly all alternative forms of maintenance
recognize it.

Society must make various choices concerning these aged and
their maintenance. It must decide, for example, through the delibera-
tions of business enterprises in the "private sector" of society, what
actions will be taken with respect to the ages through which an individual will be permitted to remain in employment or, conversely,
when he will be required to retire. It must decide, for example, in
the "public sector," whether the government will underwrite a program providing alternative income maintenance for these aged.

In short, it is required that policy be formulated regarding the
aged and, in this case, their economic problems: those of mainte-

nance in "old age." Society has evolved such policy; in following the usage of this volume we may note that "social policies" have been developed and are to be found in both the public sector and in the private. In turn, these policies have been implemented by programs of various kinds.

II

Let us look briefly at the configurations of old-age policies and programs in the United States. We shall do this under a number of headings.[1]

1. The maintenance problems of the aged, specifically those of income, upon which we shall focus from now on, may be approached through two major routes: the preventive and the alleviative. In the former case one "prevents" the undesirable insecurity (the loss of income) from occurring; this is done by permitting the aged person to continue to work and hence to earn the necessary income with which to maintain himself. In the latter, the alleviative case, job separation takes place and some type of substitute or nonfactor income must therefore be provided so as to permit maintenance.

In the United States we have largely followed the alleviative route for a variety of reasons—some economic, such as the "lump of labor" notion, which holds that only so many jobs exist and the way to get youngsters into them is to retire the oldsters, and some noneconomic, such as the cultural belief that the older person is entitled to spend his declining years in retirement, which is contradicted by another belief that one should be permitted to work if he is willing and able, irrespective of age. Retirement tends to be compulsory in this country; this feature, coupled with other factors, such as the inability of many aged persons to work because of illness, has tended to minimize the preventive approach. Hence, we find in the United States primary emphasis upon alleviative programs (i.e., substitute income programs) as the means by which policy toward the aged is implemented.

The first point to note, then, is that current social policy encour-

[1] For a useful volume on many of the topics discussed in this paper, see Juanita M. Kreps (Ed.), *Employment, Income and Retirement Problems of the Aged* (Durham, N.C.: Duke University Press, 1963).

ages, in fact, in many cases compels, retirement. This is true in the first instance in the employment relationship; whether the employer is a public agency or a private business enterprise, fixed retirement ages are the rule. It holds also for retirement income programs; with some exceptions benefits are not paid unless retirement occurs. Whether this is desirable social policy—economically and psychologically—is another matter; the papers by Joseph Spengler and Juanita Kreps elsewhere in this volume point out clearly the reasons for the development of present policy.

2. Various sectors, such as the public and the private, might be expected to adopt policies with regard to the aged, and to implement these policies with specific programs. This is, in fact, what has taken place. The public sector, that is, government, has come over the last quarter-century to accept the responsibility of providing a "floor of income-maintenance protection" for the aged. In turn, the private sector is assumed to bear the obligation for building upon this floor, whether through group means, such as provided at the place of employment, or through individual methods, such as the personal annuity.

Current social policy has placed a responsibility on both public and private sectors for income maintenance programs in old age—the former in providing a floor of protection, the latter in providing a covering upon the floor. Social policy has not crystallized to the point where one can say with certainty how much income maintenance both sectors should provide. The "minimum budget" comes as close as any currently used criterion, and the accomplishments of public and private programs tend to be assessed against this standard. It can be argued that the goal of social policy should be to provide an adequate rather than a minimum standard. But at present this remains a goal.

3. Given the pluralistic economic and political philosophy of the United States, it is not surprising that the programs that have evolved to implement policies toward the aged are a complex combination of public and private, with, in turn, many diverse forms in each sector.

With these general observations behind us, let us examine in detail the pattern of programs for the aged currently existing in this country. We shall postpone until the conclusion our evaluation of the overall system and we shall need to specify our criteria for this.

III

The preventive approach in this country (that is, of keeping the aged at work) is both contradictory in nature and limited in practice; probably the latter is true because of the former. We commented above upon several facets of this problem; here we might inquire more thoroughly, supplementing briefly the more detailed economic analysis presented in this volume by Juanita Kreps.

At least two kinds of contradictions appear in the preventive approach. The first is pragmatic. On the one hand it involves a belief that those who want to work should be entitled to, irrespective of age. On the other, it faces the realistic limitation that many of the aged are unable to work because of physical or mental incapacities. Hence, "voluntary" retirement operates in important ways.

The second is more of a cultural myth, although it is not a smaller constraint. As noted above, a good deal of lip service is given to the right of the older person to work if he is willing and able. But at the same time compelling factors are at work which tend to lead to involuntary retirement (for an unwillingness to use the services of the aged), not the least of which are, on the one hand, the "lump of labor" thesis and, on the other, the administrative simplicity of the fixed-age retirement practice.

Hence, on both counts, one finds that providing for old age by continued employment is not common (though it is surprising, perhaps, how much does occur). In 1964, for example, there were more than three million persons aged sixty-five and over in the civilian labor force, of which approximately three million were employed, over a hundred thousand unemployed. Nearly fourteen million were not in the labor force. This is a participation rate of about a third of that of the population at large. Moreover, a high percentage of such employment tends to be part-time. Nevertheless, nearly 20 percent of those sixty-five and over provided for part of their maintenance by continued employment.[2]

[2] See Erdman Palmore, "Work Experience and Earnings of the Aged in 1962: Findings of the 1963 Survey of the Aged," *Social Security Bulletin*, 27 (June, 1964), 3-14, 44.

Given this kind of work-limitation philosophy, it is not unexpected that we have no federal or state programs which, in effect, require that a person be permitted to work as long as he wishes and as long as he is capable of meeting such minimum production standards as the employer may impose. Eleven states do have laws which prohibit employment discrimination on the basis of age. But seven of these laws set sixty-five as the top age, and the others are couched in language which gives the employer flexibility in his operations: he *can* set standards as long as they are neither unreasonable nor arbitrary. Insofar as the older worker cannot meet such requirements, he is not discriminated against in hiring or retention if refused work; the basis is not age, but performance.

Hence, the impacts of all these forces emphasize the alleviative route—the substitute or nonfactor income stream approach—and this, in fact, is the major path currently followed in the United States.

IV

A series of basic principles underlies the substitute income maintenance system currently in effect in this country.

1. The system is pluralistic in nature: a floor of protection provided by government, and incremental coverings afforded by private group and private individual plans. Moreover, within each of these categories, pluralism exists. In the government sector there is a basic federal program (OASDI), but there are other programs covering special groups of employees (in some of which the government is an employer): railroads, civil service, the military, as well as a plethora of separate plans at the state, county, and municipal levels. In addition, old-age assistance and public assistance provide residual forms of maintenance. In the private sector a vast miscellany is also to be found. The price paid for this diversity is the existence of a series of gaps and overlaps in the protection afforded given individuals, as well as individual income maintenance arising from many sources rather than from a unified program.

2. With the exception of private individual programs exemplified by the individual purchase of an annuity, the plans are all employment-related: the protection is provided at the place of work and through the employment nexus. We have no "universal" pension

system such as exists in certain other countries. The income stream at (and after) retirement is intended as a substitute for foregone wage and salary income; and it is the contributions (or deductions) from the wage and salary stream made during work life which provide the old-age income. Thus, the employment relationship is an important focal point in retirement income programming.

3. Current programs involve a "time lock," that is, the individual must have been covered under the plan for a certain period of time before he is eligible for benefits. In some instances the time lock is on an all-or-nothing basis. Under OASDI the individual must meet the forty-quarter (or, alternatively, the one-in-four) rule; failing this, he receives neither benefits nor a refund. In other cases, benefits (or refunds) are graded on the basis of the length of time a person has been covered with some prescribed minimum time lock for benefits. There is an actuarial logic in relating benefits to contributions. However, the all-or-nothing basis is less compelling, though there is an interesting ethic revolving about the length of labor-force attachment and the obligation society has in providing substitute income.

4. Again, with the exception of individual plans, old-age income programs are contributory in nature. This means simply that both employer *and* employee make payments on the old-age account. Technically it is true that the majority of group plans are noncontributory. But if one views employer contributions (or the employee's portion thereof) as wages or a wage increase taken in a different form, the underlying "monetary contribution" thesis is still valid. Various reasons have been suggested for the contributory principle, ranging from the economic (a greater income can be provided) to the operational (greater interest and watchfulness will be exhibited by those covered).

5. Benefits are wage- and salary-related, again excepting individual plans. In part, this is a matter of in-payments. Insofar as contributions are a percentage of wages and salaries one would expect the higher the wage or salary (to some maximum), the greater the contribution; hence, the higher the benefits. However, benefits do not tend to be related to wages and salaries on a one-to-one basis, particularly in public programs. Benefit payments involve a loading in favor of the lower wage and salary groups. For example, in 1966, the minimum individual Old-Age and Survivors Insurance retirement benefit (at age sixty-five) was not $1.00 or $10.00 but $44.00.

6. There is a mixture of compulsion and voluntarism in all programs. Public programs tend to be compulsory—one has no option as to coverage and contributions, although even here some exceptions are to be found, as in the coverage of ministers under OASDI. Negotiated private group programs have a voluntary characteristic at their introduction; in these collectively bargained plans, for example, the union *can* choose to include it in its demands. But once a plan is agreed upon, future employees may have no option. Individual plans, of course, maximize voluntarism; one is free to purchase or not to purchase an annuity or to seek to provide protection in other ways.

V

Governmental assumption of the responsibility for providing a floor of income maintenance in old age was formalized with the passage of the Social Security Act in 1935. One of the titles in this Act—in addition to those providing for categorical grants-in-aid and unemployment insurance—set up a system of old-age insurance benefits.[3]

Before the twentieth century, government assistance to the aged consisted almost entirely of direct provision of services, as through the "old-folks home." A few states made cash grants to the needy aged in the first thirty years of this century, but it was not until the Social Security Act that the federal government entered the picture on an economy-wide basis. In turn, social insurance plans for the aged originally took the form of retirement plans for persons rendering service to the government. The Social Security Act altered this and provided for a formalized old-age "insurance" system and an old-age "assistance" program (to be discussed later).

Let us look systematically at the OASDI system.

---

[3] The Act has been amended variously since 1935 and currently includes "disability" and old-age "health" protection. Hence, the abbreviation one most frequently sees is OASDI or Old-Age, Survivors, and Disability Insurance. Although the abbreviation OASI is sometimes used for the old-age and survivors portion of the program (as in the OASI trust fund), we shall employ the more common term, OASDI. It should be noted, however, that we are dealing only with the old-age income maintenance portion of the program, irrespective of the abbreviation. (With the enactment of "health" insurance for the aged in 1965, the full abbreviation becomes OASDHI. We shall still use OASDI herein.)

Basic nature. OASDI is a social insurance system (some would suggest social "assurance"), compulsory in nature (with certain exceptions to be noted), operating through the employment nexus (i.e., you cannot obtain coverage merely by sending a premium payment to the government), involving contributions by both employer and employee or by only one if self-employed (based upon a percentage of payroll up to the taxable maximum), and providing, for those qualified, retirement benefits at sixty-five (or sixty-two at reduced rates) as well as supplementary, survivor, and disability benefits (the latter of which are of minor relevance here). The 1965 health-insurance protection for the aged will become increasingly important.

Coverage. Coverage was restricted in early years to limited groups for a variety of reasons: administrative, economic, political, and others. With successive amendments, coverage has widened to the point where it is becoming universal. Up to 1965, work as a self-employed doctor of medicine was the only principal exclusion, aside from employment in federal jobs covered by a federal staff retirement system. However, amendments enacted in 1965 brought physicians also under the Act. Certain categories of employees are given the option of coverage: ministers and members of religious orders, employees of nonprofit organizations, and employees of state and local governments. In general, in the first case, an individual option is involved; in the latter, it is a group choice. In addition, where state and local governments are involved, a voluntary agreement must be entered into between the federal government and the other political unit. If current coverage were to continue and expand, it is estimated that 95 percent of those sixty-five and over would be eligible for benefits by the year 2000 and approximately 90 percent by 1975.

Qualifications for retirement benefits. One must reach sixty-five, or sixty-two with reduced benefits, and nominally retire, in the sense that earnings "limitations" apply until age seventy-two. But while these are necessary conditions, they are not sufficient; for certain requirements precedent must have been met. There are the time-lock factors we noted previously, and they require that the individual must have been in covered employment for a certain period of time. As the law read in 1965, a worker who reached sixty-five, or sixty-two for women, in 1957 will need credit for one-and-one-half years of covered payment; by 1991 or later, ten years will be required. No one is fully insured with credit for less than one-and-one-half years of work, and no one needs more than ten years of work to acquire this status. These requirements represent complex decisions designed on the one hand to extend the floor of protection as widely as possible but on the other to preserve some semblance of an "insurance" system, or to differentiate the program from one which provides a "pension" to all who reach a specified age.

Benefit levels. Currently (1966), the primary insurance benefit minimum is $44.00 a month, the maximum, $168.00 (both for retirement at age sixty-five). Supplemental payments are also provided; the wife (age sixty-five) of a primary beneficiary will receive $22.00 if the primary benefit is $44.00, and $84.00 if the primary benefit is $168.00. Actuarially reduced benefits apply in cases of retirement at sixty-two.

The entire benefit structure is wage-related. The minimum benefit noted above is payable to an individual whose average yearly earnings after 1950 were $800 or less; the maximum, to one whose earnings were $6,600. In general, the principle applied is that one's benefits are related to one's average taxable earnings under social security. Certain low-earning years may be excluded, but this does not negate the principle.

Various formulas have been used to apply to earnings so as to compute benefits. At present, tables are used for this purpose, but they are based upon a formula that provides a weighting (or loading) in favor of the lower-earnings group. Congress has periodically raised the benefit structure to adjust payments to increases in the cost of living. Taking into account the increase in the tax base and hence taxable wages upon which benefits are based, benefits have kept pace with price level increases until recently. However, the increases have not been automatic in the sense of being tied to some price index (as are certain other plans discussed below); rather, they have required congressional action in each instance. But since such action has occurred only periodically, there have been short-term lags, one of which the benefit structure is currently facing.

Financing. OASDI is financed by means of employer and employee contributions. The tax was 1.0 percent each in 1937; currently it is 4.2 percent each (6.15 percent for the self-employed); and in 1968 the current schedule calls for a rate of 4.4 percent (6.4 for the self-employed). Of the 4.2 percent rate currently in effect, .35 percent is to finance the hospital benefits included under OASDI.

The tax base upon which these rates are levied was $3,600 from 1937-1954; for 1955-1958, $4,200; for 1959-1965, $4,800; and from 1966 on, $6,600. Unlike the tax structure, which is scheduled for another step increase in 1967 (and another in 1969), the tax base has no built-in schedule increase.

The amount and timing of increases in the tax base and tax structure represent judgments reflecting a series of factors: on the one hand, the "actuarial" need for increases given increased coverage and, more importantly, the rising benefit schedules; on the other hand, the desire to avoid the adverse economic and political impacts of sudden and marked changes. This approach is considered feasible since benefit payments are considerably lower now than they are expected to be in the future. Over the years, in-payments have exceeded benefits with the result that an OASI trust fund (invested in U. S. Government obligations) has been built up; in recent years the fund has approximated $19 billion. This fund is technically not the equivalent of the "reserve" of a private insurance carrier. For example, had OASI been terminated in 1960, the $20 billion in the trust fund would not have been sufficient to pay the approximately $82.5 billion current value of old-age and survivor benefits to current recipients. However, since it is not anticipated that the system will discontinue operations, the analogy to a private sector counterpart is not necessarily relevant.[4]

Administration. OASDI is administered by the Social Security Administration, which is a component part of the U. S. Department of Health, Education, and Welfare. Tax collection and trust fund supervision are administered separately, essentially through the Treasury Department. The Social Security Administration has regional and district offices located throughout the country. Well-defined procedures have been established for record keeping, benefit application and payment, and like matters.

[4] For a detailed discussion see Robert J. Myers, *Actuarial Cost Estimates and Summary of Provisions of the Old-Age, Survivors, and Disability Insurance System as Modified by the Social Security Amendments of 1961* (Washington: U. S. Government Printing Office, 1961).

Operational details. Tables 6-1, 6-2, and 6-3 present selected data with respect to the income maintenance aspects of OASDI. The tables do not require elaboration, though one or two additional factors may be mentioned.

TABLE 6-1

NUMBERS OF BENEFICIARIES AND AMOUNTS OF
BENEFITS PAID AT END OF YEAR, 1940 AND 1964

YEAR	NUMBER OF BENEFICIARIES IN CURRENT STATUS AT END OF PERIOD[1]			OLD-AGE AND SUPPLEMENTARY BENEFITS (IN MILLIONS) IN CURRENT STATUS AT END OF PERIOD[1]		
	Total	Old-Age	Wife (Husband) Children (Supplementary Beneficiaries)[2]	Total	Old-Age	Wife (Husband) Children (Supplementary Benefits)
1940	149,000	112,000	37,000	17.2	14.8	2.4
1966 (Jan.)	14,381,000	10,182,000	4,199,000	$14,496.0[3]	$10,262.0[3]	$4,234.0[3]

Source: Social Security Bulletin, Annual Statistical Supplement, 1962, pp. 27 and 73; *Social Security Bulletin,* October, 1964, p. 37.

[1]These are "current-payment" status figures, that is, the numbers of beneficiaries receiving payment at the end of the period in question. The "total" number of beneficiaries would be larger; the average (presented in Table 6-2) lower.

[2]Estimates made by the writer. This section of Table 6-1 indicates for 1940, for example, that 112,000 retired workers were receiving primary benefits at the year's end and, in addition, a total of 37,000 wives and children of these retirants were receiving supplementary benefits. Thus, in effect, 112,000 persons plus members of their families were receiving income maintenance monies as a matter of right.

[3]Estimates made by the writer.

Table 6-1 includes income maintenance data for the retired worker and his family *if and only if* the retirant were still living. If

TABLE 6-2

CASH BENEFITS AND BENEFICIARIES UNDER SOCIAL
INSURANCE PROGRAMS, 1940 AND 1962[1]

Year	Total Amount of Benefits (in thousands) OASDI	Beneficiaries (monthly averages) OASDI
1940	$ 17,152	77,200
1963	10,794,622	13,038,100

Source: Social Security Bulletin, Annual Statistical Supplement, 1962, p. 6.

[1]Does not include disability data.

TABLE 6-3

AVERAGE MONTHLY BENEFITS BY TYPE OF
BENEFICIARY, 1940 AND 1964

Beneficiary	Average Benefits in Current-Payment Status at End of Period		Average Benefits Awarded During Period[1]	
	1940	1965 (Dec.)	1940	1965 (Dec.)
Aged individuals				
Retired workers	$22.60	$83.92	$22.71	$88.25
Wives or husbands	12.13	43.63	12.15	43.53
Widows or widowers	20.28	73.75	20.36	73.11
Parents	13.09	76.03	13.09	85.23
Children of retired workers	9.70	32.06	10.60	40.68

Source: Social Security Bulletin, April, 1966, pp. 55-56.

[1]Average benefits awarded during the period tend, with some exceptions to be
higher than benefits in current-payment status, since the former are calculated on
more recent wage experience, and insofar as wages increased throughout this period,
they are as expected. (This is apart from any changes in the law which influenced
benefits — changes such as increases in the tax base.)

one is interested in the income maintenance problems of the widow or widower (and family) of said worker, the figures must be adjusted upwards since benefits also are payable to those living persons. A 20 percent increase in the number of recipients and a 15 percent increase in total payments would approximate the additional income maintenance provided were widows, widowers, and their families to be taken into account.

What percentage of the aged receive income maintenance assistance via OASDI benefits? In 1940, the number was seven per 1,000 of those sixty-five and over; by 1950, it had reached 164; by 1960, 616; by 1962, 674; and currently it is over 700.[5]

A concluding comment. We shall discuss more fully in the concluding section the role of OASDI in meeting the budgetary needs (the income maintenance problems) of the aged. For the moment, let us note impressionistically that it does provide a floor of protection.

VI

The other public programs paying retirement benefits as a matter of right include the following: (1) railroad retirement; (2) public employee retirement, including (a) Federal Civil Service, (b) other federal employee, and (c) state and local government; and (3) veterans' program. In the first of these, the government is not an employer; in the next three it is; and in the last, it can be viewed as a former employer.

These programs are a conglomeration of varying kinds, but a number of generalizations can be made about them.

1. In some cases they tend to be closer actuarially to private insurance than is OASDI; in other instances, there is an even greater degree of social "assurance" than some analysts use to characterize OASDI. This is perhaps a euphemistic way of stating that some plans have been financially unstable in terms of unfunded obligations. The situation has improved markedly through the years, but these unfunded obligations have loomed large at times.

[5] *Social Security Bulletin, Annual Statistical Supplement 1962* (Washington: U. S. Government Printing Office, 1962), p. 13.

2. Like OASDI, the plans are provided through the employment relationship. Coverage is compulsory for the employee.

TABLE 6-4

CASH BENEFITS AND BENEFICIARIES UNDER SOCIAL INSURANCE AND VETERANS PROGRAM, BY RISK AND PROGRAM, 1940 AND 1962

	Amount of Benefits (in thousands)		Beneficiaries (in thousands)[1]	
	1940	1962	1940	1962
Retirement	$330,819	$13,374,952[2]		
OASDI	17,150	10,161,892	77.2	12,248.2[3]
Railroad retirement	83,342	638,350	102.0	474.1
Public employee retirement	206,210	2,542,983	193.8	1,214.5
Federal Civil Service	49,069	659,664	47.4	304.0
Other federal employee	54,141	743,319	33.4	245.4
State and local government	103,000	1,140,000	113.0	665.0
Veterans' program	24,117	31,727	33.8	24.3

Source: Social Security Bulletin, Annual Statistical Supplement, 1962, p. 6.

[1] For OASDI, average monthly number; for others, number on rolls June 30.

[2] In 1965 this had increased to $16,368,000.

[3] In 1965 this had increased to $14,177,000.

3. Qualifications for benefits tend to be less restrictive in certain ways than under OASDI. For example, under the Civil Service Retirement Act of 1962, an employee can retire at age sixty-two after five years of service with a full annuity terminating at death, or at age sixty with thirty years' service. Retirement programs for policemen and firemen frequently permit retirement with full benefits at even earlier ages, such as sixty or fifty-five. Here retirement tends to be a function of length of service, such as twenty-five years.

4. Benefit levels tend to be higher than under OASDI. This is to be expected since OASDI is viewed as affording a floor of protection, while the programs in question are frequently not only the floor but also the coverings upon it. In the case of the railroads, the government is not an employer, but this program is not supplemented by

private group plans. In all other instances, the government is an employer—present or past. (One of the reasons why certain groups of public employees have been reluctant to have their agencies enter voluntary coverage agreements under OASDI is the fear of benefit dilution, as well as qualification tightening.)

As an example of a benefit structure, in the Federal Civil Service, the maximum annuity an individual can obtain is 80 percent of "average" salary (highest average annual basic salary during any five consecutive years). This compares with a current flat primary benefit high of $168 under OASDI, granted that supplementary benefits could double that total. Survivor benefits tend to be available, commonly for the spouse whether death is before or after retirement, less commonly for children.

One innovation introduced in the Civil Service Retirement Act of 1962, and subsequently in military retirement, is the automatic cost of living increases in annuities. This was the first provision in federal law tying benefit amounts to living costs. Annuities are to be adjusted upward whenever a cumulative rise of at least 3 percent in living costs occurs. The adjustment is based upon the actual increase, rounded to the nearest $\frac{1}{10}$ of 1 percent. The effective date is April 1 of the year following the comparison years. Thus April 1, 1965, would be the effective date for an increase if a comparison of 1964 with 1963 showed a 3 percent or greater increase. The amount of annuity increase will reflect the living cost increase. On the benefit side, this provision reflects the "variable annuity" approach (discussed below), but the method of financing is quite different.

5. Financing is customarily joint, with both employer and employee contributing. Contribution rates tend to be higher than under OASDI (which is one reason for the higher benefit structure). For example, Federal Civil Service rates are 6½ percent of basic salary each for employer and employee, compared with 4.2 percent under OASDI. It is true that included in the OASDI rate there is a .35 percent health-insurance charge, but the comparison is not completely inappropriate.

Since OASDI is a nationwide program, vesting is not a basic problem. (Vesting involves giving employees with a certain number of years of service the right to draw benefits at retirement age whether or not they stay with the company until then.) Most other public programs provide some kind of vesting, or alternatively, contribution refunds. For example, with less than five years of service, plans permit a refund of accumulated contributions, although employer contributions are not necessarily refunded in all cases. With more than five years, or some variant thereof, a choice of a refund or a deferred annuity may be given.

6. Administration is undertaken by a plethora of units of varying kinds, customarily involving some type of retirement board. Some program interchanges are found at the federal level. A worker with less than 120 months of railroad service has his earnings for railroad work after 1936 considered in computing OASDI payments. With at least 120 months of railroad service he could receive benefits under both railroad retirement and OASDI, providing he has additionally qualified under the latter. Military service is computed directly after 1956 for OASDI; after September 15, 1940, and before 1957, OASDI credits of $160 a month may be given under certain circumstances.

7. Operational data for various public systems for the years 1940 and 1962 are shown in Table 6-4, with OASDI included for comparative purposes. Two items stand out in this table: (1) the sizable increase over a quarter-century in the income payments made on account of the aged, and (2) the very marked increase in the importance of OASDI in the income maintenance system.

Again we shall defer evaluation until the concluding section.

VII

Private income maintenance programs provide the covering upon the OASDI floor of protection. The covering arises from two sources: (1) group plans customarily provided through the employment relationship, and (2) individual policies.

Contrary to the fears of some, public insurance programming has not driven private enterprise from the field, but probably has acted as a stimulus to the growth of such plans. Certainly, as we shall see shortly, the increase in protection has been sizable.

VIII

Group plans providing income maintenance during retirement can be characterized simply: they are—irrespective of variations in detail—"mass merchandized," which makes them economical. Dollar for dollar, they provide more income than individual plans (or conversely, a dollar of retirement income can be purchased more cheaply), simply because one "sale" covers many individuals.

Group plans are found in a variety of employment relations. They may cover the employees of one employer, or they may involve the employees of a number of employers. Examples of the latter include the plans of the International Brotherhood of Electrical Workers, the United Mine Workers of America, and the respective employers with whom they bargain collectively.[6]

Group pension plans—on an insured basis—go back to the early 1920's and, in turn, arose out of experiences with group life-insurance programs initiated in 1910-1912 by Montgomery Ward and Company.[7] These early plans (up to World War II) were largely introduced unilaterally by employers, that is, they did not result from collective bargaining. The major impetus toward expanded growth arose from union interest in and pressure for retirement programs initiated during and after World War II. Two factors aided this development: (1) the establishment of the United Mine Workers Retirement Plan, which became effective in 1947 and provided benefits of $100 per month to workers aged sixty who had completed twenty years of service; and (2) the decisions by the National Labor Relations Board and the courts in the Inland Steel case (circa 1947-1949) in which pensions, among other health and welfare plans, were held to be issues subject to collective bargaining.

Let us now look at such programs in the same way as we did OASDI.

Coverage. A recent survey indicates that in 1962 some 23.1 million private sector wage and salary workers were covered under employee-benefit retirement plans.[8] This constitutes 45 percent coverage of wage and salary workers in private industry, compared with 31 percent in 1954. Coverage tends to be compulsory for all employees in the employing unit and starts either upon completion of a

[6] See Joseph J. Melone, *Collectively Bargained Multi-Employer Pension Plans* (Homewood, Ill.: Irwin, 1963).

[7] See Louise Wolters Ilse, *Group Insurance and Employee Retirement Plans* (Englewood Cliffs, N. J.: Prentice-Hall, 1953), Chapter II.

[8] See Joseph Krislov, "Employee Benefit Plans, 1954-62," *Social Security Bulletin,* 27 (April, 1964), 6.

probationary period or some time thereafter, such as after the completion of a year of employment.

Qualifications for benefits. For rank-and-file employees, two conditions must be met in order to qualify for benefits. First, the employee must have reached "retirement" age. Sixty-five is the age most commonly specified ("normal" retirement). "Compulsory" retirement—at a later age such as sixty-eight or seventy—is also provided for in some situations, but the employee's right to continue working to such ages is almost without exception at the discretion of the company. "Early" retirement—at sixty-two, sixty, or even fifty-five —is becoming increasingly more common.[9] This trend is a consequence, in part, of taking productivity gains in the form of earlier separation from employment, and hence of increased leisure in one's advanced years. But it is also a reflection of the "lump of labor" thesis: that one way to provide younger people with jobs is to get older people out of them.

Second, the employee must have had a certain number of years of service with the company. Fifteen years is the most frequent figure, although ten is becoming increasingly common; to the contrary, twenty is found in a number of plans.

Benefit levels. Benefits are commonly calculated using one of the following:

(1) The "money purchase" formula, in which the benefit is that amount which can be provided on the basis of an annual contribution to the plan equal to a percentage of the employee's earnings. This plan is not common, in part because the benefits are difficult to "explain," and in part, because they decrease rapidly as the age of the entrant increases.

(2) The "definite or unit benefit" formula, in which the benefit is a flat amount for all retirants or more commonly a specified function of age, service, earnings, or some combination of these. An example would be 1 percent of average monthly earnings during the

[9] A U. S. Department of Labor survey covering 15,818 private retirement plans embracing 15.6 million employees found that 13,000 plans covering 12 million employees provided for early retirement. See Walter W. Kolodrubetz, "Early Retirement Provisions in Private Pension Plans," *Monthly Labor Review*, 87 (October, 1964), 1165-1170.

last 120 months or $2.60 times the number of years of service up to thirty-five.

(Early retirement is usually accompanied by a reduction in the pension unless one of the purposes is to get the employee out of the labor force, in which case a higher benefit may be payable. We shall treat this shortly.)

OASDI benefits tend to be integrated in one way or another with private payments. Various alternatives are used here: (1) deduct social security benefits from the private pension benefit, (2) exclude earnings under $4,800 or $6,600 from the private plan, or (3) apply a smaller rate of benefit to the earnings under $4,800 or $6,600.[10]

Current benefit levels (for rank-and-file employees) show wide variations, with $75 a month being a common figure. However, the automobile contract settlements of late 1964 show considerably higher benefits. For example, the revision of the Chrysler Corporation plan provides for a payment of $4.25 a month (*in addition* to OASDI benefits) for each year of service. Thus, a thirty years' service retirant (age sixty-five) would receive $127.50 per month, the highest figure in any basic industry at that time.

In this plan, however, a special incentive is provided for early retirement (age sixty). This involves the "incentive retirement bonus." Here, an individual can retire at sixty; if he has thirty years of service, his monthly benefit would be $381. At age sixty-five, it would drop to $316 (including OASDI) for life. Various other early retirement alternatives and examples could be given, including retirement as early as fifty-five. These early retirement approaches appear to reflect an increasing concern about providing jobs for younger individuals.[11]

Unlike OASDI, "supplementary" benefits are uncommon, but the use of survivorship payments is increasing. Where such payments are made, a common figure is 55 percent of the basic benefit.

"Executive" pensions tend to be much more liberal, both in

[10] See Dan M. McGill, *Fundamentals of Private Pensions*, 2nd ed. (Homewood, Ill.: Irwin, 1964); and D. C. Bronson, *Pensions* (New York: McGraw-Hill, 1958).

[11] See "Chrysler-UAW Settlement," Bureau of National Affairs, *Collective Bargaining—Negotiations and Contracts*, Extra Edition Bulletin, No. 504, September 28, 1964. See also the comments of Walter Reuther on "Phased Retirement as a Way to Create Jobs," *The New York Times*, February 16, 1964, Sec. 1, p. 75.

terms of percentage of salary available for retirement benefits and in the absence of ceilings, except insofar as they are salary related. A recent study indicates that in 1963, the median pension for various salary levels ranged from 33 to 37 percent of salary, as against 23 to 30 percent six years earlier in 1957.[12]

A pressing retirement income problem since the end of World War II has been that of benefit erosion brought about by rising prices. Many administrative approaches have been made to this problem: congressional increases in OASDI benefits, supplements of one kind or another made by employers, and so on. The Civil Service Amendments of 1962, noted above, are one of the few attempts, how-ever, to provide for automatic adjustment.

Another ingenious approach was developed by the Teachers Insurance and Annuity Association in the early 1950's. This was the so-called variable annuity. This system is based upon the hypothesis that living costs and common-stock prices tend to rise and fall in parallel fashion. Hence, if one invests his retirement funds in com-mon stocks, one can hedge against the inflationary erosion of benefits. The details of the plan are too complex for summary presentation here, but the logic is not. If one invests annual sums in a portfolio of common stocks and some years later, upon retirement, finds that prices (hence living costs) have increased, one should also find his stocks worth equivalently more. Therefore, one has increased assets sufficient to meet the price increases.[13] Although TIAA was for some years the only carrier underwriting this type of annuity, other com-panies increasingly have been given legal sanction to enter the field.

Financing. The majority of group plans currently are noncon-tributory, with employer contributions forming about 85 percent of the total. While various arguments can be made for employee con-tributions (for example, if employees contribute they will be more interested in the plan), other factors are more pertinent. For one thing, employees have increasingly taken portions of wage increases in the form of fringe benefits. Hence, the employer contribution may simply be viewed as a type of wage increase and a component in the

[12] See Harland Fox, "Top Executive Pensions, 1957 and 1963," *The Con-ference Board Record*, 1 (October, 1964), 7-10.

[13] See William C. Greenough, "Pensions—Meeting Price Level Changes," in D. M. McGill (Ed.), *Pensions: Problems and Trends* (Homewood, Ill.: Irwin, 1955).

wage payment. For another, it is more economical for the employer
to make the full payment, particularly since it is tax-deductible as a
cost of production. One corporation executive is said to have declared
that the bookkeeping costs of handling employee contributions were
greater than the contributions, that is, it was cheaper for the company to pay the full cost.

Various funding media are used. A plan may be "self-insured" by
the employer or insured with an insurer. Under the former, if it is a
trusteed plan, a consulting actuary advises the employer who transfers funds periodically to a trustee such as a bank. The trustee invests
the monies and handles the benefit payment operation. This approach
is highly flexible, particularly with respect to the types of investments
that can be made. Under an insured plan the contributions are paid
to an insurer who administers them in one of several ways: a pension
trust, a group annuity plan, deposit administration plan, immediate
participation guarantee contracts, segregated asset plans. The major
variations arise from the type of contract and the form of investment.

Vesting is a more serious problem in group plans than under
OASDI. As noted previously, there are some multi-employer plans in
existence. Here an employee can transfer from one company to another with no loss of coverage. But the employee moving from an
employer with one plan to another with a different plan faces serious
problems unless he has some retirement income rights built up with
the first employer. While vesting does exist in the private sector, it
is considered less than desirable; a presidential commission reporting
in January, 1965, recommended minimum vesting standards for plans
to be eligible for favored federal tax treatment.[14]

Administration. A variety of administrative procedures is to be
found. In insured plans, the insurer, in effect, assumes administration
via contractual agreement. In self-insured plans, practices vary more
widely, with the employer, and the union if involved, assuming a
greater degree of control. The Labor Management Relations Act of
1947 requires that welfare and pension plans established after 1945
in which a labor representative is involved and in which the employer makes contributions be administered by a board of trustees

[14] See the *Report* of the President's Committee on Corporate Pension
Funds and Other Private Retirement and Welfare Programs (Washington: U. S.
Government Printing Office, 1965).

representing management, labor, and the public. Abuses developed, however, resulting in (1) reporting requirements enacted in some six states, (2) the Welfare Pension and Disclosure Act (Federal) of 1958 (amended in 1962), and (3) a fund-bonding requirement in the Labor-Management Reporting and Disclosure Act of 1959. Private insurers are closely regulated by the states. The result of this legislation has been to reduce irregularities.

Operational details. Tables 6-5 and 6-6 present certain details of group plans. Several facts stand out from these tables.

(1) Growth has been marked. Under insured plans, for example, the number of persons covered has increased more than tenfold from 1940 to 1966. The increase in self-insured (noninsured) plans was considerably larger; even though no reliable estimate is available for 1940, it must have been small—well under a million, or even under five hundred thousand of numbers of persons covered.

(2) While the number of beneficiaries and the benefit totals are only about 20 percent of the comparable OASDI totals, the numbers are by no means insignificant. Moreover, beneficiaries are likely to increase at an accelerating rate for a period, given the recency of introduction and the time-lock qualifications involved (such as ten years minimum).

(3) The relative importance of self-insured (noninsured) plans is evident from the tables. This results not only from greater general flexibility, but also from the fact that investment regulations are less restrictive and hence equities can be more readily purchased.

IX

Individual annuities can be described in two basic ways: (1) the method of purchase, and (2) benefit payment arrangements.

With respect to the method of purchase, two options are open. In the "immediate annuity" case, the buyer goes to the insurer with an accumulation of assets (cash) and purchases a contract for which the payments begin immediately. Mutual funds have become an important method of accumulation. In the deferred annuity, the purchaser undertakes his accumulation by making regular payments to the insurer.

TABLE 6-5

GROUP PENSION PLAN DATA FOR SELECTED YEARS

YEAR	COVERAGE	
	Employees Covered (in thousands)	
	Insured Plans	Noninsured Plans
1940	700	No reliable estimate
1962	5,200	17,900

YEAR	CONTRIBUTIONS (IN MILLIONS)			
	Employer Contributions		Employee Contributions	
	Insured Plans	Noninsured Plans	Insured Plans	Noninsured Plans
1940	$ 720	$1,030	$200	$130
1962	1,240	3,500	310	510

YEAR	NUMBER OF BENEFICIARIES (END OF YEAR, IN THOUSANDS)	
	Insured Plans	Noninsured Plans
1950	150	300
1962	620	1,470

YEAR	AMOUNT OF BENEFIT PAYMENTS AND RESERVES			
	Benefit Payments (in millions)		Reserves — End of Year (in billions)	
	Insured Plans	Noninsured Plans	Insured Plans	Noninsured Plans
1950	$ 80	$ 290	$ 5.6	$ 6.1
1962	500	1,650	21.6	39.0

Source: Joseph Krislov, "Employee-Benefit Plans, 1954-62," *Social Security Bulletin,* (April, 1964), Table 5, 16.

TABLE 6-6

PENSION PLANS IN THE UNITED STATES INSURED WITH
LIFE INSURANCE COMPANIES (DOLLAR AMOUNTS
IN MILLIONS)

PLANS IN FORCE AT END OF YEAR

1940	Deferred Annuity	Deposit Adminis-tration	Individual Policy Pension Trusts	Other Plans	Total
Number of plans	770	20	440	315	1,545
Number of persons covered	575,000	65,000	15,000	40,000	695,000
Payment into plans in year	NA	NA	NA	NA	NA
Reserves end of year	NA	NA	NA	NA	NA
Annual income provided	NA	NA	NA	NA	NA
1963					
Number of plans	6,660	5,360	30,630	4,810	47,460
Number of persons covered	2,305,000	2,555,000	725,000	475,000	6,060,000
Payment into plans in year	$ 790	$ 590	$ 325	$ 240	$ 1,945
Reserves end of year	$13,125	$ 2,400	$ 2,400	$ 2,100	$23,300
Annual income provided	$ 1,535	$ 735	$ 735	$ 380	$ 3,420

Source: *Life Insurance Fact Book*, 1964, p. 34. Data for 1964 and 1965 exhibit
growth rate in line with recent trends.

Regarding benefit payment arrangements, alternatives have been
developed to meet the needs of the retirant. In the "single-life" annuity, the payee receives an income during his lifetime. After his
death, payments cease. If he has not used up his accumulation, two
alternatives exist. In one case no refund of the unused balance is
provided for and the monies go to meet the needs of those who live

longer than the average, that is, those who outrun their accumulation. This type provides the largest benefit per dollar of input. In the other case, a refund of the unused balance or a portion thereof is payable to a designated party.

The joint-and-survivorship annuity provides a benefit payment to two parties and, upon the death of one, continues the benefit (at the same or a reduced level) during the lifetime of the other. Again, the refund or no-refund alternatives are possible.

Per dollar of input, the benefit amount depends upon (1) the benefit option selected, (2) mortality, (3) the rate of return upon investment, and (4) "loading"—the expense charge of the insurer.

TABLE 6-7

ANNUITIES IN FORCE IN U.S. LIFE INSURANCE
COMPANIES (IN THOUSANDS)

YEAR	INDIVIDUAL ANNUITIES		SUPPLEMENTARY CONTRACTS[1]		TOTAL	
	Number	Annual Income	Number	Annual Income	Number	Annual Income
1940	940	$475,000	75	$ 30,000	1,015	$505,000
1963	1,104	585,000	502	257,000	1,606	842,000[2]

Source: Life Insurance Fact Book, 1964, pp. 36-37. Data for 1964 and 1965 conform to trends of recent years.
[1]These contracts provide life income through the settlement of the benefits of life insurance.
[2]This represents payments on 23 percent of the annuities in force. In future periods payments would begin on the other 77 percent.

Table 6-7 provides selected data on individual annuities. One striking fact stands out: the small growth over the years of this layer of income protection for the aged. In part, this has resulted from the fact that annuities have never been as popular as, for example, life insurance; in much larger measure, it is a result of the alternative, and more economical, protection provided by group approaches.

X

What of the aged individual or couple who has no OASDI benefits, group pensions, individual annuities, or other income (or not enough income from any source)? The answer is to be found in old-age assistance, or in that residual form of aid known as general or public assistance. Let us look at each of these in turn.

Old-age assistance (OAA) is one of the categorical grant-in-aid programs legislated in the Social Security Act of 1935 and since amended variously. Its basic characteristics are three in number. First and fundamentally, benefits are granted only on the basis of need, not as a matter of right as is true under OASDI. Second, it is a federal-state program—in effect, it is enabling legislation. The federal government spells out certain minimum specifications, and the states are encouraged to develop programs which incorporate these standards. Third, if the states so act, they are eligible for federal monies in the form of grants-in-aid to help defray the costs of the programs.

The federal specifications are detailed.[15] In essence, they involve matters of coverage, age, citizenship, residence, need, rights of appeal, and administration. These requirements are all designed to promote equity, ethics, and efficiency of operation. All states now have such laws.

Under the Public Welfare Act amendments of 1962, the federal government contributed, via the grant-in-aid method, the following portion of the *average* monthly pension provided under an approved state program: 29/35 of the first $35, plus 50 to 65 percent of the next $35, and in addition will pay 75 percent of certain expenses such as for rehabilitation, plus 50 percent of "other" expenses. The 50 percent grant-in-aid for the second $35 is paid to states with "above average" per capita income; the remaining range of 50 plus to 65 percent is applicable to other states, depending upon their income levels. This sliding scale is designed to afford a certain equalization and favors the poorer states; the overall formula also aids

[15] For a discussion, see John G. Turnbull, C. Arthur Williams, Jr., and Earl F. Cheit, *Economic and Social Security*, 2nd ed. (New York: Ronald, 1962), pp. 68-72.

those wealthier states which make a large number of low average grants. (Subsequent amendments have increased these figures.)

As noted, OAA is predicated on the basis of need. The states are free in this respect to set their own definitions. In general, an applicant is considered needy if he has insufficient income or other resources to provide reasonable subsistence compatible with decency and health. Some states consider a person needy if his income or other resources are less than a specified dollar amount; some require children to support their needy parents and withhold or reduce assistance if it is not forthcoming; some require support from children but do provide assistance if the children do not help. Almost all states set upper limits on the amount of property an applicant may own and still be viewed as needy.

General assistance is the residual support program, classed by some as the residuary legatee of the poor laws. Actually, little assistance to the aged goes to them in the form of money payments—the bulk is used for other needy. Most of the assistance given those aged who do not qualify for other programs takes the form of institutional care, and here the needy are frequently ailing as well as being old.

Table 6-8 illustrates selected trends in OAA and general assistance. A number of facts stand out in this table.

1. As OASDI and group and individual programs have developed, the numbers of OAA recipients and general assistance cases have tended to decline. In 1950, for the first time, the number of OASDI recipients exceeded those of OAA. By 1966, over 15 million individuals were receiving OASDI payments while OAA, which had "peaked" in late 1949 and early 1950 at some 2.789 million, counted less than 2 million.

2. Several medical programs for the aged begin to appear: vendor payments for medical care in 1951, and Medical Assistance for the Aged (MAA) in 1960. These provide supplements to other kinds of nonfactor income for the aged. With Medicare, as enacted in 1965, one may expect a sizable increase, if not in average payments, in total payments and numbers of recipients.

3. Average payments vary widely by state. In July, 1964, the high OAA state was Minnesota ($113.74 average payment for money payments plus vendor payments for medical care); the low, Mississippi ($38.34). The high general assistance jurisdiction was the Dis-

trict of Columbia ($70.71 average per recipient), and low, Arkansas ($4.47).

TABLE 6-8

OLD-AGE ASSISTANCE AND GENERAL ASSISTANCE — SELECTED DATA

Year	Number of Recipients–OAA (thousands)	Number of Recipients– Medical Care–Aged (thousands)	General Assistance Cases (thousands)
1936	1,106	–	1,510
1940	2,066	–	1,239
1950	2,789	–	413
1960	2,332	15	431
1962	2,226	110	353
July, 1965	2,145	266	306

	AVERAGE MONTHLY PAYMENTS OAA			GENERAL ASSISTANCE (PER CASE)
Year	Total	Money Payment to Recipients	Vendor Payments for Medical Care	Medical Assistance for Aged	
1936	$18.79	$18.79	–	–	$24.13
1940	20.26	20.26	–	–	24.28
1950	43.95	43.95	–	–	46.65
1960	68.45	58.00	$10.45	$192.98	71.62
1962	75.36	60.83	14.53	212.20	66.80
July, 1965	80.43	62.46	17.97	185.30	65.91

Sources: Social Security Yearbook, Annual Statistical Supplement, 1962, pp. 106-110; Social Security Bulletins.

What can be said about the scope and usefulness of these programs? They do provide a last line of income defense for the aged.

And the aggregate sums dispensed are not insignificant: total OAA was running at a monthly rate of $172 million (per month) in July, 1964; MAA, $36 million; and general assistance, $24 million.

But these programs tend to come in for severe criticism by many welfare specialists (to say nothing of an opposite type of censure, as witness that arising in the Newburgh, New York, situation). The necessity to prove need, the rigid residence laws, lack of interstate reciprocity (though some exists), have all tended to cause many critics to voice strong protests over these systems.[16] A serious student of the subject proposed twenty years ago that a general pension be provided for the aged whose income was substandard.[17]

But, as another specialist has suggested, "public assistance is here to stay."[18] Given this, and the fact that eligibility requirements are deterrents designed to keep these programs in bounds as far as taxpayers are concerned, it is nevertheless true that improvements could be made: greater uniformity, increasing reciprocity, and the like. Other programs—the public OASDI, the private group and individual approaches—need further expansion. But if some poor people will always be with us, these assistances form a necessary and useful line of support.

XI

What do all these programs add up to in terms of income maintenance for the aged?[19] Table 6-9 provides a summary of this information. A number of explanatory comments will be useful.

1. The "frequency," that is, the probability, of reaching old age (sixty-five and over) is increasing. As infant mortality decreases and as people live through the pre-sixty-five years, the absolute numbers and relative proportions of the aged increase.

[16] One study has suggested that some 100,000 persons are able to meet OAA criteria and yet are not on the rolls. See Floyd Bond et al., *Our Needy Aged* (New York: Holt, Rinehart and Winston, 1954), p. 249.

[17] See Edith Abbott, "Abolish the Means Test for Old Age Assistance," *The Social Service Review,* 17 (June, 1943), 213.

[18] Valdemar Carlson, *Economic Security in the United States* (New York: McGraw-Hill, 1962), p. 101.

[19] These materials have been adapted from John G. Turnbull, *The Changing Faces of Economic Insecurity* (Minneapolis: University of Minnesota Press, 1966).

TABLE 6-9

AGGREGATE INDEXES OF ECONOMIC INSECURITY AND SECURITY: OLD AGE

The Economic Insecurity of Old Age	Ideal	1910	1960	2000
Frequency (probability, age 14, of reaching 65)	100	58	69	?
Severity (indicated only directionally)	0			
Economic Security: Protection Against Old Age[1]				
Prevention (through continued employment)	All those who can/want to work = 100	65	30	25 or less
Alleviation (for total number of the aged)				
Public programs (income as a matter of right)	50% of budgets for the elderly (non-deferrable budget)	0	38%	50%
Private programs (and private means; income as a matter of right)	50% of budgets for the elderly (non-deferrable budget)	15-20%	22%	30-40%
Total	100% of budgets for the elderly (non-deferrable budget)	15-20%	60%	80-90%

[1]These are global data and apply to *all* the aged irrespective of the degree of coverage under public and/or private programs.

2. The income maintenance requirements associated with old age are becoming more severe as time passes. This is in part due to a rising plane of living which requires more things to have in old age; it is also markedly influenced by the fact that as medical science pro-

gresses, more older people can have their lives prolonged, but only at increasing costs.

3. The preventive route (income maintenance through continued employment) will continue to decrease in importance. Irrespective of its desirability, there appears to be an inexorable trend toward lowering the age of retirement. The recent reduction in retirement ages for males under OASI (sixty-five to sixty-two) and the "early retirement" provisions negotiated in the automobile industry in late 1964 are illustrative.

4. With respect to alleviation, we have used as a retirant's budget that one developed by the Social Security Administration.[20] This elderly-couple budget was priced out in the latter part of 1959 for twenty large cities; the low was $2,641 for Houston; the high, $3,366 for Chicago. We employed in the table a median of $3,000, and regarded the total as "nondeferrable"; that is, there were no purchases that could be deferred, this unlike a young couple who could postpone the acquisition of capital items.

5. We assumed that the government floor of protection should provide 50 percent of this budget, private means the rest. The table shows such income provision for three dates: 1910, 1960, 2000. The improvement in income maintenance (received as a matter of right) is marked.

6. In using "global" figures as well as "averages," the table tends to understate the problem in several respects. For example, in 1960, the median money income of a two-person family with a head sixty-five or over was $2,897, or almost equivalent to the elderly-couple budget. But the income of the head was only about $1,900, indicating that other family members make a relatively large contribution. Moreover, a substantial proportion of older families had incomes of less than $2,000. This last does not explicitly take into account the "impoverished" and their problems. For example, "poor families" where the head was sixty-five and over numbered 3.2 million in 1962, out of 6.8 million total families. Thus, some 47 percent of the aged families could be classified as "poor," the largest percentage of any

[20] See Molly Orshansky, "Budget for an Elderly Couple: Interim Revision by the Bureau of Labor Statistics," *Social Security Bulletin*, 23 (December, 1960), 26-36. See also earlier discussions by Lenore Epstein in the same journal. For a general discussion, see John J. Corson and John W. McConnell, *Economic Needs of Older People* (New York: Twentieth Century Fund, 1956).

age group.[21] For single individuals sixty-five and over, the problem is not much different.

7. How are the residual, economically insecure aged cared for currently? That is, for those whose incomes are insufficient (indicated in Table 6-9), what alleviative programs are available? The answer is found in old-age assistance, public assistance, relatives, friends, charity. But these all tend to be offered on the basis of need rather than as a matter of right. And while "nobody starves [many of the aged] rub along on a standard below minimal."[22]

8. Yet withal, progress in income maintenance is being achieved, and as OASDI and private group benefits become payable to more individuals as time passes, the picture will improve still further. One may even wonder, paraphrasing the old cliché mentioned earlier, whether the aged poor will always be with us.

XII

What can be said by way of evaluating social policy and programs for the aged discussed above? This depends, of course, upon the criteria one selects and applies in making such an appraisal. Let us look first at currently existing public and private programs (including under the latter all those cases in which governments act as employers), and subsequently discuss the problems of the goals of social policy.

1. One of the broadest categories of criteria has been developed by Kenneth Boulding.[23] Four standards are proposed: economic progress, economic stability, freedom, and justice. We shall return shortly to the first two; let us here look at the latter pair. Boulding views "freedom" as the power to make decisions. Insofar as OASDI is financed in part by employee contributions, the individual's free-

[21] See *Economic Report of the President, 1964* (Washington: U. S. Government Printing Office, 1964), p. 61. See also Dorothy McCamman, "Low Incomes of the Aged: An Actual Fact or a Statistical Myth?", U. S. Congress, United States Senate, Special Committee on Aging, *Developments in Aging, 1959 to 1963* (88th Congress, 1st Session, 1963), Appendix D, and Lenore S. Epstein, "Income of the Aged in 1962: First Findings of the 1963 Survey of the Aged," *Social Security Bulletin*, 27 (March, 1964), 3-24.

[22] Paraphrased from Dwight Macdonald, "Our Invisible Poor" (Book Review), *The New Yorker*, January 19, 1963, pp. 82-132.

[23] Kenneth Boulding, *Principles of Economic Policy* (Englewood Cliffs, N. J.: Prentice-Hall, 1958).

dom is restricted by this payment—he has less purchasing power than he would have in the absence of the tax. But, at that point at which benefit payments begin, the individual's freedom is increased—he has more power to purchase than he would have in the absence of such benefits. On the basis of the "compensation principle," the utility of the benefit payments at this time is greater than the summation of the disutilities arising out of the contributions made over time. Hence, OASDI comes off positively in this respect. In the case of the assistances, the problem is more complex since interpersonal utility comparisons are involved (between taxpayer and assistance recipient). But here one could conjecture at least that the results are not negative.

"Justice" is related to the distribution of worldly goods and services (and to political discontent) and involves society's obligations to the individual on the one hand, and the individual's claims upon society on the other. We would conclude with Boulding that these economic security programs increase rather than lessen "justice."

Hence, on the philosophical (rather than economic) grounds of freedom and justice one may conclude, even if only with less than complete certainty, that programs providing nonfactor income in old age are positive in their contributions and impacts.

2. If we move to the economic sphere, several approaches can be utilized. The broadest of these involves the application of "welfare economics" criteria. Unfortunately, little if anything has been undertaken by way of analysis in the area at hand. Jerome Rothenberg has contributed to our general understanding, but not pointedly to the particular problems we are commenting on.[24] In allied fields some "applied" work has been done by, for example, Kenneth Arrow.[25] One is almost forced to conclude with Valdemar Carlson (not a welfare economics specialist in the sense in which this term is customarily applied) that, "The programs of economic security have been established on the conviction that they will promote the efficiency of the economy or at least not make it less efficient.[26] In

[24] Jerome Rothenberg, *The Measurement of Social Welfare* (Englewood Cliffs, N. J.: Prentice-Hall, 1961). See also the bibliography at the end of the volume.

[25] Kenneth Arrow, "Uncertainty and the Welfare Economics of Medical Care," *American Economic Review*, 53 (December, 1963), 941-973.

[26] Carlson, *op. cit.*, p. 214. See also his useful discussion of welfare economics, Chapter 14.

FEDERAL AND STATE PROGRAMMING

the narrower economic sense, income maintenance programs for the aged are not economically neutral. Basically they involve the following problems: the impacts of contributions (taxes) collected; the issues associated with investment as when trust funds are accumulated; and the impacts of benefit distribution (payments). A systematic presentation of the income redistribution and the deflationary-inflationary impacts of these situations can be worked out depending upon the combinations chosen. One specific impact worthy of particular note relates to the question of the "automatic stabilization" features of such programs. One writer concludes that OASDI does possess such characteristics.[27] On the other hand, Boulding has suggested that they may work in reverse; he indicates that the imposition of OASI taxes was largely instrumental in setting off the depression of 1937-38.[28]

In the same vein, do old-age programs contribute to economic progress? Economic stability? As to economic progress, Boulding concludes that we are adrift on a large sea of ignorance, but he further indicates that social security makes little difference. As to stability, he suggests that the impacts may be procyclical rather than countercyclical, as in increasing the benefit structure when inflationary pressures were already strong.[29]

Summing up all of the above one might venture the tentative conclusion that nonfactor income programs for the aged at worst make little difference, as in the case of economic progress; at best they, via the compensation principle, do provide an income stream *when required* increasingly on the basis of right rather than need.

3. Operationally, the various public programs can be evaluated in terms of purpose and accomplishment. Here one would use

[27] See Wayne Vroman, "An Econometric Analysis of Social Insurance," unpublished paper presented at the Chicago Meetings of the Econometric Society, December 28, 1964.

[28] Boulding, *op. cit.*, pp. 246-247.

[29] Boulding was writing at a time (1945-1955) when the memory of deflation and the currency of inflation were much more evident than today. We suggest that the stabilization features of OASI are more positive than Boulding would indicate. That important problems still persist, however, is indicated in a report of the Social Security Advisory Council (released January 2, 1965). The Council, in recommending a health-care program and an increase in the base to $7,200 and in the tax structure, notes its concern over the possible deflationary impacts if benefits are not raised. It is indicated that if taxes are increased but benefits not, a surplus of about $4 billion annually would start to accumulate in 1968. See *The New York Times*, January 3, 1965, Sec. 1, p. 68.

criteria relating to coverage, qualifications for benefits, benefits themselves (adequacy and flexibility), financing, and administration.[30] Were we discussing unemployment insurance or workmen's compensation, we would have a good many critical comments to make. OASDI, however, has a better record. Coverage is almost universal. It is not easy to decide objectively what qualifications for benefits should be. But OASDI has become increasingly liberal in this respect. If one views the government floor of protection as providing 50 percent of the elderly-couple budget, OASDI is also moving in this direction. We would prefer to see benefits adjust automatically to living costs (as newly done under the Civil Service program), and we have some misgivings about the earnings tests and disqualifications (up to age seventy-two), which is a latent function of OASDI. On balance, however, the program receives a good mark. Insofar as one can specify a criterion, contribution rates do not seem excessive, all factors taken into account, although they could become burdensome in a later period. Administration also receives a high mark; OASDI is very well managed.

Old-age assistance and public assistance should be evaluated differently. As residual programs, they serve different purposes; ideally, they should work themselves out of existence. The major problem here appears to center on eligibility: residence, assets, income, and so on. Given our cultural and moral outlook toward the indigent, one might suggest that we have come a long way over the past half or full century and that further betterment will occur.

4. Private programs—group or individual—also require a different frame of reference. Individual plans are most easily disposed of. The individual has freedom to purchase or not to purchase, as well as to select the annuity form desired: eligibility involves only the purchase price; benefits are actuarially determined; costs are related to the type of annuity and benefits desired; and administration is carried out by the insurance company. In essence, the individual gives up present purchasing power in exchange for an income stream beginning at retirement, and the details of this process are undertaken by the insurance carrier.

Nevertheless, this approach has not proved to be the answer

---

[30] For an extensive discussion, see Eveline M. Burns, *Social Security and Public Policy* (New York: McGraw-Hill, 1956).

to all of the nonfactor income problems of the aged. Coverage has not been widespread; that is, the numbers of such contracts sold has been small relative to the total number of the aged, and growth has been slow. (It is, of course, difficult to say what would have happened in the absence of OASDI and the sizable growth of group plans.) Benefits have not been flexible with regard to cost of living increases, although the introduction of the variable annuity offers some promise. To the contrary, insurance carrier competition (plus "objective" actuarial factors) have kept costs in line. Administration is likewise open to little criticism; between competition and regulation the record is good. While individual contracts are an important covering upon the floor of protection, one might hazard the view that if left to individual initiative, income programs for the aged would not be anywhere near the magnitude we find today.

Group plans are of a still different order. Coverage is spotty, although broader than the collective bargaining relationships in which these plans were introduced. Coverage tends to be compulsory in those cases where group plans exist. Eligibility for benefits is becoming increasingly liberal both in terms of the time lock involved (ten years employment will frequently qualify an individual) and retirement age (early retirement at, say, fifty-five). Median benefits tend to be lower than OASDI, though improving; but the interlock with the OASDI floor of protection affords an increasingly meaningful level of nonfactor income. Benefits do not tend to be automatically flexible, although frequently negotiated upwards, with ex-post adjustments for past retirants. It is more difficult to appraise the cost-benefit relationship since many group plans are of the noninsured type yet to be tested in the long run. Vesting is not nearly as widespread as it should be, though it is increasing.

Incomplete coverage is the price paid for "free collective bargaining," or an equivalent in nonunion cases, for the employer's right to determine his wage package. One might ask about the propriety of individual A being covered by a group plan and individual B (working for another employer) not having this protection. But to ask this question is to ask why any employee should be better off than another working elsewhere. The latter question we have seldom seen raised. At the other end of the spectrum, past administration of group plans has been less than wholly satisfactory, although as a consequence of recent legislation the picture is much improved.

XIII

Factually, we may summarize as follows the threads of discussion in this paper.

1. A nearly universal floor of old-age income protection is increasingly being provided by OASDI. Covering on this floor is far less widespread, though improving.

2. By any standard, eligibility requirements can be viewed as liberal whether one looks at the time lock required or the retirement age. (In fact some critics with whom the writer has discussed these questions have viewed early retirement as undesirable in terms of the loss of national product. The lump-of-labor thesis rears its head! We shall reexamine this shortly.)

3. Benefit adequacy is more open to debate, but two answers are that (a) society is limited by its productive capacity as regards the level of nonfactor income it can provide, and (b) society has "chosen" the present levels as consonant with other needs. Certainly the benefit structure will improve as time passes, not only absolutely but also relatively. Benefit flexibility could be increased, although improvements are occurring as via the variable annuity.

4. Financing is undertaken in a variety of ways: contributory under OASDI, largely noncontributory under group programs, and self-financing under individual plans. The actuarial relation of costs and benefits is difficult to appraise because of the variety of programs. Certainly, at the moment, OASDI is a "good buy." It will become less so as time passes (although its social assurance aspect will probably assure its continued desirability). In individual plans one "gets what one pays for"; in group programs, this is probably also true, though the newness of many of these types makes it more difficult to draw any firm conclusion.

5. OASDI's exemplary administration is also true of private carriers operating individual or group plans. The record of the latter is, however, less laudable, though legislative controls, as well as internal policing, are improving the situation.

In the larger sense one might note the following:

1. Applying the criteria of freedom and justice, one might suggest that old-age income programs rate well (though we shall have a final comment to make about "freedom").

2. Old-age programs are not economically neutral. There is not much evidence as to their effect upon economic progress; concerning stability they are built-in stabilizers (though some critics such as Boulding have suggested they may be procyclical rather than countercyclical). In this paper we have not sought to touch upon other specific impacts, such as the macroeconomic impacts of taxes and benefits and the accumulation of reserves, but these are certainly of consequence.

In conclusion, then, on programs:

1. We have a vast and complex arrangement of old-age programs. This creates gaps and overlaps and many other kinds of problems. Given the reduction in administrative costs that would occur, it would undoubtedly be cheaper simply to have some type of universal pension system for the aged. But this would not square with our cultural notions about the desirability of a pluralistic approach. Hence, desirable or not "economically," it is not likely that this development will take place.

2. Current old-age programming involves a shift from individual choice to group choice. As Carlson has noted, "programs of economic security transfer some of the responsibility of making provisions for an individual's welfare from him to social organizations."[31] But insofar as this approach still provides for consumer free-choice in the expenditure of nonfactor income, and insofar as it substitutes for the dismal service approach of the old-folk's home, it cannot be judged other than positive.

In essence, our current system may not be viewed as optimal (however one would define that term), but it exists, is steadily improving, and cannot be regarded as anything but an improvement over what existed fifty or one hundred years ago.

XIV

Throughout this chapter, we have focused upon existing programs. Are such programs optimal or do they fall short of a set of goals for older people? The answer, of course, depends upon the goals that one selects, and here value judgments play an important role.

[31] Carlson, *op. cit.*, p. 212.

Rather than constructing here a set of goals, the reader is referred to the chapter in this volume by Donald P. Kent in which he spells out objectives and goals for older people. We would accept his presentation and his statement that what he sets forth "represents a growing consensus of national purpose and conscience."

If we measure current programs against these goals, accomplishment falls short—more so in some areas, less so in others. But, without being falsely optimistic, we would suggest that "progress" is being made and that the situation at any time represents a compromise of conflicting interests of many kinds.

More specifically, let us look at the basic postulates underlying current old-age policy and programming. These include (1) "compulsory" retirement; (2) a floor of protection provided by government with covering afforded by private action; and (3) a pluralistic approach to old-age income maintenance, which postulate is actually contained in (2).

We would take issue with the compulsory retirement practice for two reasons. First, we cannot help but believe that many older people would find it psychologically advantageous and economically rewarding to continue to work. Second, we likewise believe that the economy could use the additional gross national product that would be generated by such additions to the labor force. To alter the tide of compulsory retirement would, however, be no easy matter. For one thing, the practice is becoming culturally ingrained to the point where its reversal would be difficult. As a matter of fact, there appears to be an increased belief in the desirability of reducing still further retirement ages.[32] For another, until the economy can show that it needs the services of the older worker, it is not likely that he will be demanded. The assumption that younger people can get jobs only if old ones retire is most strongly evident, as Juanita Kreps has clearly indicated in her paper.

Who should provide all the income protection for old age—the government or private initiative? Again this depends upon one's value judgments as to the relative role the respective parties should play. If one accepts the view that the individual should work out his own destiny, one would emphasize private means. If one believes

[32] See the Gallup Poll report on retirement as reported in the *Minneapolis Tribune,* March 31, 1965.

that all of the responsibility should be shifted to social organizations, the government would act as the prime agent. Our prejudices lead us to believe that total commitment to a single source is undesirable. Hence, we would accept the pluralistic approach, although it makes for gaps and overlaps, leads to diversities, and is less economical in terms of dollars and cents (though it may be much the more valuable philosophically).

But what of adequacy, irrespective of source? There is little doubt that income maintenance is inadequate for sizable numbers of the aged. But so it is for even larger numbers of the non-aged, in absolute though not in relative terms. What standard does one use in deciding the "proper" share of the gross national product to be allocated to various groups—in this case, age groups? In no small measure this is a political problem, as Fred Cottrell has pointed out in this volume. If the aged unite in order to seek a larger share, how quickly would they breed anti-groups? While it would take only a small increase in the share of the national product going to the aged to solve the income adequacy problem, could this be done without making the same provision for other age groups? And this would require the diversion of a larger share. In large measure, the answer is only to be found in increased productivity, and this is a function of time. Paraphrasing Lord Keynes, in the long run we shall all be provided for.

BIOGRAPHICAL NOTE

JOHN G. TURNBULL was born in Milwaukee, Wisconsin, in 1913 and was educated at Denison University, University of Chicago, and Massachusetts Institute of Technology (Ph.D.). He is now Associate Dean of the College of Liberal Arts and Professor of Economics at the University of Minnesota. He is the author of articles and monographs in the field of economic security and labor relations and is senior author of *Economic and Social Security*. Professor Turnbull has served as consultant to various public and private agencies in the areas of economic security, economic education, and economic research.

7

Social Services and Social Policy

Donald P. Kent

This paper is concerned with social services for the aged and the social policy that has guided their development. By their nature such services are geared to meet "problems," and these in turn have a cultural specificity. The social context in which problems are incurred will be considered, followed by a discussion of the nature of social policy vis-à-vis the aged, and an overlook at its historic development. A set of objectives toward which our social policy is directed is posited, and this is followed by an assessment of responsibility and a critique of present policies.

I

Concern for the well-being of those in need is probably as old as the human race itself. However, the forms this concern has taken have varied greatly from time to time and from place to place. Never has it been of the importance envisioned by Mr. MacKenzie King when he said, "The era of freedom will be achieved only as social security and human welfare become the main concerns of men and nations."[1]

In historical perspective the reasons for this concern have been as varied as their overt manifestations. Social problems are culturally defined, as are also the causes and the remedies for them. What is a personal problem in one era or society is accepted as the normal run of events in another, and in yet another the same circumstance is re-

[1] W. L. MacKenzie King, Canadian Prime Minister, Toronto, Canada, October 9, 1942.

garded as a grave social concern. Underlying these differences are differences in social circumstances, social values, and economic conditions.

It would be an error to assume that concern for social problems is a recent development, and it would be equally erroneous to assume that modern attitudes and practices are relatively unchanged from those of our remote ancestors or even from close kin. It is one of the fundamental theses of this essay that there have been major social changes in recent times with respect to the problems of the aged. The task of the behavioral scientist is to identify both the common aspects of social behavior and those that are unique in time and space.

All societies take care of those whose neglect would endanger the group. Thus the English Poor Law of 1388 provided aid to the poor to restrain the wanderings of paupers chiefly to protect the citizenry from itinerants. The Elizabethan Poor Laws were not inspired solely by compassion for the poverty-stricken, and the reforms of Bismarck were not unrelated to his desire to "steal the thunder" of Socialists and thereby cement the state's power.[2]

As members of a society become increasingly more interdependent, the area of social concern must inevitably expand. The web of modern social relations makes it inevitable that many problems once considered to be purely personal are now social problems. This is not to deny that changes in values are also operative. Obviously human behavior is motivated not only by social necessity but also by social values.

Throughout the greater part of human history personal and social problems have been accepted as the inevitable lot of man. To be born is to suffer; this is the inexorable law of life. Given this attitude, the remedy was amelioration by those more fortunate. "It is the duty therefore of righteous living and of complete citizenship to carry the burdens adequately, generously but hopelessly."[3] This view stands in sharp contrast to the very recent one that has been characterized as the "constructive approach."[4] This view holds that it is always possible to do something.

[2] John D. Hogan and Francis A. J. Ianni, *American Social Legislation* (New York: Harper & Row, 1956), pp. 489-490.
[3] James H. S. Bossard, *Social Change and Social Problems* (New York: Harper & Row, 1938), p. 14.
[4] *Ibid.*, p. 15.

Psychologically the constructive ideal rests upon the confidence of modern students in the extreme modifiability of human nature; sociologically it is based upon a conviction that social sciences can understand and achieve as effectively as the physical sciences have made possible; historically it is inspired by the success and illustrated by the failure which every parent, teacher, and case worker has had during the ages of man's history; logically it finds its basis in that need of man's faith in man without which man ceases to be a proper companion for man.[5]

Present policies toward services for older people are grounded in this belief. As a consequence, a number of things follow: rehabilitative services are encouraged, retraining is advocated even for those in advanced years, and the ever-present hope is strong that independence is indeed possible for virtually all. Given this view, there follows logically an emphasis upon prevention. We justify the cost of housing specifically designed for older persons on the ground that it will maintain independence. We advocate homemaker services, home-care programs, and similar social services on the basis that they will prevent persons from entering institutions.

Implicit in this viewpoint is an assumption that the cause of social ills is known. Prior generations assumed that poor health, poverty, and the infirmities of age were the inevitable lot of man. We assume a natural cause that can be overcome. There is a maxim in medicine, "No cure without understanding the cause." The philosophy applies equally to "social engineering," even if the etiologic knowledge is far less developed. The services presently provided would indicate that the bulk of the problems are assumed to be caused by external factors, such as retirement or lack of income.[6]

This approach is an optimistic one, and certainly the spirit of optimism runs high throughout both the American view of aging

[5] *Ibid.*, p. 15.

[6] The natural corollary of the growth of a view of problems as externally caused was a shifting of responsibility for solutions from the individual to society. This changed philosophy is basic to an understanding of present mixed feelings about social welfare services. A former commissioner of the Social Security Administration notes, "The lack of a comprehensive public program or plan to provide economic security was not due to neglect or indifference. It reflected an important and affirmative American philosophy: a philosophy which placed on the individual the responsibility for his own welfare. Nevertheless, the fact of economic insecurity—the clear evidence of poverty and suffering—was shattering the faith of many in the ability of persons to take care of themselves." (Charles I. Schottland, *The Social Security Program in the United States* [New York: Appleton-Century-Crofts, 1963], p. 24.)

(which is often a denial) and the programs developed. This optimism is understandable, for there has been progress. The problems of earlier generations centered around survival itself; those of today center upon making life richer. The very few descriptions of old age before the nineteenth and twentieth centuries may be attributed to the small numbers who reached old age. However, those references that do exist paint a gloomy picture. The concern is not with housing boasting grab bars and nonskid floors, but with protection from the elements; not with an imbalanced diet, but with starvation; not with retirement, but with increasing toil when one is weary with age; and certainly not with that "gravest of modern problems," meaningful activity to occupy leisure.

Here again we see the culmination in our times of trends that have a long history, but are of such magnitude that quantitative difference becomes a qualitative difference. The principle of relative deprivation has long been operative, even if the jargon is relatively new. Mankind has consistently raised its sights; as one problem is met, another emerges. The problems of old age were never greater, even though those of basic maintenance have been met in a manner far exceeding the expectations of social reformers as recently as the early part of this century.

This view has indeed become a part of public policy by dint of a statement of the Supreme Court decision upholding the constitutionality of the Social Security Act. Justice Cardozo states, "Nor is the concept of the general welfare static. Needs that were narrow or parochial a century ago may be interwoven in our day with the full being of the nation. What is critical or urgent changes with the times."[7]

However, as one's standards rise, a number of things happen. The less severe the problem, the greater the number of cases. For example, the need for meaningful free-time activities has been noted by gerontologists as being a nearly universal problem among the elderly. As standards rise, prevention can also become increasingly emphasized, because the circumstance in question is less severe. This, too, is characterized by the current approaches in social geron-

[7] Helvering vs. Davis, 301 United States 619, 57 Supreme Court 904, 81 L. Ed 1307 (1937). In the words of the first commissioner of the Social Security Administration, "Social Security will always be a goal, never a finished thing, because human aspirations are infinitely expansible—just as human nature is infinitely perfectible" (September, 1945).

tology. Modern social welfare services are frequently geared to prevention, and as standards rise there is a great increase in the number of problem cases whose discomfort is defined in psychological terms.

If social welfare is not paramount it is at least among our major concerns. En route to America the Pilgrims bound themselves to promote "the common good." It has been sufficiently engraved in our life that a cabinet officer could say "responsibility for our fellowman is of the essence of the American way."[8]

II

It is perhaps both unrewarding and irrelevant to seek for motives for social policies. Suffice it to say that there is not one reason but many reasons for any policy, and the important fact is the nature of the policy rather than the reasons for it.

To establish the nature of social policies in America (or in any complex society) is not easy. While social policies are sometimes enunciated in legislative acts, court decisions, and executive messages, more often the policy remains unarticulated in a formal sense. Social policy usually must be inferred from actions; for social policy means the set of guidelines which people use in selecting courses of action and, by and large, these guidelines are not explicitly stated. Thus the passage of the Social Security Act and subsequent growth of public support are reflections of a policy that retirement income preferably should be provided by a system of social insurance rather than public assistance. And our system of cash payments reflects a policy that such payments are preferable to vendor payments or a vast system of services.

In fact, at the outset it is important to recognize that in the United States our approach (one could almost say our policy) of meeting the needs of older people has been through the income route rather than the service route. This is not true with children. As early as the beginning of this century there were extensive child welfare services, and this century has seen a steady expansion of these services and the organizations necessary to deliver them. On the other hand, if one looks at the monetary payments under the Aid to De-

[8] Abraham Ribicoff, Secretary of Health, Education, and Welfare. November 18, 1961.

pendent Children program, one is struck by how meager they are. As low as old-age assistance is, it is far higher in most states than the financial assistance given to children.[9] Having selected the income route to meet the needs of older persons, the tendency in America, at least at the federal level, has been upon retirement income, disability payments, and provision of health insurance, rather than upon the expansion of a vast array of services.

In a democratic society, clear social policies emerge only when there is virtual consensus. Prior to this there must be action; but the patterns of action tend to be designed to fit immediate situations and vary widely throughout the country. It is also apparent that consensus only comes (1) when there is a convergence of patterns of thought and action, and (2) when these become congruent with basic social values.

More than a century ago that most perceptive observer of the American scene and character, Alexis de Tocqueville, noted the American taste for physical well-being: "In America the passion for physical well-being is not always exclusive, but it is general; and if all do not feel it in the same manner, yet it is felt by all. The effort to satisfy even the least wants of the body and to provide the little conveniences of life is uppermost in every mind."[10] This basic orientation is probably in part responsible for the fact that American social welfare has been almost exclusively concerned with economic well-being.

Once, in response to a child's query, Mrs. Bronson Alcott indicated that they "indeed were poor" but they "did not think poor." Until very recent times our concern as a nation has been with the physical rather than with the psychological aspects of poverty and deprivation. And our social welfare policies in the past paid scant attention to their psychic implications. These values, coupled with a system that emphasizes the primacy of the states, make it inevitable that the social service policies of America will follow a set pattern. An individual is distressed by the conditions of his fellows. He seeks out others with like feelings. They band together for action as an association. When this fails, they seek to involve the state govern-

[9] The nearest "income approach" for children is the survivor's benefits that are a part of the Social Security Act designed initially for the aged.

[10] Alexis de Tocqueville, *Democracy in America*, The Henry Reeve Text, Vol. II (New York: Knopf, 1948), p. 128.

ment, enlisting labor unions or other groups as allies in this process. "At some stage, the revelations of commissions and general dissatisfaction with state activity result in pressure for legislation to meet on a national basis the need for which the state legislation was devised."[11]

III

As with most other aspects of our civilization, social welfare policies derive from three basic taproots: Hebraic social thought, Greco-Roman philosophy, and Christian ethics. The Middle Ages melded these and added its own distinctive world outlook, which was in turn seen through the prism formed by the Renaissance, the Reformation, and the discovery of the New World. The early settlers to America came with this heritage, which was transmitted to us with modifications resulting from settling a new continent, the rise of urbanism and industrialism, and the twentieth century energy revolution. While each of these influences has been described in detail by social historians, at least a sketch of them is necessary here to understand the present position of social welfare services in the United States.

Those leading social thinkers of the human race, the prophets of Israel, began with God. They assumed his complete rule, and they also assumed his great concern for man. Man is made in God's image and acquired his dignity and worth merely from being in God's image and being an object of God's concern. Justice and love are indications of God's concern. A concern that embraces the children and also the aged was voiced: "Cast me not off in old age, desert me not when my strength faileth." It was assumed that God would neither cast one off nor desert one, and man was to behave in a similar way. The Mosaic injunction still rings clear: "Honor thy father and thy mother, that your days may be long in the land which the Lord your God gives you." Here again the injunction is a very strong one, and it holds a promise of God's benefaction *if* you indeed honor the elderly.

On the other hand, the Greeks began not with God but with man; yet their conclusions come out not too distant from those of the

[11] Hogan and Ianni, *op. cit.*, pp. 488-489.

Jewish prophets. Humanism (respect for the dignity of the individual), freedom, and rationality are all logical outcomes of their philosophy. Plato says through Socrates, "There is nothing which for my part I like better, Cephalus, than conversing with aged men; for I regard them as travelers who have gone a journey which I too may have to go, and of whom I ought to enquire, whether the way is smooth and easy, or rugged and difficult." And Socrates asks the aged Cephalus, "Is life harder towards the end, or what report do you give of it?" And the venerable patriarch, speaking from the Greek view of age, replies:

I will tell you, Socrates, what my own feeling is. Men of my age flock together; we are birds of a feather, as the old proverb says; and at our meetings the tale of my acquaintance commonly is—I cannot eat, I cannot drink; the pleasures of youth and love are fled away: there was a good time once, but now that is gone, and life is no longer life. Some complain of the slights which are put upon them by relations, and they will tell you sadly of how many evils their old age is the cause. But to me, Socrates, these complainers seem to blame that which is not really in fault. For if old age were the cause, I too being old, and every other old man, would have felt as they do. But this is not my own experience, nor that of others whom I have known. . . . The truth is, Socrates, that these regrets, and also the complaints about relations, are to be attributed to the same cause, which is not old age, but men's characters and tempers; for he who is of a calm and happy nature will hardly feel the pressure of age, but to him who is of an opposite disposition youth and age are equally a burden.

But Socrates calls his attention to the fact that he is wealthy and that there are some who attribute his happiness to his riches. The aged philosopher replies:

You are right . . . there is something in what they say; not, however, so much as they imagine. I might answer them as Themistocles answered the Seriphian who was abusing him and saying that he was famous, not for his own merits but because he was an Athenian: "if you had been a native of my country or I of yours, neither of us would have been famous." And to those who are not rich and are impatient of old age, the same reply may be made; for to the good poor man old age cannot be a light burden, nor can a bad rich man ever have peace with himself.[12]

The Christian ethics of love and brotherhood have been a wellspring for most social services. Thus early services to the aged in Europe in the decades following the introduction of Christianity stem from this motive. Individuals cared for older people because they were living with the ethics of Jesus. This eventually became institutionalized, with the church providing hospitals and hospices for care of the aged. The alms to the aged and the home for the aged were church-organized and church-supervised.

With the secularization that came with the close of the medieval period, the responsibility for aid which had initially rested with the individual and then was transferred to the church was in turn given to the community. That it was still recognized as a special responsibility was unquestionably due to the Christian ethic, but it was discharged in a very different manner when it became a community responsibility.

The American experience reworked this viewpoint of life and man's obligation. In the first place, work took on a new meaning. The rewards were greater, the necessity for it was greater, and the dignity of it was vastly increased. At the same time, those who suffered misfortune were viewed with less sympathy. The attitude toward work was reinforced by our attitude toward individualism and belief in each man's taking care of himself. Counterbalancing this, however, was a feeling that everyone should be happy and taken care of. Ralph Barton Perry writes, "They [Americans] do not regard unhappiness as the necessary lot of man, to be accepted as a fatality and sublimated in tragic nobility. Every sin is regarded as curable; if not by divine grace, then by psychoanalysis."[13] Yet another complicating factor was an attitude toward government and toward association. On the one hand, government has long been and is still greatly distrusted by Americans. "That government is best which governs least" may be an erroneous view, but it is widely held. Coupled with it is a faith that somehow or other local government is much less repressive than state government, and the latter in turn

[12] Plato, *The Republic*, trans. by B. Jowett (New York: Modern Library, n.d.), pp. 5-7.
[13] Ralph Barton Perry, *Characteristically American* (New York: Knopf, 1949), p. 12.

less ominous than federal government. This belief, too, is one that is widely held, despite the fact that all the evidence throughout our history would indicate that probably the reverse of this is more often a true statement of fact.[14]

At the same time there is a widespread faith that voluntary groups are good and that association other than government is a very desirable thing. The astute De Tocqueville notes:

> Americans of all ages, all conditions and all dispositions constantly form associations. They have not only commercial and manufacturing companies in which all take part but associations of a thousand other kinds—religious, moral, serious, feudal, general or restricted, enormous or diminutive. The Americans make associations to give entertainments, to form seminaries, to build inns, to construct churches, to diffuse books, to send missionaries to the antipodes. In this manner they found hospitals, prisons and schools. If it is proposed to inculcate some truth or to foster some feeling by the encouragement of a great example they form a society. Whenever at the head of some new undertaking you will see the government in France or a man of rank in England, in the United States, you will be sure to find an association.
>
> As soon as the several of the inhabitants of the United States have taken up an opinion or a feeling in which they wish to promote the world they look out for mutual assistance and as soon as they have found one another they combine. From that moment they are no longer isolated men but a power seen from afar.[15]

IV

Various attempts have been made over the past fifteen or twenty years to develop goals, objectives, and policies to guide the nation and its communities in creating conditions essential to secure and meaningful life throughout the later years. There have been exercises of the states, of scores of conferences including two national forums, of the Council of State Governments, of the United States Congress and state legislatures, and of numerous voluntary organizations. The

[14] Throughout American history two disparate views of government have contended. While that expressed above may have been a majority view, a goodly number, including many of the academic community, shared the view that our society suffers not from paternalism but from undergovernment; that government ought not to restrain the forces of society, but instead provide the means for them to operate freely.

[15] De Tocqueville, op. cit., p. 106.

statement which follows represents an attempt to report the essence
and the principal particulars of these efforts. Essentially, what is
set forth represents a growing consensus of national purpose and
conscience.

The objectives are offered within a framework of biologically
and culturally based needs and drives. Although these needs and
drives are assumed to persist throughout life, the marked extension
of life and the changes associated with it may warrant their re-
identification and reevaluation. Relative strength or intensity of
drives may change with age, and methods of satisfying needs differ
from one stage of life to another, particularly in old age. The proto-
type for this classification is obviously the W. I. Thomas formulation
of the four wishes. In the decades that have elapsed since their promulgation, many more elaborate systems have been developed. It
was felt, however, that for the purposes of this exposition, a relatively
simple system was preferable.

Security: the basic need and objectives. The basic need of
middle-aged and older people, hence the objective underlying all
others, is for security of income, of physical and mental health, of
suitable housing and living arrangements, and, as indicated later on,
of relatedness and opportunity to participate significantly in family
and community life. Objectives aimed to free older people of concern
for basic securities include the following:

(1) Guarantee of sufficient money purchasing power over the
    later stages of life to afford equality of opportunity for ob-
    taining adequate food, clothing, health care, shelter, trans-
    portation, and the necessary incidentals of living.

(2) The establishment of minimum levels below which no in-
    come may be permitted to fall and of systems of insurance
    and subsidized services to meet needs which cannot be
    individually predicted.

(3) The availability of retirement income beyond the minimum,
    which recognizes differential earning capacities during the
    working years, variations in health and responsibility for
    dependents, and differences in customary patterns of living
    and activity.

(4) Sources of regular income free from the maladies of inept

and dishonest manipulation, proof against inflation, and independent of means tests, and a reasonable amount of savings and property ownership.

(5) A retirement income system which enables older people to share in the rising national income for which they helped to lay the basis during their economically active years.

(6) Ready access to health education, preventive health services, prompt medical treatment, and restorative services based on the most advanced knowledge and techniques available, for all older people without regard to income.

(7) A wide range of housing and living arrangements located, designed, and priced in keeping with the changing health and social characteristics, needs, and interests associated with the processes of aging.

(8) A complement of community social welfare facilities and services available to all older people in their own homes and in institutions, so organized as to permit prompt utilization as needs arise.

(9) Services to protect all older people from exploitation through false claims, frauds, quackeries, unnecessary services, and unreasonable charges, and to provide special assistance to those unable to manage their own affairs.

Recognition and individuality as needs and goals. The processes of aging may dim but certainly do not extinguish the universal need for recognition as a significant member of society and as an individual with a separately identifiable personality. The needs for recognition and individuality are threatened in the middle and later years by completion of parental and work roles, gradual physical and mental decline, reduced income and mobility, widowhood, and relative lack of positive expectations for older people on the part of society. Among the goals which will promote and preserve individuality and recognition are the following:

(1) Full cooperation on the part of the family, community, and society in helping older people in their search for significant roles and in developing positive societal expectations for the postparental and retirement years.

(2) Guarantee of freedom of choice in the utilization of in-

come, in the pursuit of interests, and in housing and living arrangements.

(3) Opportunity for maximum independence and privacy, consistent with physical and mental capacities, in housing, living arrangements, and medical care facilities.

(4) Recognition of individual circumstances, needs, and preferences when a protected living or medical environment becomes necessary.

Goals to satisfy needs for response and relatedness. The needs for response and relatedness find satisfaction in family relationships, companionship, friendships formed out of association with others, and through opportunity to serve one's fellowmen. Earlier developed patterns for satisfying these needs are threatened or disrupted by changes and events of later life. Individual initiative supported by appropriate social action is essential if new modes of satisfaction are to be established. Frequently stated goals to support the needs of older people for relatedness and response are the following:

(1) Warm, mutually satisfying, dignified family relationships born out of freedom from forced dependence on adult children and relatives, other than husband or wife.

(2) Opportunity for participation in organizations and for developing contacts and friendships in social and activity centers, clubs, congregate housing, foster homes, and long-term care facilities.

(3) Creation of opportunities for paid and unpaid voluntary services in community agencies and to people of any or all age groups.

(4) Provision of institutional and medical care, community and protective services, and care and attention to the home-bound by personnel sympathetic toward the aged and trained to work with them.

Creativity and goals for satisfying the need. The principal benefit of longer life is probably the opportunity it affords for fulfillment of the need for creativity. The creative need is perhaps a cultural overlay, built and sustained on the psychobiological drives for stimulation or activity. The origin of the need notwithstanding, nearly everyone short of extreme old age appears to have a basic desire for exploration and expression of his capabilities, for improving the environment of his living and that of his children, for creating something new, or for doing something better than it has been done. Objectives and goals aimed at enabling middle-aged and older people to satisfy the creative need have been defined as follows:

(1) Providing income sufficient to permit older people to utilize the educational, artistic, scenic, and recreational opportunities in their communities and in the country.

(2) Provision of facilities and programs in which older adults can fulfil their desires for education, creative self-expression, adventure, and recreation.

(3) Bringing these activities to home-bound older people, to those who are in institutions, and to those with restricted mobility living in retirement housing and communities.

(4) Involving older adults in planning and conducting programs and services for them and for others in their communities.

V

Any policy statement which defines objectives or goals calling for social action must necessarily include some assignment of responsibility for that action. Responsibility for initiating action on behalf of older people is obviously a shared responsibility. It involves older people themselves, younger people, families, governmental agencies at all levels, and voluntary associations and organizations. The paragraphs which follow set forth national policy with respect to the responsibilities of older people and of governmental and voluntary organizations.

Whenever a society vouchsafes rights or guarantees benefits to its members or to any segment of them, it does so in return for contributions which it expects will accrue to the total society. Conversely, those who accept such guarantees obligate themselves to discharge certain responsibilities to the society. In extending rights and benefits to youth, society is, in part, equipping young people for contributions expected from them in the future. In the case of older people, the extension of rights and benefits is, to a considerable extent, compensation for contributions already made. On the other hand, there are responsibilities which society expects its members to carry throughout life. And there are certain contributions which older adults are peculiarly equipped to make.

Delegates to the White House Conference on Aging in 1961 balanced their lists of "Rights of Senior Citizens" with a list of "Obligations of the Aging." The obligations were stated as follows:

(1) To prepare himself to become and resolve to remain active, alert, capable, self-supporting, and useful so long as health and circumstances permit, and to plan for ultimate retirement.

(2) To learn and apply sound principles of physical and mental health.

(3) To seek and develop potential avenues of service in the years after retirement.

(4) To make available the benefits of his experience and knowledge.

(5) To endeavor to make himself adaptable to the changes added years will bring.

(6) To attempt to maintain such relationships with family, neighbors, and friends as will make him a respected and valued counselor throughout his later years.

In our culture these are reasonable expectations, generally consistent with the desires of older people; hence, they properly have a place in a definition of national policy with respect to senior citizens.

Much has been debated and written regarding responsibilities of families for their older members. A majority of the states have statutes which, if enforced as they sometimes are, require adult children to support parents who are in financial need. A good deal of evidence has accumulated, however, which indicates that these requirements may (1) deprive young children of the support needed for their development and education, (2) give rise to antagonism and guilt feeling on the part of the adult generations, and (3) prevent middle-aged adults from saving for their own retirement years. In all likelihood, these problems are growing more acute as more older people—sometimes two generations—survive into the retirement years and as standards for the education of children rise.

In view of these considerations, sound national policy dictates that younger generations be free from any societally imposed responsibility for financial or other support for parents, grandparents, and other older relatives. Further, experience suggests that when such responsibilities are not imposed, the older and oncoming generations are more likely than not to develop mutually satisfactory relationships based on kinship ties. Thus, among the several generations, family members are able to find love and affection, preservation of dignity and mutual respect, and, frequently, mutual exchanges of services and financial contributions voluntarily made.

All men have created social mechanisms to aid them in achieving objectives not attainable through individual action. As societies have become more complex, their members have traditionally invested their governments and other agencies with broader functions and greater responsibilities with respect to matters lying beyond individual capabilities and control.

Consensus is now well molded into national policy that the proper functions of governments at various levels with regard to older citizens include (1) guarantee of sufficient income to enable older people to live in decency and self-respect; (2) regulation of private actions which are essential or potentially dangerous to life, health, or welfare; (3) protection of rights and property, especially of those who are declining in strength, health, and mental capacities; (4) establishment and enforcement of standards of performance for services and facilities, as with reference to rental housing and total-care institutions; (5) utilization of the federal taxing power and other resources to stimulate—through education, incentives, and subsidies—the development of facilities, programs, and services, and to secure equality of their distribution and opportunity for their use throughout the country; (6) provision of facilities and services by state and local public agencies when needs are too great or widespread to be met by individuals and private groups; and (7) education of the public as to needs and problems of older people and the promulgation of reliable and up-to-date knowledge on methods of dealing with needs.

Much of this nation's strength derives from the eagerness of its citizens to act on their own volition and to advance and secure their personal welfare through the medium of voluntary organizations. Currently, as in the past, some older people have been wont to create organizations of their own to aid themselves in meeting their needs and in seeking solutions to their problems. The freedom of action constitutionally permitted private citizens offers the latitude to pioneer, to demonstrate new approaches, to protest inequities, and to advocate changes in law and in public and private practices.

Although public agencies are now encouraged and expected to develop new approaches and experimental programs and to recommend legislative actions, it is in the interest of national welfare that voluntary organizations be encouraged and sometimes assisted to perform services supplemental to those of governmental agencies and to perform such functions as may be inappropriate to public agencies. Sound national policy directs that organizations of senior citizens be encouraged to assess and make known the needs of all older Americans. Their right to press for measures to meet their needs and alleviate their problems is recognized.

VI

Knowledge of most aspects of aging has been growing rapidly over recent years, through systematic research and through evaluative studies of service facilities and programs. Yet more remains to be known than has been revealed thus far; and much that is known is not being applied to the benefit of older people.

Beyond this, both the United States and the position of older people are changing with unprecedented rapidity. Thus it becomes necessary, insofar as possible, to forecast future social and economic conditions in the country and the changing circumstances of older people. Only in this way can the lag between discovery and application of knowledge be shortened, and the needs of present and future generations of older people and of the total society be adequately served. National policy, therefore, calls for increasing investments in research, in the training of personnel for research, teaching, and professional service, and in systematic and long-range planning.

Whatever is done for the benefit of older people should also be of advantage to the nation as a whole. Benefits provided to the seniors in the population should be proportioned to their needs but also in relation to the needs of those who are in the earlier stages of the life cycle. Equitable allocation of the nation's resources among the various elements of the population is not an easy matter. The young must be properly prepared for adulthood and for the responsibilities they will inherit. Those in the middle generations in a country which has the wealth, productive capacity, and resources of the United States are entitled to share fully in all the satisfactions which can be derived from them.

At the same time, it must ever be borne in mind that a deprived, disgruntled older population suffered to exist on charity can only be a burden on the conscience of the nation and a drag on its social health and well-being. Finally, when the younger members of a society tangibly express concern for the present generation of older people, they are, in all likelihood, improving the environment in which they will live their own later years.

VII

With the passage of the Social Security Act, the nation may be said to have assumed its stance with reference to meeting the needs of its older citizens. Virtually everyone sixty-two years of age and over is now receiving or could be receiving some income under government programs. Research has yielded a good deal of information about chronic diseases, health information and medical care are increasingly available, and there is no longer a one-to-one relationship between long life and invalidism. A start has been made in the area of retirement housing, and there is rising concern over the quality of care in nursing homes and homes for the aged. A few institutions of higher education and a few more libraries and public school systems are offering educational programs to the middle-aged and the retired. Several hundred senior activity centers and several thousand golden age clubs are providing opportunities for social, recreational, and creative experiences. Persistent efforts are being made to provide job opportunities for those who wish to remain in the work force, and thousands of older people are engaged in voluntary services of one kind or another.

Nearly a dozen federal agencies have one or more programs for older people. Their expenditures from general revenue in 1965 amounted to $1.5 billion for public assistance and to approximately $1.2 billion for health services, housing, food distribution, research, and employment programs. Approximately $14.5 billion was distributed among older people from various federally managed trust funds. Federal tax benefits to older people amounted to about $0.8 billion. State and community expenditures add considerably to some of these totals. The nation has moved far indeed from the position that total responsibility for the aged rested with themselves, their families, churches, and private charity.

These advances notwithstanding, it is common knowledge that the circumstances and the environment of older people today fall far short of the goals set forth in the preceding section. A brief review will serve as a reminder of the distances remaining to be traveled.

Older people probably represent the least secure group—certainly the least secure age group—in the population. More than 40 percent of the older couples and approximately 75 percent of nonmarried older persons have incomes below levels which afford only stringent living at best and which make no provision for long-term, expensive illness. The incomes of three-fifths of the older couples and upward of nine-tenths of the nonmarried are below the modest goals of $3,500 for couples and $2,500 for individuals.

It is apparent from these figures that the assumption that retired people would have sufficient income beyond social security levels has turned out to be mostly wishful thinking. The assets picture is no better. Median assets beyond equity in a home amount to about $3,000 for older couples and about $700 for the never-married and the widowed. Yet another unfavorable aspect of the income picture is that in recent years there has been an erosion of the income principle. Increasingly one can cite instances where older persons are receiving subsidies such as reduced fares, tax concessions, food stamps, and housing supplements in lieu of receiving increased incomes. It is here contended that such service payments are less desirable than monetary payments, for they tend to restrict the freedom of choice of individuals, and in a sense place them outside the market economy in which most Americans live. In effect, this makes them "different" and, conceivably, somewhat second-class.

Although the health picture has its positive side, four-fifths of those sixty-five and over and practically all of the one million who are eighty-five and over suffer from one or more chronic physical or mental pathologies which divert energy and attention from external interests. Forty percent of those sixty-five and above are physically unable to carry on their major activity, and one-half of these have difficulty getting around alone or are, for all practical purposes, confined to their homes or institutions. Sixty percent are edentulous.

Students of aging report that the overriding fear of older people is that of long-term illness without proper care or the ability to pay the costs. Currently, public welfare policy is resulting in the discharge of thousands of old people from mental hospitals into circumstances—nursing homes, foster homes, and the homes of children—which no one has dared to evaluate. Some health insurance is held by three-fifths of the older population, but complete coverage is restricted to a tiny minority. Medical Assistance for the Aged is equally inadequate in nearly all states. Health and medical facilities are generally insufficient and lack the coordination essential for proper utilization.

The population sixty-five years and over includes something above 5.5 million husband-wife households and upward of 5 million households headed by an older, unattached person with no children present. Approximately 4.5 million older people are sharing living quarters with an adult child and, often, with grandchildren, frequently because of insufficient income or need for personal care.

Thirty percent of the older population live in housing which is substandard structurally or deficient with respect to such commonplaces as an inside flush toilet, hot and cold running water, and bathtub. It has been estimated that one-half of older household members are in need of housing designed and priced with reference to their low incomes, health-restricted activity and mobility, or social deprivation. Yet the total number of dwelling units built with the aid of federal funds and occupied by older people stands at less than 50,000. The great majority of these house either high-income or low-income older people, there being as yet no federal assistance program suited to the needs of the middle-income elderly, who constitute perhaps one-fourth of the older population.

Several countries of Western Europe and a number of cities in the United States have demonstrated the value of community kitchens and home-delivered meals, homemaker services, companions to the elderly, visiting nurses, reassurance services, loan of sickroom equipment, and protective guidance and help in enabling physically and mentally frail older people to remain in the community with some degree of security and some satisfaction of the need for independence and individuality. Yet in most American communities these services are totally lacking or minimally available.

Means tests, residence requirements, and relative's responsibility statutes insult the dignity of hundreds of thousands of older people, deprive some of almost their total savings, and cause many to do without assistance they need.

The question of how much activity and participation older people desire is moot. There is wide variation among people, of course, in their capacities and preferences. Nevertheless, as suggested in an earlier section, there is ample evidence of the continuing need of the organism for activity and of the individual for relatedness and for a feeling of some usefulness to others, for opportunity for expression of his personality, and for recognition as an individual.

This is probably the area of aging in which society is demonstrating its greatest shortcoming. Although some efforts are being made to involve older people in voluntary service and in social activities, American society has yet to face seriously the questions of meaningful use of the retirement years and the place of older people in the community. Most are forced to the realization that they are abandoned to a marginal existence in a future-directed, youth-oriented society. This is probably particularly true of older retired men and of older widows who constitute 28 percent and 30 percent, respectively, of the population sixty-five and over.

Clubs and centers for seniors have been developed by the hundred; but with only monthly or weekly meetings they constitute no more than a gesture toward providing a locus of interest and activity for those who have no other attachment in the community. A good many of the centers are crowded into buildings which have become useless for other purposes and are ill-suited to the old. Many are unable to attract significant numbers of older people because they are insufficiently staffed or directed by individuals who have no knowledge of how to work with older people.

Although there is wide recognition that planning for meeting the total needs of older people at state and community levels is a major and continuing process, efforts to obtain federal grant funds have been practically without avail; and support in most of the states is meager.

The need for personnel with specialized knowledge of aging has been stated for years but, as of today, there are few university-based programs aimed at turning out individuals with a broad knowledge of aging and with competence in planning and community organization. Similarly, there are few career training programs in the country designed to prepare personnel for managing housing for older people and homes for the aged. State or even regional institutes of gerontology which might train professional personnel, conduct research in the social aspects of aging, and provide advisory services to legislatures, program agencies, and community planning groups are entirely lacking, as are sources of support for them.

Any description of social policy that deals only with the material conditions of the aged quite misses the plight of the aged in America. The lack of a philosophy of life which offers psychic compensation for the decrements of age, the lack in our social structure of formal institutional supports for the transitions in the later parts of the life cycle, and the lack of empathy and respect for those who have aged are more serious deficiencies than the lack of adequate material comforts. There are signs that our social policies may correct the latter; there is less reason to be optimistic with regard to the former. Our hope here lies in the fact that there is an integration of life. We shall not be able to accomplish our goals without viewing the total person in a total situation. The values and genius of our society will insure that the modern age revolution is carried to its logical conclusion.

BIOGRAPHICAL NOTE

DONALD P. KENT was born in Philadelphia, Pennsylvania, in 1916 and was educated at West Chester State Teachers College, Temple University, and the University of Pennsylvania (Ph.D.). Before becoming Chairman of the Department of Sociology and Anthropology at Pennsylvania State University, Mr. Kent was Director of the Office of Aging of the U. S. Department of Health, Education, and Welfare. He is a sociologist by training, and in addition to university teaching, he has been an active participant in state government. Mr. Kent has published a number of articles on governmental and community programs on aging and is the author of *The Refugee Intellectual*. He is a fellow in the Gerontological Society and the American Sociological Association.

8

Some Special Problems and Alternatives in Housing for Older Persons

Daniel M. Wilner
Rosabelle Price Walkley

It is perhaps a sign of the relative affluence of the United States that we can speak of somehow meeting the housing problems of one age group as distinct from meeting those of another. Only a culture which has generally achieved a fairly high economic level would be in a position to be concerned about the housing provisions for older persons as an issue distinct from provisions for younger people. Yet sensible concern has been made evident in the literature on this topic in the past several decades culminating in perhaps the first half of the present decade, 1960-1965.[1] There have been national professional meetings, a White House Conference, legislative hearings, and attendant study and recommendations on local, state, and federal levels drawing attention to the nature and purported increasing seriousness of the matter.[2] The expressed feeling is that housing

[1] Wilma Donahue (Ed.), *Housing the Aging* (Ann Arbor: University of Michigan Press, 1954). Clark Tibbitts and Wilma Donahue (Eds.), *Social and Psychological Aspects of Aging* (New York: Columbia University Press, 1962); especially E. E. Ashley and M. C. McFarland, "The Need for Research Toward Meeting the Housing Needs of the Elderly," G. H. Beyer, "Living Arrangements, Attitudes, and Preferences of Older Persons," and W. S. Lake, "Housing Preferences and Social Patterns," all in *ibid*. Also see Walter K. Vivrett, "Housing and Community Setting for Older People," in Clark Tibbitts (Ed.), *Handbook of Social Gerontology* (Chicago: University of Chicago Press, 1930).

[2] President's Council on Aging, *Action for Older Americans: 1964 Annual Report of the President's Council on Aging* (Washington: U. S. Government Printing Office, 1964). United States Senate, Special Committee on Aging, *A Report of the Subcommittee on Housing for the Elderly* (Washington: U. S. Government Printing Office, 1962).

for older persons is in short supply and inadequate on a number of counts; the situation is often viewed as improper to the orderly course of life in later years.

The purpose of the first part of this paper is to review briefly the data and analysis of facts that underlie general discussions of housing for the elderly. This will be followed by consideration of the relationships between housing and the fabric of life, with emphasis on the role of housing in the later years, culminating in a discussion of some major alternatives of housing provisions. Reference will be made to some data from the California Study of Retirement Housing,[3] regarding the nature and extent of special, group housing for older persons in one state in which the actual number of older persons is among the highest in any state in the nation and in 1965 probably exceeds two million persons.

I

The facts of the rise in older populations in Western societies are well known. In some countries the world over, the population sixty years of age and over is at least 10 percent of the total population; in a few countries the proportion is more than 15 percent.[4] In these same countries this represents a substantial increase both in numbers of these persons as well as in percentage of population in the same age bracket over, say, the situation in 1900. The reasons for this spectacular rise in older populations are generally agreed to lie in the decreasing morbidity and mortality resulting from control and prevention of infectious and communicable diseases and to the great improvement in sanitation, standards of living, and medical knowledge and care.

The 1960 census showed that in the United States, the population of persons sixty years and over was approximately 23.3 million persons, with another 8.5 million persons in the age range from fifty-five to fifty-nine,[5] making perhaps 32 million Americans either al-

---

[3] An investigation supported in whole by Public Health Service Research Grant MH-01358 from the National Institute of Mental Health.

[4] United Nations, *Demographic Yearbook, 1961* (New York: United Nations, 1961).

[5] U. S. Bureau of the Census, *U. S. Census of Population: 1960, Detailed Characteristics*, "United States Summary," Final Report PC(1)-1D (Washington: U. S. Government Printing Office, 1963).

ready included in thoughts about housing arrangements for older persons or within five or ten years of being so. Because of cohorts of population with greater life expectancy in the offing, estimates are that by the year 2000, the number of persons sixty and older will have risen to almost 42 million, so that some 55 million persons at that future date must be considered in thoughts about housing for older persons.[6]

These projections have obvious massivity about them, compared to the period of, say, 1900. They are commensurate with the overall expected rise in the general population in the next few decades. Although population increases ordinarily bring certain hazards to mind, giving rise, for example, to substantial questions about congestion in our cities, they are ordinarily cause for optimism and satisfaction in housing circles simply because they augur well for continuing housing demand. In connection with older persons, however, the population rises just cited are most often viewed with apprehension and alarm. Some of the reasons for these feelings will be discussed below.

II

Perspective regarding housing for older persons in the United States may be gained through a brief discussion of some data from the 1960 decennial census. In 1960, there were 53 million organized housing units. Of these, 16 million (30.1 percent) had persons sixty years and older as residents, with almost 10 million units inside standard metropolitan statistical areas (SMSAs) and about 6 million outside SMSAs.[7] The 16 million units housed 22.2 million persons sixty years of age and older. Of these, 19.3 million persons age sixty years and older (87 percent) lived in households in which the head of the household was himself (or herself) age sixty or older. In other words, the preponderant majority of older persons in the United States live independently in their own dwellings. In these units an

[6] U. S. Department of Labor, Bureau of Labor Statistics, *Projections to the Years 1976 and 2000: Economic Growth, Population, Labor Force and Leisure, and Transportation* (Washington: O.R.R.R.C. Study Report 23, 1962).

[7] U. S. Bureau of the Census, *U. S. Census of Housing: 1960*, Vol. VII, *Housing of Senior Citizens* (Washington: U. S. Government Printing Office, 1962).

older person is head of household despite the fact that there may be some measure of assistance from children. Among the 19.3 million persons in households just mentioned, approximately 3.8 million (20 percent) live alone in one-person arrangements—room, apartment, or house. Of the remaining 15.4 million, most (10.3 million) live in two-person households (mainly husband and wife), while the rest live in three-person households (3.1 million), or in households with four or more persons (2.1 million). Threading further through other census data regarding household composition, we find that there are approximately 7 million married couples age sixty and older in "independent" circumstances, and 6.1 million heads of household without spouses, mainly widows or widowers.

Not quite 3 million persons sixty and older live in households in which the head is under sixty. These persons tend, of course, to be related to the head of the house or his wife and are most likely to be parents of one or the other. In these cases, the older person is most often the only such person in the household (married older couples are only rarely found living with children or other relatives) and is most likely to be a woman.

III

Attention has time and again been brought to the precarious economic condition of many older persons in the United States, a fact that warrants consideration in discussions of housing for this portion of the population.[8] Income level is at least one important factor in limiting the degrees of freedom of older persons regarding housing.

Of the 16 million American households with persons sixty years of age and older, more than half have incomes below $4,000. Table 8-1 shows the income distribution for various subgroups. Among two or more person households, 65.7 percent of those with heads under sixty have incomes of $5,000 or more compared to 38.0 percent of those with heads age sixty or over. (For the latter, the median is $3,800, with almost 4 million households having incomes under

[8] Ying-Ping Chen, "Poverty: The Special Case of the Aged" (University of California at Los Angeles, Department of Economics), mimeo; presented at the Interdisciplinary Seminar on Aging, UCLA School of Public Health, April 20, 1965.

$3,000.) Most serious of all is the situation for the older person living alone, with median income of $1,100 (1.7 million with income under $1,000 per year). As might be suspected, medians decline still further in successively older age groups.[9]

TABLE 8-1

HOUSEHOLD INCOME FOR HOUSEHOLDS WITH MEMBER 60 YEARS OLD OR OVER

| | TWO OR MORE PERSON HOUSEHOLDS | | | | ONE PERSON HOUSEHOLDS, 60 YEARS OR OVER | |
| | Head under 60 years | | Head 60 years or over | | | |
Income	Number	Per-cent	Number	Per-cent	Number	Per-cent
Less than $1,000	120,655	4.5	1,084,304	11.4	1,706,637	45.6
$1,000 - $1,499	75,764	2.8	818,617	8.6	639,092	17.0
$1,500 - $1,999	75,823	2.8	787,037	8.3	336,637	9.0
$2,000 - $2,499	87,491	3.2	711,887	7.5	249,359	6.6
$2,500 - $2,999	89,258	3.3	591,696	6.2	142,756	3.8
$3,000 - $3,999	218,441	8.1	1,016,328	10.7	226,557	6.0
$4,000 - $4,999	260,594	9.6	886,071	9.3	154,690	4.1
$5,000 - $5,999	297,868	11.0	792,790	8.3	105,207	2.8
$6,000 - $6,999	275,097	10.2	614,496	6.5	60,654	1.6
$7,000 - $9,999	608,813	22.6	1,113,041	11.7	72,205	1.9
$10,000 or more	592,221	21.9	1,099,001	11.5	61,536	1.6
Total	2,702,025	100.0	9,515,268	100.0	3,755,330	100.0

Source: Adapted from U.S. Bureau of the Census, U.S. Census of Housing: 1960, Vol. VII, Housing of Senior Citizens (Washington, D.C.: 1962), Table A-3, p. 6.

Of course, one of the major factors contributing to the income condition of persons in their later years is that of withdrawal from the labor force, either complete or partial. For the individual already at retirement, little increase can be expected except, perhaps, from

[9] U. S. Census of Housing: 1960, Housing of Senior Citizens.

rises in social security payments. For future retirees, the situation may be more hopeful; for example, cohorts of persons coming to retirement age in future years may have increased social security benefits, and may have a greater likelihood of being included in private pension plans.

Thus at present, although not all persons in the later years are at the poverty level, a substantial proportion are. And all—relatively well-off and poor alike—remain highly vulnerable because of the vagaries of personal experience. For example, in a population segment for whom morbidity rates are two and three times what they are at age thirty for many conditions, medical embarrassment can make irretrievable inroads into financial position.[10] With hospital costs (exclusive of physicians' services and care following illness) averaging $50.00 per day in some cities, only the most extensive (and expensive) insurance coverage can adequately protect against the most serious inroads on the older person's assets.

Finally, of some importance from the point of view of capability with regard to housing, is the difficulty older persons experience in commanding credit, due to sharply reduced income after retirement. Banks are reluctant (and from their viewpoint properly so, perhaps) to extend credit to older persons, even when income is above the poverty level.

IV

Related to the foregoing economic considerations are several factors pertaining to the housing units per se, which involve tenure,

[10] In 1960, the National Health Survey showed that about three-quarters of noninstitutionalized persons of age sixty-five and over had one or more chronic conditions (U. S. Department of Health, Education, and Welfare, Public Health Service, *Health Statistics: Older Persons, Selected Health Characteristics, United States, July 1957-June 1959* [Washington: U. S. Government Printing Office, 1960]), and a study of 500 older subjects in the Kips Bay-Yorkville Health District of New York in 1954, found that 77 percent had one or more health-connected complaints, some chronic ailment being reported by 53 percent of the sample (Bernard Kutner, David Fanshel, Alice M. Togo, and Thomas S. Langner, *Five Hundred Over Sixty* [New York: Russell Sage Foundation, 1956]). Thus, "with older adults the incidence of chronic disease rises, and there is a small likelihood that any person over 65 picked at random is free of diagnosable conditions." See James E. Birren, "Principles of Research on Aging," in James E. Birren (Ed.), *Handbook of Aging and the Individual* (Chicago: University of Chicago Press, 1959).

property values, rent levels, and age and condition of the dwellings. The 1960 decennial census showed that, of the 13.2 million housing units in the United States in which the household head is in his sixties or older, 9.1 million (68.3 percent) are owner-occupied (essentially the same percentage in which the household head is under sixty).[11] Of these 9.1 million units (housing a majority of older persons in the nation), 73 percent were built in 1939 or earlier, and only 6 percent were built in the five years preceding the census year (1960). Some idea of the value of these houses may be gleaned from Table 8-2, which gives the distribution of house values for 8.4 million

TABLE 8-2
VALUE OF OWNER-OCCUPIED UNITS

Value of Unit	HEAD UNDER 60 YEARS OLD		HEAD 60 YEARS OF AGE OR OVER	
	Number	Percent	Number	Percent
Less than $ 5,000	153,197	9.6	1,265,770	18.8
$ 5,000 - $ 7,400	182,217	11.5	1,097,721	16.2
$ 7,500 - $ 9,900	206,764	13.0	1,044,652	15.4
$10,000 - $12,400	241,091	15.1	1,032,198	15.2
$12,500 - $14,900	211,511	13.3	713,456	10.5
$15,000 - $17,400	182,089	11.5	536,448	7.9
$17,500 - $19,900	129,805	8.2	328,536	4.8
$20,000 - $24,999	137,588	8.7	348,213	5.1
$25,000 or more	145,222	9.1	410,390	6.1
Total	1,589,484	100.0	6,777,384	100.0

Source: Adapted from U.S. Bureau of the Census, *U.S. Census of Housing: 1960,* Vol. VII, *Housing of Senior Citizens* (Washington, D.C.: 1962), Table A-7, p. 52.

owner-occupied, single-unit properties. The houses tend to the modest side in estimated value, half of those with heads in the sixties being valued at less than $10,000.

In the same 9.1 million owner-occupied housing units, 41.9 per-

[11] *U. S. Census of Housing: 1960, Housing of Senior Citizens.*

cent of the household heads had been living in the house prior to 1939. Finally, housing quality data reveal that, although crowding is not an issue in these same dwelling units (97.4 percent having one or fewer occupants per room), in 20.4 percent there is dilapidation or lack of plumbing facilities.

For the 4.1 million renter-occupied housing units in which the head is sixty or older, the situation is even worse regarding both the age of the structures and their condition. In 81.2 percent of the units the structure was built in 1939 or earlier, and in 29.0 percent of the units there was dilapidation or other major defect. Some idea of the monthly rental may be derived from Table 8-3, which shows that, compared to household heads under sixty, those aged sixty and over are much more likely to pay lower rentals and less apt to pay higher rentals, the trends being consistent throughout the entire range of rents. Thus, 42.6 percent of the older household heads who rent pay

TABLE 8-3
GROSS MONTHLY RENT

Rent	HEAD UNDER 60 YEARS OLD		HEAD 60 YEARS OF AGE OR OVER	
	Number	Percent	Number	Percent
Less than $20	8,940	1.3	109,672	2.7
$ 20 - $ 29	17,921	2.6	251,394	6.3
$ 30 - $ 39	31,185	4.6 } 26.0	378,967	9.4 } 42.6
$ 40 - $ 49	49,109	7.2	465,367	11.6
$ 50 - $ 59	70,131	10.3	506,622	12.6
$ 60 - $ 79	165,276	24.5	871,179	21.8
$ 80 - $ 99	130,868	19.3 } 65.5	510,311	12.7 } 47.0
$100 - $149	119,187	17.6	381,131	9.5
$150 or more	27,502	4.1	120,885	3.0
No cash rent	57,550	8.5	418,885	10.4
Total	677,669	100.0	4,014,413	100.0

Source: Adapted from U.S. Bureau of the Census, U.S. Census of Housing: 1960, Vol. VII, Housing of Senior Citizens (Washington, D.C.: 1962), Table A-6, p. 50.

less than $60 per month, in contrast to 26 percent of the younger heads.

It would appear that the housing of older persons tends, by American standards, to be relatively old and to some extent in a state of disrepair. By and large, owner-occupied housing of older persons tends somewhat more to be dilapidated than that of comparable younger household heads, but appears to be less crowded in general. This suggests housing that was once in better repair but which, with the passage of time, has deteriorated and also indicates the departure of children from houses once large enough to provide shelter for larger families.

For the owner-occupied group it remains unclear what personal financial equities exist in the houses that might represent assets, a matter of considerable importance in attempts to estimate financial capability of older persons in connection with housing markets. In any event, it should be borne in mind that housing equity is in most market areas not a liquid asset.

A further consideration which census data only imperfectly illuminate is the fact that the dwellings of older householders—whether owned or rented—in addition to being relatively old structures are also often located in neighborhoods that have lost their fashion. These neighborhoods tend to lie in the central core of cities and are very apt to have slum characteristics and low residential property values. In the ordinary course of housing marketability, residents would move outward—and probably upward socially. However, it is suggested from the data for older home owners, at least, that they do not move. Moreover, older persons who own houses are only minor participants in new housing purchases, compared to the home-owning population as a whole (6.2 percent compared with 18.5 percent, respectively).

V

A voluminous literature exists, only occasionally concerned with older populations per se, which calls attention to an association between the character and quality of housing and the prevalence of physical, social, and psychological disorders of the residents. The general conclusion from such studies is that when housing is demonstrably inferior—that is, suffering dilapidation or major deficiency— it is more likely than housing of better quality to be the site of physical and social pathology. Regrettably, the preponderant majority of such studies rely on cross-sectional data, which do not in general permit a valid conclusion that the housing was the cause of the pathology.

Recent longitudinal research, employing matched test and control groups, and measuring families before and after the move from slum to good housing, confirms the causative role of housing quality mainly in connection with (1) infectious disease and the communicable diseases of childhood, thus suggesting the role of sanitation, and (2) with accidents, calling to mind cramped quarters, high density of population in the slum, and general dilapidation.[12] It remains to be demonstrated satisfactorily that improvement in the quality of housing (dilapidation, deficiencies, and so on) has detectable effect on issues such as morale, self-esteem, and tension levels, when other deleterious influences remain unchanged. Many changes are observable in the move from bad to good housing. But it remains an open question whether, without attempting to alter other conditions of life as well, housing betterment itself has the intrinsic seeds of psychological and social amelioration.

While confirmed proof is absent that aspects of housing are principal causative factors in long-term adjustment trends, common experience suggests ways in which intrinsic housing characteristics are pressed into the service of long- and short-term objectives of life. For example, status-accruing elements of the well-fixed dwellings in "good" neighborhoods are well known, and they presumably bolster self-esteem.[13] Housing can also be perceived in negative ways, and can intrinsically represent burdensomeness and fall from status. More extrinsically, but commonly as well, housing is the site of the myriad pleasant and unpleasant experiences of life, and in the later years may be the constant reminder of fondly dwelt-on happiness on the one hand and demoralizing unhappiness on the other.

[12] D. M. Wilner, R. P. Walkley, T. C. Pinkerton, and M. Tayback, *The Housing Environment and Family Life: A Longitudinal Study of the Effects of Housing on Morbidity and Mental Health* (Baltimore: Johns Hopkins Press, 1962).

[13] In this context, housing aspects can also serve clearly pathological ends, as, for example, in the American play of the 1920's *Craig's Wife* by George Kelly.

One aspect of housing which has been shown to affect certain behavior is architectural arrangement of dwelling units. The role of dwelling unit juxtaposition and proximity of residents has been revealed to be important in determining the nature and extent of mutually promotive contacts enjoyed among neighbors in student housing,[14] in slum dwellings, and in high-rise buildings,[15] and as factors in the development of interracial attitudes.[16] In this connection, dwelling unit proximity, associated with the factor of similarity and difference in personal characteristics of neighbors, has recently been emphasized as being important in the maintenance of social contacts and morale among elderly persons.[17]

It is in the service of these other objectives of life that individuals and family units, particularly in the United States, sometimes seek to change their housing. The 1960 decennial census reveals how normal residential mobility is for Americans; the nation over, 47.3 percent of the population had lived in different dwelling units five years earlier;[18] this is a substantial proportion, even discounting the newly formed households occurring in the period 1955-1960. Many factors account for the high mobility,[19] including movement into proximity of employment, the search for larger quarters to accommodate growing families, and the search for congenial neighborhoods.

For older persons, a particular set of situational factors may provide motives for residential change. It is important to keep in mind that not all factors operate simultaneously for all older persons; nevertheless, the likelihood is high that more than a single factor is present. Among the instigations to move are the following:

(1) Reduction in family size through the growing up of children, making the present dwelling, whether owned or rented, too large or too expensive to maintain.

[14] Leon Festinger, Stanley Schachter, and Kurt W. Back, *Social Pressures in Informal Groups: A Study of Human Factors in Housing* (New York: Harper & Row, 1950).

[15] Wilner, Walkley, Pinkerton, and Tayback, *op. cit.*

[16] D. M. Wilner, R. P. Walkley, and S. Cook, *Human Relations in Interracial Housing* (Minneapolis: University of Minnesota Press, 1955).

[17] Irving Rosow, *Housing and Social Integration of the Aged* (Cleveland: Western Reserve University, 1964), mimeo.

[18] *U. S. Census of Population: 1960, Detailed Characteristics*, "United States Summary."

[19] Peter H. Rossi, *Why Families Move* (New York: Free Press, 1955).

(2) Death or institutionalization of spouse, with similar effect on size and expense in maintaining the dwelling.

(3) Loss of kin and/or neighbors from the environs through movement or death.

(4) Physical changes in the neighborhood, including the disappearance of familiar landmarks, the general deterioration of structures, and, following urban trends, the rezoning and commercialization of neighboring buildings.

(5) Forced dislocations, as a result of demolition for a variety of civic improvements such as highways, public housing, urban redevelopment projects, or commercial buildings.

(6) Loosening of responsibilities for others and inclinations toward venturesomeness.

These reasons for movement are at the same time accompanied by two principal inhibitions to making the change: generally sharp reduction in income and, as time passes, reduction in physical energies, accompanied by actual increasing illness and impairment. The great dilemma occurs when the need (sometimes very urgent) or desire for residential change arises, but satisfactory alternatives to the present quarters either do not exist or are sharply limited.

It is in this context that we must seek elements of public policy toward housing for older persons. A viable policy depends to a great extent on the weighing of the force of the issues just enumerated and on the consideration of the realistic, but at the same time socially promotive housing alternatives generally open to persons in later years. Sooner or later all persons are faced by losses of the near and dear through death and dispersion, resulting in a general loss of familiar affectional relationships. All are faced sooner or later by loss of the statuses held in younger years, as well as by impairments of health and the threat and inroads of disease. It is against these perils to the personal, economic, and psychosocial security of individuals that housing solutions can reasonably be directed.

VI

There are at least three major alternative solutions to the problems posed by older persons searching for adequate housing arrangements. Each has purported advantages; each has drawbacks and deficits. Regarding each, so far as older persons have their own preferences and voice in the matter, there are known or suspected inclinations and disinclinations. The matter is clouded over by inevitable uncertainties, particularly where the alternative settled on is relatively new on the scene, and for which accumulated experience is slight or nonexistent. Furthermore, in the age group under discussion, because of both financial limitations and energy levels, there is a certain irreversibility of the decision. It is a testimonial to the spirit that much imperfection is endured at this age, as well as at any other.

Living with children. One alternative arrangement in the later years is living with one's children. While satisfactory arrangements exist, it is the rare setting in which older parents can live with adult children, themselves in the process of raising families, and have things go smoothly. Differences often exist among generations in goals, values, customs, energy levels, and physical and psychological sensitivities that are difficult to reconcile. Often, too, there is redintegration of older feeling states regarding independence itself that mar relationships. For older persons, perhaps nowhere are feelings of powerlessness more plainly apparent than in households in which for many reasons they are not the sources of guidance and direction. The dwelling unit itself, possibly too small and improperly arranged, is not conducive to satisfaction in this arrangement. It is the rare dwelling unit in which a parent can satisfactorily be physically accommodated even in family settings that in other respects can be expected to nurture satisfaction. Nevertheless, family ties are strong, and the gains in security for the older person cannot be entirely overlooked, despite the fact that the whole fabric may be marred by various tensions.

Independent living arrangements in unplanned settings. Perhaps no single issue is as clear-cut as that of the forces—economic, social, and psychological—pressing toward the maintenance of independent living arrangements. In youth we seek separate households as visible manifestation of our independence and individual destinies. In our middle and later years, the designation of "household head" signifies our continued status as independent arbiter of our own fate. These strivings for independence have the deepest psychological roots and are buttressed at all stages by folklore and social institutions. We desire sufficient independence to insure the promotion of our personal wishes. It would seem that separate living arrangements, although not guaranteeing, are at least the sine qua non of such promotion.

For older persons, one type of independent living arrangement in unplanned settings consists of living in dwelling units (houses, apartments, or rooms) dispersed throughout many different kinds of natural neighborhoods. Such neighborhoods would typically have the same age groups represented as are found in the general population, and all the residents would share the realities and by-products of the neighborhood's social and economic circumstances. Another type which also occurs in natural neighborhoods, often in the central core of a city, consists of the spontaneous assembly of older persons in multi-unit structures (apartment houses, hotels, rooming houses). Such "assemblies" are often the result of social and economic forces which leave older persons as the principal occupants of certain buildings, the latter sometimes old and dilapidated. By and large, in either type of living arrangement, whether dispersed or spontaneous assembly, the elderly resident has available only the services and facilities that exist naturally in the neighborhood, without special, planned provisions. For the elderly poor, there exists the economic issue of whether income is sufficient to maintain the independent living arrangement in housing of good quality. For all, the impending possibility exists that the independent living arrangement would become difficult or impossible to maintain if a long-term disabling illness were to occur.

As has been reviewed above, for a great many reasons independent living in natural settings will undoubtedly remain the modal arrangements for persons in later years. Yet, as has been suggested, forces are at work systematically making inroads on this as the primary solution.

Planned congregate arrangements. In recent years, a new version has emerged of the assembly of older persons in dwelling units in one or more buildings. This is the planned congregate arrangement under management control, in which older persons are the modal or exclusive occupants. The buildings are often clearly demarcated from the rest of the buildings in the environs, and often some deliberate attempt has been made to provide facilities or services appropriate to older persons.

Until a generation or two ago, congregate arrangements of this sort were generally unthought of except in connection with enfeeblement or illness. Today institutions still exist, in continually mounting number, for older persons who are thought unable to lead truly independent lives and who need varying degrees of assistance in their everyday activities. And as age and enfeeblement proceed, nursing homes provide further aid to the increasingly dependent.

Congregate assemblies of older persons in their late fifties and sixties—the "younger" old—are among the new developments taking place. We are here referring to facilities for persons of retirement age, catering generally to persons capable of managing their own affairs and living independent lives. Yet in recognition of special needs and desires of older persons, these facilities provide a variety of services, programs, and opportunities that are thought to have special attraction. Planned group-housing arrangements for these essentially well elderly persons are increasing in number the country over, the nationwide figure being difficult to approximate at this time, although national estimates will emerge in time.[20] A census of such housing sites in California has recently been undertaken, and selected data from this study will be discussed shortly.

VII

Forces affecting the building of group housing for the elderly. The very recent history of special group-housing facilities in the United States notes several principal sources of instigation for building and operating the sites. First may be singled out church and fraternal groups, labor unions, and voluntary associations interested in providing their elderly membership with housing at appropriate cost. The major American religious denominations (Protestant, Catholic, and Jewish) are substantially involved in this activity, catering thus far principally to persons in the late sixties and older.

Second are the facilities instigated by entrepreneurship. In

---

[20] For example, the National Council on the Aging is currently gathering this information.

various states a number of builders and real estate subdividers have been attracted to special group housing for older persons; this has apparently been found to be a highly marketable commodity if preceded by careful market analysis and planning and promoted through motivational appeals. Entrepreneurs are engaged in building housing for all segments of the elderly population, including sites appealing initially to the "younger" elderly, that is, persons in the late fifties to the middle sixties (e.g., the "retirement village"), as well as sites appealing to persons of more advanced years.

The third instigating force is the federal government, which, through the Housing and Home Finance Agency (HHFA), has taken an active role in stimulating the construction of dwelling units for the elderly, principally some kind of special group housing.[21] There are three major programs under the jurisdiction of the Housing and Home Finance Agency to help meet the housing needs of older persons, and a fourth in the Farmers Home Administration for those who live in rural areas. One of the HHFA programs provides for "low-interest-rate, long-term loans to private nonprofit corporations, consumer cooperatives, or public bodies or agencies . . . which sponsor rental or cooperative housing and related facilities for older families and persons."[22] The second HHFA program insures lenders against losses on mortgages for construction or rehabilitation of rental accommodations for older persons. The third program provides for low-rent public housing for the elderly which is planned, built, and operated by local housing authorities, through financing by means of the public sale of new bonds. "Any deficits in the debt service charges on these bonds, which cannot be met out of rental income, are provided by annual contributions from the Public Housing Administration."[23] Following its mandate to provide housing for persons in dire need and of limited finances, the PHA is currently allocating approximately half the dwelling units to be built in the next few years as "housing for the elderly."

[21] Housing and Home Finance Agency, *16th Annual Report* (Washington: U. S. Government Printing Office, 1962).

[22] President's Council on Aging, *Report to the President* (Washington: U. S. Government Printing Office, 1963).

[23] Additional information on these HHFA programs for housing the older people, and a summary of the provisions of the Housing Act of 1964 which assist in meeting the housing needs of the elderly, appear at the end of this chapter. See also, *Report to the President*.

General characteristics of group housing for the elderly. As the result of these various sources of stimulation, a variety of subtypes of special group housing for older persons (the well elderly) is emerging. The housing facilities provide both rental and purchase opportunities for living in detached, semidetached, or row (that is, "garden") arrangements; high-rise buildings as well as low-rise and combinations of both; in the center of cities and in all distances from urban centers; resembling the other buildings in the surrounding area or strikingly demarcated; sumptuously or more modestly appointed depending on the income group being sought as residents. Costs and rents vary, being low in public housing and from there ranging upward in nonpublic housing sites to a sum clearly geared to the very well-off.

There is variation also in the degree of independence being fostered in different sites. In those intended for persons in their late fifties and sixties, residents are expected to shift for themselves, personal maintenance chores, food purchase and preparation, and housekeeping being the responsibility of the inhabitant. For older age groups, meals are served centrally, and food preparation and housekeeping responsibilities are either light or the function of management.

In many instances, special features inside the dwelling units are clearly designed for the older person: weight-sustaining grab bars at strategic places, electricity outlets several feet from the floor, wide doorways (anticipating wheel-chair necessity).

In the last several years, a number of sites, including a few of those intended for the "younger" elderly, have organized and offered outpatient medical facilities on the premises in response to the known higher incidence of illness—particularly chronic diseases—among persons in later years. In one facility, for example, the charge for this service is a flat fee, plus a fraction of the doctor's usual visit charge. One entrepreneurial group in particular is extending the concept to include the presence of hospital facilities on the site. Medical facilities, both outpatient (clinic) and inpatient (hospital), apparently have been found to have sales appeal to persons in their later years.

The question sometimes arises as to whether all sites housing older persons in groups should be licensed by appropriate state or local health or welfare agencies. Concern is expressed about the existing or potential resident population who might need the protection special licensure provides. Policy on this issue will undoubtedly be developing with the passage of time, particularly as cohorts of residents in the age range sixty to sixty-five grow older and as more special group housing comes into existence.

The 1964 California survey. In recent years, heightened activity in the construction and organization of special group-housing facilities for older persons has occurred in several states, including those enjoying mild climates, for example, Florida and the states in the Southwest. The situation in California is of particular interest; in this state, with, in 1964, approximately 2 million persons sixty years and older, and with an aggressive economy, there has been evidence of a great deal of interest in the housing of older persons.[24]

In 1964, a series of studies was undertaken to examine the import of various housing environments on the fabric of life of older persons. As the first phase of this study, a statewide survey[25] was undertaken of special housing facilities for the well elderly in California.[26] The intent of the survey was to provide certain baseline information about the status of development of these sites, partly as useful backdrop for later studies of life-style of residents, and more particularly as documentation of community reaction to perceived residential requirements of persons in the middle and later years.

[24] In 1960, in California, there were approximately 5 million occupied dwelling units (U. S. Bureau of the Census, *U. S. Census of Housing: 1960,* Vol. I, *States and Small Areas,* "California," Final Report HC(1)-6 [Washington: U. S. Government Printing Office, 1962]), of which approximately 1 million dwelling units housed one or more persons age sixty and older (*U. S. Census of Housing: 1960, Housing of Senior Citizens*). Living in the dwelling units were 1.9 million persons in that age group; here, as with the national figures cited earlier, 87 percent (1.6 million persons) lived in dwellings in which an older person was himself head of the household, and 13 percent (232,000 persons) lived in circumstances in which a younger person was household head. Two-thirds of older persons lived in owner-occupied houses, the remainder as renters. In all, 442,000 (22.5 percent) lived in one-person households, that is, lived alone. While household income for older residents in California is not available in published census materials, comparison of annual incomes of *heads* of households in which older persons reside reveals a $300 differential (U. S. median: $1900; California median: $2200).

[25] R. P. Walkley, W. P. Mangum, Jr., S. R. Sherman, Suzanne Dodds, and D. M. Wilner, *Retirement Housing in California* (Berkeley, Calif.: Diablo Press, 1966).

[26] Acknowledgment is made of the contribution of the other members of the senior staff of the California Study of Retirement Housing, in the conduct of the survey: Wiley Mangum, Jr., Suzanne Dodds, and Susan Sherman.

The survey obtained information (as of midyear, 1964) on four types of sites that were formally[27] in the business of providing residence for older persons of generally good health: two varieties which were licensed directly or indirectly by the California Department of Social Welfare to provide personal care and service, that is, institutions and boarding homes for aged persons; and two varieties which were not so licensed, that is, fixed-dwelling-unit sites (retirement villages, high-rise apartment buildings, retirement hotels and mobile-home parks. Altogether, a total of 3,874 group-housing sites were identified throughout California, including more than 600 fixed-dwelling-unit facilities, mobile-home parks, and aged institutions; and 3,245 boarding homes for aged persons (Table 8-4).[28] Following

TABLE 8-4

1964 CALIFORNIA SURVEY: TYPES AND NUMBERS OF HOUSING FACILITIES

Not Licensed by California Department of Social Welfare	Number of Facilities
Fixed-dwelling-unit facilities	159
Completed or under construction	(131)
Planned new construction	(28)
Mobile-home parks	171
Licensed by California Department of Social Welfare	
Aged institutions	299
Already licensed	(284)
To be licensed	(15)
Boarding homes for aged persons	3,245
Total	3,874

[27] Beyond census information, data were not obtained about residences for older persons in "natural" neighborhoods.

[28] Included among the several thousand sites were fifty-seven *federally* assisted housing facilities: thirty-three under FHA 231; fourteen under CFA 202; and ten under PHA. Among the FHA-231 sites, twenty were nonlicensed, fixed-dwelling-unit facilities, and thirteen were licensed aged institutions; of the CFA-202 sites, thirteen were nonlicensed fixed-dwelling-unit facilities, and one was a licensed aged institution.

is a summary of the characteristics of these sites as shown by the survey findings.

1. Corresponding to the population distribution in the state, a majority of sites was located in southern California with particularly heavy concentrations of mobile-home parks and aged institutions occurring in this region (Table 8-5). Related data revealed that about 55 percent of the fixed-dwelling-unit sites and 80 percent of the aged institutions were located in the various "urbanized areas" of the state; however, two-thirds of mobile-home parks were situated outside such urban centers.

TABLE 8-5

1964 CALIFORNIA SURVEY: PERCENTAGE OF TOTAL SITES IN REGIONS OF CALIFORNIA

	FIXED D.U. FACILITIES				
	131 Completed or Under Construction	28 Planned New Construction	171 Mobile-Home Parks	284 Aged Institutions	3245 Boarding Homes for Aged Persons
Southern California	62%	64%	83%	73%	61%
Northern California: Central	37	36	13	27	33
San Francisco Bay area	(31)	(32)	(11)	(19)	(21)
S.F. Bay area outer ring	(2)	(4)	(1)	(4)	(10)
East-central area	(4)	(−)	(1)	(4)	(2)
Northern California: North	1	−	4	−	6

2. One-fifth of mobile-home parks and aged institutions enumerated were in some phase of construction, principally additions being made to existing sites. Fixed-dwelling-unit sites showed the greatest

activity, with about half the sites either still being completed or in some stage of planning.

3. The large majority of sites had fewer than 200 dwelling units (Table 8-6). The notable exceptions were among the fixed-dwelling-

TABLE 8-6

1964 CALIFORNIA SURVEY: SIZE OF SITES IN TERMS OF THE FINAL TOTAL NUMBER OF DWELLING UNITS OR MOBILE-HOME SPACES (IN PERCENTS)

Final Number of Dwelling Units or Mobile-Home Spaces	FIXED D.U. FACILITIES			
	131 Completed or Under Construction	28 Planned New Construction	171 Mobile-Home Parks	284 Aged Institutions
24 or fewer	11% } 24%	— } 4%	20% } 45%	56% } 70%
25 to 49	13	4%	25	14
50 to 74	11 } 22	14 } 28	19 } 32	6 } 10
75 to 99	11	14	13	4
100 to 149	12 } 19	14 } 21	12 } 15	5 } 10
150 to 199	7	7	3	5
200 to 299	11 } 16	7 } 14	4 } 5	4 } 6
300 to 499	5	7	1	2
500 to 999	5 } 17	7 } 33	— } 1	— } —
1,000 or more	12	26	1	—
No answer	2	—	2	4

unit facilities, where one-third of the sites completed or under construction and almost one-half of the planned new construction sites already had or would ultimately have 200 or more units. Already built and occupied, for example, was one "retirement village" with more than 6,000 dwelling units (10,000 residents), and some sites in the process of planning or occupancy had even larger numbers of dwelling units as the objective. Eighty percent of mobile-home sites and aged institutions had fewer than 100 spaces and units, respectively; only 6 percent of each category of facility had 200 or more. Half the boarding homes were licensed to accommodate fewer than five residents, with 19 percent having a capacity of from seven to fifteen residents, the latter being the maximum size.

4. At the time of the survey (midyear, 1964), approximately 59,000 residents were in fixed-dwelling-unit facilities, mobile-home parks, and aged institutions, and an estimated 16,000 residents were in boarding homes for aged persons, making a total of about 75,000 older persons in all four categories of facilities combined.

When dwelling units in sites under construction, in the process of addition, or in planning were totaled, they came to approximately 152,000 units (Table 8-7). Based on an estimate of about 1.3 persons

TABLE 8-7

1964 CALIFORNIA SURVEY: NUMBER OF DWELLING UNITS BY STATUS OF CONSTRUCTION (OR NUMBER OF MOBILE-HOME SPACES BY STATUS OF PREPARATION)

	Fixed D.U. Facilities	Mobile-Home Parks	Aged Institutions	Total
Built (or prepared)	21,267	11,118	12,966	45,351
Under construction (or preparation)	67,120	1,883	1,244	70,247
Planned new construction	35,217	–	1,636	36,853
Final Total	123,604	13,001	15,846	152,451

per dwelling unit, approximately 198,000 residents could ultimately be accommodated; adding boarding homes at full capacity (about 17,600 accommodations) results in an estimated 215,600 persons as possibly living in group-housing arrangements for older persons in the next few years.

The age of the residents spanned the later years, including on the low end a relatively small proportion of persons below age sixty and extending into the eighties and nineties for many. As might be expected, modal age varied among the types of sites. Fixed-dwelling-unit sites and mobile-home parks housed the "younger" old, with average age in the middle sixties; persons in the aged institutions and boarding homes averaged about fifteen years older (average age of eighty).

5. Dwelling-unit type, sponsorship, financial arrangements, and costs varied among the sites. Three-fifths of the dwelling units among all the fixed-dwelling-unit facilities (completed or under construction) were apartments; about one-quarter, each, were houses or rooms. There was an even more marked trend toward apartments among the planned new construction fixed-dwelling-unit sites. All the boarding homes provided rooms, and 95 percent of the units among all the aged institutions were also rooms, although some aged institutions tended to depart from the tradition by offering other types of dwelling units instead or in addition. General types of financial arrangements with the residents are given in Table 8-8 for the various kinds of sites.

TABLE 8-8

1964 CALIFORNIA SURVEY: ALL TYPES OF FINANCIAL ARRANGEMENTS AMONG FACILITIES

| | FIXED D.U. FACILITIES | | | | | |
| | Completed or Under Construction | | Planned New Construction | | Aged Institutions | |
	Number	Percent	Number	Percent	Number	Percent
Any purchase[1]	43	33	9	32	–	–
Any rental:						
Meals not included	61	46	22	78	2	1
Meals included	26	20	1	4	247	87
Any life care[2]	–	–	–	–	35	13
Any life lease[2]	–	–	–	–	17	6
All units free	5	4	–	–	3	1
Total Sites[3]	131		28		284	

[1]Meals not included in financial arrangement.
[2]Meals included in financial arrangement.
[3]Numbers add to more than "Total sites" and percentages add to more than 100 because some sites had more than one type of financial arrangement.

Fixed-dwelling-unit sites. In about one-third of the fixed-dwelling-unit facilities, some or all of the units were for purchase, generally requiring the customary down payment and mortgage payments, although in some instances cash purchases were made. While involving a minority of the sites, this category involved the largest number of dwelling units (88 percent of all units completed or under construction), because purchase arrangements most often prevailed among the largest sites (for example, retirement villages). In other words, a large majority of the units becoming available as a result of the "boom" in retirement housing in California are for purchase. Purchase costs appeared similar regardless of whether the dwelling units were apartments or detached houses. All sites taken together, the minimum purchase price averaged about $14,200, with these minimums ranging from $9,000 to $29,500 depending on the facility and the accommodations. Maximum prices averaged about $20,000, with the upper limit reaching approximately $40,000 (except for one site which had a maximum purchase price of $90,000). Depending on the required down payment (at least 10 percent), principal, interest, maintenance, and other charges often were in the range of $100 to $225 per month, with higher and lower costs possible in some sites.

In the remaining two-thirds of the sites in this category, dwelling units were for rent (with meals included in one-fifth of the sites, generally in hotel-like arrangements). For the facilities which did not include meals in the rental, mainly sites which had apartments only, the lower bound averaged about $75 per month (ranging as high as $225 per month), and the upper bound averaged $110 per month (ranging as high as $605 per month). Rooms with meals, as in the case of retirement hotels, had minimum rates averaging about $115 per month and an average maximum of about $175 per month, the upper bound of both being in the neighborhood of $350 to $400 per month.

Private enterprise dominated the development of the larger sites, almost completely for the very largest, and in three-quarters of the medium-sized sites (75-199 final dwelling units); church, fraternal, or philanthropic sponsorship, public housing, and other nonprofit corporations were responsible for three-fifths of the smaller sites.

Aged institutions. The situation on almost all counts was substantially different among aged institutions. In the vast majority of cases, payments at aged institutions were made as rentals; in about 20 percent, some form of life care or life lease arrangement was possible. Most rentals included meals, and the minimum monthly rent averaged $150 (ranging up to $400); the maximum averaged $245 (ranging up to $650). Life care and life lease arrangements required substantial initial fees. Average minimum lump sums for life care arrangements ranged from $7,500 to $16,500; average maximums from $22,000 to $58,000. Lump sum averages for life lease arrangements were from $5,000 minimum to $15,000 maximum (the highest maximum was about $43,000).

Average size of aged institutions is, of course, smaller than among fixed-dwelling-unit sites. Most of the very smallest aged institutions were generally administered for profit by private operators. Nine-tenths of the larger sites (seventy-five or more final dwelling units) were nonprofit; two-thirds were sponsored by church groups.

Mobile-home parks. Among mobile-home sites, all but two had spaces for rental only, with median monthly costs ranging between $32 and $40; upper bounds in some sites were as high as $100 and $250, respectively. In the two sites with spaces on a purchase basis, the prices ranged from $4,500 to $7,500 at one site; and from $4,000 to $6,000 at the other. Current costs of mobile homes range from $4,500 to $10,000, estimates placing the national average at about $5,500.

Boarding homes for aged persons. In boarding homes, rental was the rule for the room (sometimes shared), with meals included. Monthly rentals had a median minimum of $150 (resembling aged institutions) and a median maximum of $186. Upper bounds were $375 and $600, respectively (again resembling aged institutions).

6. Provisions for leisure and recreational activities were offered in all types of sites, but with varying frequency as shown in Table 8-9. Several general trends were detectable from the survey data. The larger the site (whether fixed-dwelling-unit site, mobile-home park, or aged institution), the greater was the likelihood for provision of programs and services (data not shown). This was presumably related to the possibility of spreading the cost of providing and supervising the facility or program over a large number of dwelling units (including, for example, the provision of buildings or rooms at the site for these purposes, swimming pools, and golf courses in some instances).

TABLE 8-9

1964 CALIFORNIA SURVEY: PERCENTAGE OF TOTAL
SITES WITH RECREATIONAL, CULTURAL, AND OTHER
PROGRAMS AND SERVICES ON THE PREMISES

	FIXED D.U. FACILITIES			
	131 Completed or Under Construction	28 Planned New Construction	171 Mobile-Home Parks	284 Aged Institutions
Recreation programs	47%	100%	42%	52%
Cultural programs	37	64	15	42
Educational programs	19	46	8	16
Self-government	34	64	17	13
Facilities for religious services	28	54	3	56
Swimming pool	35	54	35	5
Golf course	21	46	5	2
Special recreation building	43	50	50	12
Special recreation room(s)	32	50	4	50
Commercial enterprises	21	46	5	10
Off-premises transportation	17	*	–	62

*Not applicable; question asked was whether or not management *now* provides
off-premises transportation.

Recreational opportunities abounded, particularly in the larger
sites: about three-quarters of the larger installations of each type of
site had such programs. Next most frequent were cultural and educational programs, in that order. At least two-fifths of the larger sites in
each category reported having some type of resident self-govern-
ment. Facilities for religious observance occurred with highest frequency in aged institutions and least often in mobile-home parks.
The smaller sites in each category tended at most to offer one or two
of the various programs.

A trend toward greater provision of programs and services in newer sites was observed among the fixed-dwelling-unit facilities; a progression occurred from sites completely built to those under construction, and from the latter to those in the construction-planning stages. Of the planned new construction sites, *all* reported provisions for recreation, and half or more were making provisions for each of the other programs enumerated.

About half the aged institutions featured some systematic medical scheme, three-fifths of these being associated with a facility that was licensed by the California Department of Public Health to provide medical care. In a majority of these sites the cost of some type of medical care was included in the residents' basic payments or rentals. Of the aged institutions that did not have medical provisions (51 percent), most had arrangements for obtaining medical help, many undoubtedly with informal arrangements in the community. Only twelve, or 9 percent, of the fixed-dwelling-unit sites (completed or under construction) had some sort of medical provision, ranging from one or more specific types of facility or service to health insurance only. However, an additional 52 percent of the sites indicated that the management was prepared to take some type of action in case a resident became seriously ill. Among mobile-home parks, which had no medical provisions on their premises, three-quarters indicated that the management would take some action such as calling a doctor, hospital, ambulance, or fire department, taking the resident to a medical facility, or calling the resident's family.

Implications of group housing. Whether or not group arrangements are appropriate or satisfying solutions to the housing dilemmas of older persons requires careful further assessment in ensuing years before guidance for policy will be unequivocally clear regarding the priority that should be accorded this form of housing provision. Recent trends have raised several questions to which answers are needed if rational coping with the problems of housing the elderly is to proceed.

First, is it psychologically sound to encourage the assembly of older persons, exclusively, in a housing site? On the negative side are arguments that regular association and daily interaction with younger persons foster continued socialization and maintain continuity in the lives of older persons, thus preventing a narrowing of interests and excessive concentration on the problems of age and aging. An extension of this argument suggests that in the exclusive company of other older persons there is high visibility of illness and death, and that the constant reminder of this fact is damaging to morale and conceivably conducive to extra sensitivity to one's own ills.

On the positive side are the arguments that special group housing may be a possible ideal solution to the social-psychological needs of older persons. Based on evidence that society is age-graded and that the working class (to which the bulk of the aged belong) is strongly dependent on neighbors for its associates, it is reasoned that living in normal neighborhoods only insures alienation, isolation, and demoralization for older people. "With the attrition of family, friends, and other former ties, the dispersal of their age peers in a normal neighborhood reduces the number of potential new associates around them. The field of eligible new friends is thin and scattered, and the effects of this are intensified by any decline in health or mobility. Except under special circumstances, then, normal neighborhoods may attenuate the possible axes of social integration of older people."[29] Special group housing, it is argued, serves to "concentrate rather than diffuse the field of potential friends and support, thereby maximizing the conditions of social integration."

Second, to what extent are group-housing sites within the financial means of the general population of older persons? The ultimate answer to this question will, of course, help to determine the answer to a corollary issue, namely the social utility of group housing for the elderly.

The earlier discussion of the income status of the older population and the data presented in Table 8-1 have indicated that there exists a stratum of older persons in such financial straits that they probably could not on economic grounds gain entry into many of the existing group-housing sites without subsidy of some sort. The California survey showed that the costs associated with a particular type of financial arrangement—rental, purchase, life care, or life lease— varied widely among and even within sites. But the findings also suggested that, with only a few exceptions, residents of the group-housing facilities surveyed probably did not come from the lowest income groups. For this population, the only type of subsidy cur-

[29] Irving Rosow, "Retirement Housing and Social Integration," in Tibbitts and Donahue, *op. cit.*

rently available is that afforded by public housing, mentioned above as a factor in the retirement housing movement.[30] At the other end of the economic spectrum are older persons who are probably clearly in a position to rent or purchase dwelling units in most of the group-housing sites already or soon to be available. The economic capability of older persons between these extremes is in question and is still the subject of debate principally centering around the nature and convertibility of assets. Without more precise information derived from economic analyses, it may rest as an empirical matter in the long run to understand the breadth of the appeal and feasibility of group housing for all economic segments.

Third, is there an optimal type of financial arrangement for the elderly resident to undertake with the group-housing facility? One characteristic of the developing movement toward group housing is the purchase arrangement, either on a cash or on a mortgage basis. It will be recalled that the California survey found a vast majority of units in fixed-dwelling-unit facilities for purchase (mobile homes, of course, are also for sale). The most stringent financial commitment for the elderly resident occurs, of course, in connection with a cash purchase; this is somewhat less true if the purchase is on a mortgage basis. In either case, however, the resident risks a financial loss —greater or less depending on the type of commitment—if disability and enfeeblement force a move to a different type of housing, and if demand for this type of housing suffers decline in the next few years. Rental arrangements avoid this possible hazard, but they do not forestall the problems that would arise for the elderly resident on a fixed or declining income who is confronted with a rent increase. Life lease arrangements provide some protection in this respect, but they generally require a considerable initial cash outlay and, like purchase arrangements, there is not always an automatic financial adjustment provided which forestalls loss to the resident in case a move is necessary. The type of financial arrangement which probably

[30] A bill passed (and partially funded) by the 89th United States Congress as part of the Housing Act of 1965 would materially alter previous conceptions of housing subsidies. One section of the bill deals with outright rent subsidy for an older person displaced from a dwelling unit because of urban renewal activity. Under rent subsidy, the difference between rent asked and 20 percent of the older person's income will be paid to the landlord by the local housing administrator. Another section of the bill provides for outright grants, *not* loans, to persons in urban redevelopment areas to bring individually owned homes up to code and thus prevent condemnation and demolition.

provides the greatest security for the elderly residents is life care, entered into on a contract basis and insuring the individual of dwelling-unit occupancy and personal care for the remainder of his life. However, like life lease arrangements, life care contracts often involve large initial cash payments, which would place this type of financial arrangement beyond the reach of many older persons.

The foregoing comments would suggest that present customary financial arrangements made between elderly residents and the housing facility often do not cover a complex of contingencies such as the individual's present and long-range economic capability and his present and long-range health status.

Fourth, is there an optimal size for group-housing sites? The size of the group-housing site may be expected to have economic consequences for both the operator and the resident. It has been suggested by the President's Council on Aging[31] that an optimal range of size is from twenty-five to thirty units to as many as 250. The lower bound is based on an estimate of the efficiency of operation of the site, although it has been said that efficiency may decline with fewer than fifty units. The upper bound of 250 units is based on considerations of avoiding the impersonal anonymity which may occur in very large sites.

The economics of size of site are also apparent in the relationship between costs to the resident and management's provision of programs and services. The California survey findings revealed that the residents in large sites—whether fixed-dwelling-unit facilities, mobile-home parks, or aged institutions—had available a considerably wider range of programs and services than did the residents in smaller sites. Yet the costs at large sites of all kinds taken together appeared to average out to about the same as those at smaller sites. It would appear, then, that the residents in large facilities were receiving more for their money, at least with respect to the availability of various programs and services—the exception being medical care provisions which were, with several exceptions, generally lacking in fixed-dwelling-unit sites and mobile-home parks. For aged institutions, size of site and financial motivation of the sponsor appeared to be codeterminants of what the resident received for his money. In the large nonprofit aged institutions were found the greatest provision of programs and services of all kinds including medical care,

[31] *Report to the President.*

as well as the greatest likelihood of the provision of the kind of personal care and service that is offered under life care contracts.

For all group-housing facilities included in the California survey taken together, the size of the sites varied enormously, from a very few dwelling units to several thousand. This would indicate that if a theory of optimal size of site exists, it has not as yet been uniformly applied. The existence of small sites raises economic questions about efficiency and costs of operation and about the adequacy of provision of programs and services for the residents. The existence of very large sites, although more likely to provide solutions to economic problems, raises psychological questions about the possible creation of an anonymous and impersonal atmosphere and the effect this might have on the psychological well-being of the residents.

Fifth, is there an optimal age composition for group-housing sites? If group housing for older persons has created basic age segregation, the findings of the California survey would imply that it has also generated a type of "age subsegregation." Thus the "younger" old were found to predominate in fixed-dwelling-unit sites and mobile-home parks, with the "older" old predominating in aged institutions and boarding homes for aged persons. This is not surprising inasmuch as the two former types of sites provide independent living arrangements appropriate for essentially well and still vigorous persons, and the two latter types provide more protected environments for those in declining health and with reduced energy levels.

The desirability of this apparent group housing trend toward "age subsegregation" may be open to question, however, and more age intermixture is a possible preferable alternative. It seems doubtful that the sites which are presently "young" because they are inhabited by the "younger" old will remain so indefinitely. Present age cohorts will continue to age, and in order for a site to remain "young," replacements as vacancies occur would, on the average, have to be of a younger median age than the original settlers, a generally unlikely possibility. More age intermixture in group housing facilities might be accomplished through greater diversification of types of dwelling units, some for independent living and some for protected living, with programs and services geared appropriately to persons in the different independent-dependent statuses.

Sixth, what kinds of facilities and services are appropriate and desirable for group-housing arrangements? Underlying this question is the possibility that, by virtue of physiological factors and personal and social adjustments, older persons have special housing requirements. Considerable attention is paid in the newer group-housing sites to the provision of special design features and facilities inside the dwelling unit which are thought to be needed and wanted by older persons. However, aside from a relatively few considerations, such as dwelling unit size being commensurate with family size and certain provisions for declining health, it is possible that good design for older persons is not much different from that for younger age groups, the goal in either case being the optimal promotion of safety, comfort, convenience, and conservation of energy. Of greater importance than special design features and facilities may be psychological considerations, such as the preservation of the privacy, individuality, and dignity of the elderly resident.

Successful adaptation to the housing environment could be expected to be related to several physical characteristics of the housing site, including its geographical relationship to an urban center, its proximity to needed everyday services and facilities (that is, stores, banks, and other commercial enterprises), and its provisions on the premises for leisure and recreational activities. What kind of and how many leisure and recreational activities and facilities should be provided remain matters for speculation, and the issue is highlighted by the emphasis placed on "leisure" as a way of life in various retirement housing promotional efforts. Meaningful activity is needed to fill the void resulting from no longer being employed or involved in the raising of children; but at the same time, a life of nothing but "fun and games" goes against some deeply ingrained cultural directives as well as conceivable energy limitations.

From the California survey data it would appear that a substantial, if somewhat diffuse, effort is detectable in group-housing sites to make various social, cultural, educational, and recreational programs and facilities available on the premises. Most pronounced efforts seem to be in the direction of recreational opportunities, often involving considerable expenditure in the form of recreation centers ("clubhouses"), swimming pools, and, in some instances, golf courses. In more modest sites, rooms or sets of rooms are designated for recreational purposes. It is difficult to say how much of the present effort to provide social and recreational programming is sales "gimmick" and how much is perceptive understanding of the needs of persons in their later years. Particularly in the larger retirement villages the effort appears in some respects to attempt to pattern after the "country club" model, with some notable differences related to the middle-class economic level of the residents. Thus, not only are there golfing and swimming, but also socials, trips to places of interest, opportunity for the pursuit of hobbies, and so on.

Even where there is conscious sponsor awareness of the utility of providing various programs and services, several opportunities are only minimally taken advantage of. First is the possibility of supportive services. Granted that, by and large, the middle-class residents of retirement communities have had little prior experience with or even need of social-work assistance broadly interpreted, such persons entering the mature periods of their lives might well profit from availability of such help. For example, problems related to personal adjustment, family, and other interpersonal relationships suggest the utility of psychological or psychiatric counseling. Moreover, there may be the high desirability of financial and legal counseling even for persons who are essentially able to manage their own affairs.

A second opportunity apparently not fully realized is the provision of continuing educational opportunities for the site residents. Of the various programs and services inquired about in the California survey, educational opportunities were among those least frequently mentioned. There appeared to be little systematic provision of short-term and long-term courses and other instructional forms with content, objective, and method appropriate to age, sex, background, and interest. The objective of such programs would be to permit opportunity for continued adult intellectual development which might include not only the exploration of old interests long neglected, but also the assimilation of information about the changing world.

A third opportunity might well be the employment of older persons as teachers of others. As a fount of knowledge and skills in many topics, occupations, and professions, older persons would seem a resource of great scope. Granted that many of the skills represented are old-fashioned (in a sense, many of the skills of even younger adults are outmoded in a rapidly automating technology), many are not, and those that are may have ontogenetic value. The accumulated knowledge and skills harnessed in this manner might be disseminated in a variety of ways and to a variety of potential recipients: to the young in our society, the older residents might serve as guides and tutors; to institutions of government and business, they might serve as consultants and part-time aids; and they might communicate their knowledge to other interested site residents.

Underlying the possibilities that have just been suggested regarding the reorientation and expansion of programs and services in group-housing facilities is the recommendation for increased attention to these provisions on an appropriate scale and with motives geared to background, experience, and energy levels of the residents which would enhance and enlarge the fabric of their lives, and with supportive aspects to ensure care and nurturance when energies decline. Factors that may inhibit development of such programs include (1) on the part of management (sometimes the de facto adviser, guide, counselor, and social worker), an imprecise assessment of, inexperience with, and distrust of social work methodology broadly conceived, and timidity regarding receptivity of residents to such programming; (2) on the part of (middle-class) residents, a lack of experience with such helping ventures and general suspicions regarding "welfarism"; (3) on the part of professionals who might provide the programming, a lack of familiarity with non-indigent populations in need of promotive service; and (4) with respect to the programs themselves, a tendency to foster excessive psychological dependency in an age group especially at risk in this regard.

Besides the various facets of appropriate and desirable facilities and services for group-housing residents that have already been discussed, an additional aspect pertains to the provision of medical care. Reference was made earlier to the relatively high morbidity (particularly chronic illness) among persons in their later years. Attendant upon greater likelihood of illness is, of course, the need for medical attention for both minor and serious conditions. In group-housing arrangements for the elderly, the possibility arises for rendering at least partial services at the site, and not inconceivably of providing actual hospital facilities. The California survey revealed that half the aged institutions, only a few of the fixed-dwelling-unit sites, and none of the mobile-home parks had medical provisions on the premises. Which is the most promotive arrangement? Some observers view with dismay bringing the clinic and hospital to the dwelling doorstep, and even further bringing to greater visibility the illness and death occurring among the residents.[32] Others take

[32] Recent experience in group-housing sites for older persons in which outpatient medical services are available on the site at relatively modest cost

the point of view that ill health, as age progresses, is an undeniable fact, and that the assembly of older persons in a site provides an extraordinary opportunity to make available comprehensive medical care to a population at special risk.

All of the half-dozen questions that have just been raised specifically concerning group housing await answers. They are only part of the general problem of housing arrangements for older persons for which there is pressing urgency for solutions. The urgency becomes increasingly clear when it is considered that the hitherto generally accepted retirement age in the mid-sixties is being lowered, at least in selected industries. Policy toward housing for many older persons is, for the short run at least, dependent upon economic and social community matters. But for the long run it is tantalizing to think about the various preferable alternatives, all other considerations being equal.

Summary of Principal HHFA Programs Related to Housing for the Elderly

In the Federal Housing Administration (FHA) there are three programs directed toward the provision of congregate housing for older persons (section numbers refer to provisions of the National Housing Act).

Section 231: Loans are insured for the construction or purchase and rehabilitation of rental projects of eight or more units for elderly persons (sixty-two years or older).

Section 213: Mortgages are insured on cooperative housing projects of five or more dwelling units (sites for elderly persons sixty-two years and older are included in this program).

---

suggests that utilization of such services is perhaps twice as high as for persons in the same age group in more normal dispersed residential circumstances. One recent preliminary study of such integration of outpatient services is very suggestive: the medical records of "high" and "low" utilizers of service show little difference in the acknowledged serious chronic diseases, but show substantial difference in less serious (although apparently symptomatic) conditions. Perhaps not so surprisingly, highest use of the outpatient service tends to occur among persons living closest, physically, to the clinic—across the street or in adjacent blocks.

Section 221: Loans are insured for sale and rental housing for elderly persons relocated from dwellings displaced by
urban renewal projects.

In distinction to these loan insurance provisions of the FHA, the
Community Facilities Administration (CFA) makes direct loans under
section 202, which provides for long-term low-interest loans to private,
nonprofit, corporate sponsors for developing rental housing and related
facilities for older persons (age sixty-two years or older).

The Public Housing Administration (PHA) makes federal funds
available to qualifying local communities to buy land and build public
rental housing for families of very low income who are inadequately
housed. Local housing authorities are authorized to give preference to
elderly applicants and to waive the requirement that such tenants must
come from substandard dwellings.

Major Differences Between Provisions of Section 231 (FHA) and Section 202 (CFA)

Of the programs mentioned thus far that affect elderly persons at
present, the FHA 231 and CFA 202 are the major ones. A comparison of
the provisions of these two programs is as follows:

SECTION 231	SECTION 202
a. is a loan insurance program	a. is a direct loan program
b. covers new construction or the remodeling of existing structures (rental only)	b. covers new construction only (rental only)
c. is available to profit-motivated and nonprofit sponsors alike	c. is available to nonprofit sponsors only
d. projects not subject to rigid operational control of FHA	d. projects subject to rather rigid operational control and review of CFA
e. projects aimed at middle- to high-income older persons	e. projects aimed at low-middle-income older persons
f. projects not limited to housekeeping units only	f. projects limited to housekeeping units essentially
g. projects may involve life care, accommodation fees, admission fees, etc. May be "care" facilities.	g. projects may not involve life care, accommodation fees, admission fees, etc. Generally are not "care" facilities.

Provisions of the Housing Act of 1964*

Provisions in Public Law 88-560, the Housing Act of 1964 (approved September 2, 1964), which assist in meeting housing needs of the elderly:

1. *Low-rent public housing:* Section 403 authorized approximately 37,500 additional units of low-rent public housing. During the past two years, about half of all new low-rent housing units placed under contract have been designated for senior citizens. It is anticipated that a large portion of the new authorization also will be used to benefit the elderly.

2. *Urban renewal land for public housing:* Section 306 permits greater use of urban renewal project land for low-rent public housing.

3. *Direct loans:* Section 201 increased the authorization of funds for direct loans at below-the-market interest rates for terms up to fifty years to nonprofit sponsors of rental housing for the elderly. Fund reservations under this program have risen from less than $3 million on December 31, 1960, to nearly $200 million on June 30, 1964. The increased authorization in the new law will permit the growth of this program to continue.

4. *Single elderly persons:* Section 202 permits occupancy by single persons sixty-two years of age and older of moderate income sales and rental housing authorized by section 221 of the National Housing Act. Since almost one-half of those in the elderly population are unmarried, widowed, divorced, or separated, this amendment greatly increases the usefulness of section 221 programs in meeting housing needs of the elderly.

5. *Relocation assistance:* Section 405 requires local public agencies to assume responsibility for relocating individuals as well as families from urban renewal areas. This is a significant added protection to senior citizens, since such a large proportion of them are single and since they tend to be concentrated in urban areas subject to renewal or redevelopment.

6. *Relocation rent assistance:* Section 310 established a new program of relocation rent assistance for families and individuals sixty-two years of age or older who are displaced from urban renewal areas. The program calls for payments to those unable to relocate in public housing, of the difference between 20 percent of the displacee's annual income and the rental for twelve months of a suitable, modest dwelling unit up to a maximum payment of $500 to any one individual or family for any one move.

* United States Senate, Special Committee on Aging, *Major Federal Legislative and Executive Action Affecting Senior Citizens: 1963-1964* (Washington: 1964).

None of the payment can be made longer than five months after displacement. Section 406 establishes the same program for such individuals and families displaced from low-rent public housing projects.

7. *Rehabilitation loans:* Section 312 establishes a new program of rehabilitation loans. It authorized a revolving fund of $50 million for loans to rehabilitate homes and business properties in urban renewal areas. Home rehabilitation loans are limited to $10,000 and to a term of twenty years or three-fourths of the remaining economic life of the property, whichever is less. The maximum interest rate is 3 percent. Many elderly homeowners living on small incomes have been faced with displacement because they could not afford to make necessary improvements in their homes or have been unable to obtain the necessary financing. This program of loan assistance should enable many to improve their housing and remain in their own homes and familiar surroundings.

8. *Nursing home construction:* Section 117 made nonprofit nursing home sponsors eligible for mortgage insurance for nursing home construction on the same terms as proprietary sponsors.

9. *Physically handicapped:* Section 203 amended each of the HHFA senior citizens housing programs and the low- and moderate-income section 221 programs to include financial assistance for specially designed housing for physically handicapped families and persons. It also expanded eligibility for the handicapped in low-rent public housing. Previously, there was no specific federal program to meet this need, except for a limited program for veterans who are paraplegics. In addition, the new law provides that demonstration grants may be used in conjunction with other programs in the HHFA, including housing for the elderly, public housing, and FHA low- and moderate-income housing for people of all ages to assist physically handicapped families and persons to live in adequate housing.

10. *Rural elderly:* Section 501 extended through September 30, 1965, the mortgage insurance program of rental housing for the rural elderly administered by the Farmers Home Administration, and increased from $100,000 to $300,000 the maximum mortgage insurance available for any one project under this program.

BIOGRAPHICAL NOTES

DANIEL M. WILNER was born in Poland in 1918 and was educated at the University of California, Los Angeles (Ph.D.), where he is now Professor of Public Health. His published writings include books and articles on environmental influences on health and behavior. He is coauthor of *Human Relations in Interracial Housing, The Housing Environment and Family Life,* and *Retirement Housing in California.* Current interests include psychosocial processes in aging.

ROSABELLE PRICE WALKLEY was born in Byers, Colorado, in 1920 and was educated at Columbia University (Barnard College, New York School of Social Work, and Graduate Faculties). She is now Associate Research Behavioral Scientist and Lecturer at the University of California, Los Angeles. Mrs. Walkley is coauthor of *Human Relations in Interracial Housing, The Housing Environment and Family Life, Retirement Housing in California,* and articles on the influence of the housing environment on health and psychosocial adjustment. She is currently engaged in research on the housing of older retired persons.

9

Social Forces Influencing the Care and Health of the Elderly

Ewald W. Busse

Throughout the life-span the social environment is recognized as one of three elements that promote or damage the health of the individual. The other two are the inherent biological makeup of the individual and the physical environment. Social deprivation and other distorted social forces are believed to play a significant role in the etiology of a number of mental disorders. Attitudes of social origin underlie many criteria used to determine the existence and diagnosis of mental disease. Social relations are important in the therapy of those diseases that are primarily caused by inherent defects or physical trauma, or by defects or deficiencies within social interactions. Although our understanding of this complex matter of social forces and health is far from satisfactory, considerably more is known than will be mentioned in this presentation. The points that will be briefly touched upon are selected to emphasize the importance of the social influences as they relate to the care of the elderly patient by the medical and health professions.

The pathological consequences of social deprivation and hostile social influences upon the infant have been reported by a number of investigators, including Goldfarb,[1] Provence,[2] and Bowlby.[3] Investigation of adults indicates a relationship between lower social class and a higher incidence of disease. The possibility that this is an ap-

[1] William Goldfarb, "Psychological Privation in Infancy and Subsequent Adjustment," *American Journal of Orthopsychiatry*, 14 (1944), 162-173.

[2] S. Provence and R. C. Lipton, *Infants in Institutions* (New York: International University Press, 1962).

[3] John Bowlby, "Grief and Mourning in Infancy and Early Childhood," *Psychoanalytic Study of the Child*, 15 (1960), 9-52.

parent rather than a real correlation has been considered.[4] Possible explanations that have been suggested include differences in community tolerance, class influences on psychiatric diagnosis, and downward social mobility as a manifestation of mental disease. Although it is likely and possible that these explanations have some validity, the additional stresses encountered in lower classes do appear to be the major determinant.

Since this chapter is concerned with health and care of the elderly, brief attention will be given to the term *health* and its meaning as it relates to the elderly. It is probable that a state of complete or perfect health does not exist in any individual; if it does, it is so transient that it is difficult to measure or study. Disease, illness, and disability are usually more easily recognized as departure from health because they have persistent characteristics, that is, signs and symptoms (complaints) that identify the condition. Health is a relative state, and the parameters which measure the health of the infant are different from those which are applied to the young adult, the middle-aged adult, and the elderly person. Unfortunately, the term *health* is frequently designated as applying either to the body or to the mind. Although this separation is sometimes convenient, it obviously has no scientific justification. Health is a state or condition that exists when the individual is functioning at a high level of efficiency in all respects. The healthy individual can deal effectively with his internal needs and the variations and stresses induced by the external environment. If one is willing to accept this viewpoint, then what are the important differences between the health of the aged and younger humans? When employed as a biological or medical term, aging indicates a type of process which is manifested by an accumulation of adverse changes that decrease the ability of the person to carry out various specialized functions. Aging processes are inherent and inevitable changes which are time-related but independent of stress, trauma, or disease. It is likely that these primary aging processes are rooted in heredity. They are not identical in all people, nor do they progress at the same rate. Therefore there is greater variation in the biological age of elderly people than of children.

Primary aging is distinguished from disabilities resulting from

[4] Marc Fried, "Social Problems and Psychopathology," Symposium #10, Group for the Advancement of Psychiatry, New York, November, 1964.

disease or trauma. This is termed secondary aging. It is the problems created by the latter (chronic disease) that are foremost in any discussion of the health of the elderly.

Early in his training, the physician becomes aware of the physical phenomenon "atrophy of disuse." The scholar knows that unless he draws upon his memory and puts it into action it is not long before the value of that once-learned material declines and disappears. These common observations, plus numerous studies, lead the physician and members of the health professions to believe that there is a reciprocal relationship between activity and health.[5]

In addition, another factor is sometimes overlooked; this is diversion from pain by interesting activities. The stimuli entering the central nervous system from an exciting experience will be dominant over pain stimulus. Consequently, the members of the health disciplines accept the maintenance of mind and body by social activity and contact as a means of prevention, a method of restoration to health, and an effective way of divergence of attention from pain or unwholesome preoccupation with one's self.

I

Over the past three decades acute illnesses of various types have been reduced in frequency, severity, and duration. The acute diseases that carried a high mortality rate have been virtually eliminated. Chronic illness is the most urgent and frustrating medical problem of modern society. Although some therapeutic agents are available which can relieve the pain and discomfort accompanying chronic disorders, medical science rarely possesses the treatment measures necessary to prevent progression or to produce a reversal in the course of chronic ailments. Consequently the physician must devise a regime aimed at making it easier for a patient to live with his disease. Such a therapeutic regime contains two essential but overlapping features. The first is an attempt to prevent progression of the disease, and the second is symptom relief in order to make the patient more comfortable and to increase efficiency of functioning.

[5] F. Jeffers and C. R. Nichols, "The Relationship of Activities and Attitudes to Physical Well-Being in Older People," *Journal of Gerontology*, 16 (1961), 67-70.

If the physician is to be successful in his goal of making the patient comfortable and more effective, he must keep in mind that decreased activity parallel to the chronic disease can arise from a source other than the physical impairment. This second source is the psychosocial influences which reduce or aggravate the degree of incapacity.

Chronic illnesses are prevalent among the aged, and the incidence advances steadily with age. In young adulthood, that is, up to forty-five years of age, 45.3 percent of persons have one or more chronic conditions. Fortunately these conditions produce limitations of activity in only 7.4 percent. However, between the ages of forty-five and sixty-four, chronic conditions are present in 61.3 percent and limitations of activity in 18.3 percent. From sixty-five and over, chronic disorders advance to 78.7 percent, and disability to 45.1 percent. From a medical and social viewpoint the elderly person is seriously affected with chronic disease and disability requiring specialized medical procedures and social assistance.[6]

The pattern of chronic disease is one of exacerbations and limited remissions, but there is a progressive decline. Also, unfortunately, the speed of decline is in most instances correlated with advancing age.[7] In a recent unpublished survey of noninstitutionalized population of the United States, 2.3 percent of the aged are bedfast and 6.1 percent are confined to their rooms or living quarters. Of the remaining, 86.2 percent can go outdoors without difficulty, and the remainder (5.4 percent) must exert considerable effort in order to venture out.[8]

Of the six million disabled older people in America, two million are invalids in the commonly accepted sense of the term. One-half million are in nursing homes and similar institutions, and a quarter of a million or more are in mental hospitals. The health measures available to the various types of chronic disorders are the result of social judgments. For example, the limited funds available for retraining and rehabilitation are more likely to be awarded to the

[6] Department of Health, Education, and Welfare, Public Health Service, *Health Statistics* (Washington: PHS Publication No. 584-536, October, 1962).

[7] S. Katz and A. B. Chinn, "Some Advances Toward the Understanding of Long-Term Illness in the Elderly," paper presented at the Second National Conference of the Joint Council to Improve the Health Care of the Aged, December, 1961.

[8] Unpublished data from a survey in the United States. A full report will appear in a volume on cross-national studies of aging by Ethel Shanas, the American investigator, and others.

younger individuals who have disability resulting from damage, trauma, or from acute disease. Therefore, society does play an important role in deciding who will or who will not receive medical attention. Apparently society views this as the practical application of the principle of utilizing monies in a manner which will most likely show a financial return to society.

II

In our society the "sick role" is acceptable to the individual and to the group if it is a temporary state. The chronic occupancy of the sick role is regarded by some patients as a refuge, that is, a device for maintaining self-esteem,[9] and by others as a bondage.[10] Society is apt to reject the chronically impaired individual who does not "overcome" his handicap and in some manner participate in and give back to society. It is true that this rejection of the chronically ill or disabled is rarely recognized or admitted, and if recognized, it is likely to result in a guilt reaction, which in turn produces activity that is guilt-reducing rather than practical for the patient. Rehabilitation programs are not only geared to helping the individual restore his self-respect but are also aimed at reducing the financial strain on the community. Maintaining a balance in these two goals is tricky. For example, the patient who suspects that the rehabilitation program is more concerned with getting him off workmen's compensation than in helping him with his psychosocial difficulties is likely to become an uncooperative patient.

The individual who occupies a sick role for any length of time is gradually cut out of his established place in society; that is, his family and friends adjust their lives so that they can carry on without the patient's participation. The bridge club finds a new member to fill the vacancy created by the chronically ill person. If this pattern of living is maintained for any length of time, the living habits of the

[9] E. W. Busse, "The Treatment of the Chronic Complainer," *Medical Record and Annals*, 1 (September, 1956), 196-200. E. W. Busse, "Psychoneurotic Reactions and Defense Mechanisms in the Aged," in P. Hoch and Joseph Zubin (Eds.), *Psychopathology of Aging* (New York: Grune and Stratton, 1961), pp. 274-284.

[10] D. S. Shaw, C. R. Nichols, and M. D. Bogdonoff, "Problems in Comprehensive Medicine: A Distinction in Approaches," *The Journal of Medical Education*, 36 (1961), 148-153.

family become firmly established and resistant to change. When the physical condition of the ill person has improved to a point where he is capable of returning to his family and to society, he encounters considerable resistance, for he has either been replaced or his position has been eliminated.

Clearly the chronically ill person has a dual problem. He must adjust to his physical disability and discomfort as well as deal with the social resistances which have developed. To reestablish a place in the family or in society is particularly difficult if the family or group has discovered that it can actually function more conveniently without the person involved or if the sick person has been replaced by an individual with additional assets. The restoration of the chronically ill person requires, therefore, that the physician understand and realistically appraise the social situation. If the patient has little chance of resuming his old place in the social structure, then it is necessary for him to seek a new situation. The patient who discovers that he must find a new place in society is apt to think, "I have suffered enough, why shouldn't it be made easy for me?" or "I am accepted here in the hospital, therefore, the easiest solution is for me to remain in the medical situation." Although these thoughts are understandable, they can hardly be acceptable as a practical solution. Recognizing the social barriers which develop, the members of the health-care team must urge the patient's family and friends not to close their circle against the patient, but to preserve at some cost an opening for the patient so that he can return to his place in society. The maintenance of communication with the patient is essential, and he should continue to participate in those family and social decisions which have been his responsibility and for which he possesses the necessary capabilities.

III

Attitudes—some realistic, some biased—affect the health care of the aged. Some of these attitudes are reviewed in another portion of this chapter.[11] Apparently there is a limited number of physicians

[11] An excellent review of attitudes toward aging can be found in S. M. Chown and A. Heron, "Psychological Aspects of Aging in Man," in P. R. Farnsworth (Ed.), *Annual Review of Psychology*, Vol. 16 (Palo Alto, California: Annual Reviews, 1965), pp. 417-450.

who are capable of dealing with large numbers of chronically ill persons with sustained enthusiasm and effectiveness. If this is true, what is the possible explanation? The physician, like all people, needs to maintain his self-esteem. The criteria for measuring his worth are rooted and tied to society. Society acclaims the medical scientist who perfects a method of prevention, a drug, or a surgical procedure resulting in cure, but rarely if ever accords recognition to the skilled and devoted person who struggles to relieve discomfort and pain. Society's reaction to rewarding the person who produces breakthroughs is understandable, but it does push the highly capable medical scientist to exerting his efforts in areas where he believes breakthroughs are possible. The physician's self-esteem as a practitioner of medicine is lowered when he does not see clear improvement resulting from his efforts. Contributing to this is the fact that the chronically ill patient is not likely to express gratitude to the physician for his help. Rather, the patient frequently indicates to the physician in subtle, often nonverbal expressions that he is dissatisfied with his treatment. An explanation of this pattern of interacting will be offered. In addition, the physician is aware that many psychosocial complications disrupt his treatment plans and frustrate attainment of his goals. Often he does not understand the psychosocial complications, he does not possess the knowledge or tools to cope with them, and this compounds his discouragement.

Chronically ill patients frequently become disappointed because of their lack of progress. They become irritable and angry. Consequently, such patients find it difficult to express positive feelings toward those caring for them. In a permissive and encouraging situation a patient will express the opinion that he is not becoming better because the physician or other members of the treatment team are incompetent or are disinterested in him. This is a natural reaction to frustration, and it is essential that staff members understand it and accept it without retaliation or arguing. Many chronically ill patients report that they harbored such feelings or thoughts for a considerable duration of time but held them in check because they recognized that they were highly dependent upon the staff for their care. The patients felt that if such hostile feelings were expressed the dependency relationship might be destroyed, and this they could not afford. When such feelings are held in check, the physiological component can be a highly destructive force within the patient.

Thus it aggravates the disease. If such dammed-up feelings are permitted to be released, the disruptive element is reduced, and the energies of the patient can be directed into constructive efforts.

The reluctance upon the part of the chronically ill to express appreciation for the medical help given them has been mentioned. This observation has correctly been challenged and reconsidered. A physician charged with the inpatient care of chronically ill elderly patients reported that a number of patients did thank him. Observations confirmed his statement, but the explanation was quickly obvious. The supporting personnel of this particular unit rarely if ever interacted on a personal level with the patient, but the physician did. He felt that he had little to offer on a "professional basis." For example, one patient stated, "Doctor, I'm sure glad you talked with me—no one else does." In this instance the physician was utilizing a much-needed therapeutic approach but apparently did not recognize its significance and did not insist upon its being utilized by the ward personnel. Also the physician failed to take advantage of the positive relationship to discuss the patient's feelings with regard to his illness and his loss of status and place in society.

IV

There is always a question regarding the universality of attitudes; that is, does a segment of our society share the same views regarding the elderly with the majority of our society? For example, do physicians, nurses, and social workers, in general or as a group, maintain certain attitudes toward the elderly that are not consistent with those of most citizens? Are these attitudes maintained by the health professions positive or negative ones? What views do members of the health professions hold that result from their training and experience, and do these attitudes promote or detract from the health care of the aged? Ethel Shanas[12] says that some years ago the staff of social agencies believed that their clients were a representative sample of all older people and that on the basis of these observations they made the old person into a stereotype. She indicates that

---

[12] Ethel Shanas, "Older People and Their Families," in *The Multigenerational Family: Papers on Theory and Practical Problems and Promise* (Trenton, N. J.: Department of State, Division on Aging, 1964).

just the opposite is true. The elderly client of social agencies is unlike the majority of the aged. He is more likely to be a bachelor or to be widowed, he is more likely to be childless, and he is likely to be destitute.

Over a decade ago Tuckman and Lorge developed a questionnaire to measure attitudes toward old people. They put together a series of statements which were meant to be consistent with the stereotype of elderly people. One hundred and thirty-seven statements were included in this questionnaire. Subjects were asked to indicate whether they agreed or disagreed with a statement, and if it were not true of all old people, they were to indicate the percentage of old people to whom the statement applied. The measure was then employed to determine if attitudes toward old people could be changed by education and by experience with elderly individuals. Eisdorfer has questioned the reliability and validity of the scores, and more importantly raised the question, "Are attitudes predictive of behavior in real life situations?" Unfortunately, no systematic studies have been carried out to determine if the attitudes and beliefs that are held in regard to old people by those in the health professions influence the care that is given them. In an unpublished continuation of his investigation, Eisdorfer finds that young people (that is, nursing students and undergraduate students) do not like to believe that old people are strong. Young people expect old people to be sick and relatively weak; when they find out otherwise, it is disrupting. Observations conducted in a clinical setting suggest student nurses readily accept the dependency relationship sought by a man or a woman seventy years or more who appears to be elderly. On the other hand, the student nurse rejects dependency bids made by women in the age groups of sixty or below. Student nurses have verbalized this feeling, offering the explanation that such conflicts are related to their parental relationships.

V

It is important for an elderly person to have a role or place in society. If he is excluded from society, he is likely to become depressed and decline in health. If preservation of a role in society is important to health, the physician must concern himself with an understanding of the so-called social role, that is, the work role, sick role, retirement role, and so forth.[13] It appears that if the elderly person maintains a position of value, he is respected, that is, society agrees that the existence of the elderly person contributes to its well-being and preservation. What happens if a person is prevented from contributing to society because of illness? Will he eventually be excluded from society? A person who because of ill health has been placed in a noncontributing situation apparently must rely upon the continuation of impact of his original contributions in order to be respected by current society. The marginal contributor quickly loses his position in society. This has implications when we consider the elderly person who is apparently being rejected by his children. Our studies some years ago indicated that the rejected elderly parent was very likely to be perceived by his children as a poor parent, because in earlier life he made very little contribution to their happiness and education. When such a person becomes sick and places a burden on his children, he is likely to be rejected.

VI

In our society a belief has more or less persisted that there is a relationship between retirement and subsequent decline in health. Studies indicate that a disruption of social activities, in particular retirement, does not seem to affect health and consequently death. This conclusion is reached by McMahan and Ford[14] and by Thompson and Streib.[15] However, there is evidence that relocation of the institutionalized elderly person does have an adverse effect upon his health and can speed the approach of death. Also, there is evidence that the death rate for elderly persons increases shortly after admission to homes for the aged. However, our experience suggests that declining physical health in an elderly person often brings about the decision to enter an institution. It is our observation that an inordinate number of elderly persons applying for admission to a home

[13] Shaw, Nichols, and Bogdonoff, op. cit.

[14] C. A. McMahan and T. R. Ford, "Surviving the First Five Years of Retirement," Journal of Gerontology, 10 (1955), 212-215.

[15] W. E. Thompson and G. Streib, "Situational Determinants, Health, and Economic Deprivation in Retirement," Journal of Social Issues, 14 (1958), 18-34.

for the aged have a serious pathology that is unrecognized by them; this has not been picked up on routine medical examination and is only discovered when they have been examined very carefully. Because of this empirical observation, the idea has been entertained that the elderly person is unconsciously alerted to an impending disaster, and this influences the decision to enter an institution. Assuming this observation has some validity, the disruption of social contact with family and familiar environment would not be the major factor in rapid decline in health and death. Relocation of the aged within an institutional setting or from one institution to another does seem to play a role in death rate. The increase in death rate appears to occur within a relatively short period of time after relocation, and it does occur in the more vulnerable patients, that is, those who are physically disabled and psychologically maladjusted.[16]

VII

The extent and adequacy of the use of medical professions and health facilities are influenced by numerous factors. Some of these forces are highly personal, for example, frequent visits to the physician by the hypochondriac. However, several important factors significantly affect sizable and identifiable segments of the aged population. One of the most important determinants is family income.[17] Of course, it is highly likely that many patterns will change with the advent of the national program for medical care for the elderly. However, it is also probable that there will continue to be a relationship between family income and the type and extent of medical care.

Spending for health care is also very much influenced by family attitudes and patterns of behavior. Both high-income and low-income families that put off needed health care share somewhat similar characteristics. For example, families who buy on impulse or utilize time payment as a major device for purchasing are somewhat more likely than families not in such patterns, regardless of income,

[16] C. K. Aldrich and E. Mendkoff, "Relocation of the Aged and Disabled— A Mortality Study," *Journal of the American Geriatrics Society*, 11 (1963), 185-194.
[17] "Medical Care and Family Income—A 30-Year Trend," *Progress in Health Services*, 13:5 (Health Information Foundation, November-December, 1964).

to have their members put off medical care.[18] Although private insurance coverage has tended to even out the hospital admission rate at various income levels, admission rates to hospitals continue to mount in accord with family income. However, it is of considerable import to note that the National Health Survey indicates that patients from families with lower incomes stayed in a hospital longer than those with high incomes.[19] This suggests that low income families are incapable of providing adequate care within the home and therefore must leave the patient in the hospital for a longer period of time.

It appears that for a number of years a majority of persons aged sixty-five or over has favored a government insurance plan for paying doctor and hospital bills. A survey in 1957 indicated that 54 percent were in favor of a government plan for health protection.[20] This same survey revealed other information of significance. It indicated that a number of elderly people required medical help but had not visited a physician. Their failure to seek medical attention was not for economic reasons, but for psychosocial causes that in the years ahead will require the attention of the health professions.

In recent years the proportion of older persons in mental hospitals has increased steadily. On any given day about one out of every three beds in a public mental hospital is occupied by a person sixty-five years of age or older. In 1960, this accounted for a total of approximately 165,000 patients. The admission rate and the number of patients in the hospital population must be considered separately. Approximately one-half the persons in the sixty-five or older age group in public mental hospitals were admitted as younger patients. The other half were admitted at age sixty-five or older. Of those first admission older patients, 83 percent were diagnosed as having senile and arteriosclerotic brain damage. Most of these people are quite seriously ill, and 30 percent of them die before the end of the first year. Although these patients are physically and mentally quite ill upon admission, a relatively high percentage of those who survive

[18] "Family Spending Patterns and Health Care," *Progress in Health Services*, 9:1 (Health Information Foundation, January, 1960).
[19] "Medical Care, Health Status, and Family Income, U. S.," *Vital and Health Statistics* (Washington: National Center for Health Statistics, U. S. Public Health Service, Series 10, No. 9, 1964).
[20] "Voluntary Health Insurance Among the Aged," *Progress in Health Services,* 8:1 (Health Information Foundation, January, 1959).

respond to treatment and could be transferred to a transitional type
of facility or returned to the community, provided personnel and
facilities exist.[21] Studies strongly suggest that there is a relationship
between the appearance of organic changes at a younger age and
admission to mental hospitals. In urban settings a high percentage
of patients with organic brain disease are residents of areas characterized by socioeconomic deprivation. Persons coming from poor
living conditions are likely to develop earlier physical and mental
disabilities. [22]

A number of misconceptions are encountered in our society regarding health and the utilization of health facilities. Such distorted
attitudes and beliefs are often shared by members of the health profession who are not sufficiently informed; unfortunately these attitudes permeate and influence the care provided for the patient, for
they interfere with the cooperation with family, community agencies,
and legislators. One such misconception concerns the utilization of
state hospitals for the care of the aged. This is the belief that many
elderly people are placed in state hospitals because they are rejected
by their family or friends and that many patients with relatively mild
organic brain disorders are placed in state hospitals because their
families are not interested in taking care of them. Reporting on a
careful study of the utilization of state hospitals in New York, Goldfarb concludes that elderly patients who are admitted are likely to
have organic brain syndrome and that they "are not persons who
have been rejected by their families for social or financial reasons.
They are sick people who need comprehensive medical care and for
whom no other adequate community facility is yet available." It is
highly likely that such elderly persons would benefit by care in institutions which maximize the opportunity for continuing relationship
with family and friends; but it is also clear that such institutions are
practically nonexistent.[23]

[21] *The Aging and Mental Hospitals,* A Report of the Subcommittee on the
Problems of the Aged and Aging (Washington: Committee on Labor and Public
Welfare, United States Senate, 1960).
[22] E. M. Gruenberg, "Community Conditions and Psychoses of the Elderly," *American Journal of Psychiatry,* 110 (1954), 888-896. Also J. J. Down-
ing and E. M. Gruenberg, "Some Differentials in the Prevalence of Mental
Symptoms in an Aging Population" (New York: State of New York, Mental
Health Research Unit, 1957).
[23] A. I. Goldfarb, "Personal Communication," paper to be published.

VIII

Two psychoneurotic reactions are frequent in elderly persons. These are so-called hypochondriasis and depression. These reactions demonstrate the value in the simultaneous application of the views of Freud and Durkheim.[24] These disorders, hypochondriasis and depression, are often prevented, precipitated, and altered by psychosocial forces. Strictly speaking, hypochondriasis is not a disease entity. It is a syndrome consisting of anxious preoccupation with the body or a portion of the body which the patient believes is either diseased or not functioning properly. Bodily preoccupation can be associated with a variety of medical conditions, including neurosis, psychophysiological reactions, and personality disorders. Regardless of the underlying cause of hypochondriasis, the chronic complainer tries the patience of his medical advisers, his family, and his friends. In a study of the prevalence of hypochondriasis among the adult population of a large university medical clinic, it was found that chronic complaining was much more frequent in elderly patients. In an attempt to find a reasonable method of handling this type of reaction, a number of hypochondriacal patients were gathered together in a special clinic. In this study it was quickly recognized that social factors played an important role in the disease process. It was evident that many of these patients, particularly the elderly, were unable to keep up with society's financial and social demands. Such a patient is unable to cope with the true cause of his difficulties. Rather, he attempts to maintain his self-respect by becoming sick and demanding that society provide him with financial support and medical care because he is sick. This is not the only social factor which plays a role in the development of hypochondriasis. When the social setting does not provide adequate opportunity for rewarding experiences, a second pathological process is likely to develop. In essence, this is a withdrawal of the patient's interest from persons and his environment and a centering of his psychic energy upon himself, and in particular upon his body and its functions. Of course there are other dynamics which play an important role in the development of a syndrome of chronic complaining, but further discus-

[24] Fried, *op. cit.*

sion would force a departure from the central theme of this paper.[25]

Social attitudes, as well as the medical treatment program, influence the support from society offered the chronic complainer. The social attitude which influences the attempts of the elderly hypochondriac to achieve a level of acceptable adjustment can be rather crudely expressed as follows. Today in most Western societies, and particularly in the United States, we continue to place great emphasis upon a person's independence and achievement. It is likely that in recent years this social value has undergone some alteration, but certain essential criteria of worth are relatively unchanged. Most people in our society apparently continue to judge the worth of others by material and financial success and by achievement of positions of authority and responsibility. Our society has little understanding and appreciation for the nonachiever. On the other hand, religion and democratic ideals give the person who is physically ill the right of medical care and financial assistance. This ideal is continuing to be expanded. It is at this point that physical illness and social failure or underachievement begin to interact. When a person fails or feels he is failing in his attempt to be a success by social standards, he is fearful that he will be condemned by society as a lazy or incompetent person who has not succeeded because he has not put forth enough effort or has substandard abilities. The young or middle-aged adult is likely to attempt to maintain his self-respect by considering himself physically sick and by convincing others that his failure is the result of illness. This defense of the chronic complainer may be successful for a varying period of time, but eventually his friends, acquaintances, and business associates recognize that the excuse of illness is physically unjustified and feel that they are being exploited. Society does not permit people to "play sick" to avoid trouble and responsibility. This attitude of rejection is found to be present in members of the health disciplines. When applied to the elderly hypochondriac it may be devoid of a realistic basis, as the elderly person may have made his contribution to society but is now the victim of socioeconomic deprivation.

The second common psychoneurotic reaction encountered in the elderly is so-called depressive reaction. This type of reaction should be distinguished from the much more serious psychotic depressive

[25] E. W. Busse, "Mental Disorders of the Aging," in W. M. Johnson (Ed.), *The Older Patient* (New York: Hoeber, 1960), pp. 513-542.

illness which is a common cause for hospitalization. Periods of depression that are more or less incapacitating but do not require medical help develop in the lives of most people. Evidence indicates that such depressive periods increase in frequency and depth in the advanced years of life. In a study of "normal" community volunteers over the age of sixty,[26] it was found that a significant portion of the subjects were aware that they were experiencing more frequent and more annoying depressive episodes. It was observed[27] that there was a difference in the process leading to depression in the elderly person as contrasted with the middle-aged or young adult. Guilt and the turning inward of unconscious hostile impulses that are unacceptable to the ego are common mechanisms in the depression of younger adults. This was not the case with elderly subjects. The depressive episodes can be readily linked with the loss of so-called narcissistic supplies. The older subject becomes depressed when he cannot find ways of gratifying his needs; that is, when social environmental changes or the decreased efficiency of his body prevent him from reducing his tensions, he is likely to have a loss of self-esteem—hence, he feels depressed. In one study approximately 85 percent of the elderly subjects were able to trace the onset of most of their depressive episodes to special stimuli. The major precipitating stimuli were experiences associated with physical suffering, with lowered financial, professional, or social status, or with the loss of loved ones.

Inasmuch as depressive reactions can be related to social environment, suicide will be briefly mentioned as one manifestation of a serious depressive illness. Individuals who attempt suicide do so for many reasons. Often suicide is the result of a serious psychotic reaction or a severe neurosis of long standing. However, in all countries where adequate figures are available, statistics show that the frequency of suicide increases in late middle life or in old age. The possible explanations for this increasing incidence of suicide are worthy of consideration. Contrary to what might be expected, an

[26] E. W. Busse, R. H. Barnes, A. J. Silverman, M. B. Thaler, and L. L. Frost, "Studies of Processes of Aging. X: The Strengths and Weaknesses of Psychic Functioning in the Aged," *The American Journal of Psychiatry*, 111 (June, 1955), 896-901.

[27] E. W. Busse, R. H. Barnes, A. J. Silverman, M. B. Thaler, and L. L. Frost, "Studies of Processes of Aging. VI: Factors That Influence the Psyche of Elderly Persons," *The American Journal of Psychiatry*, 110 (June, 1954), 897-903.

elderly person with organic brain disease rarely attempts suicide. The suicidal attempt is much more likely to accompany a depressive episode that is superimposed upon a lifelong history of socioeconomic instability and deprivation. An elderly person who has had considerable difficulty throughout his life-span seems to find the added problems of advanced years too much to tolerate.[28] Although losses, disappointments, and suffering, whether due to social or physical reasons, do not explain why an individual selects suicide as the solution to his problems, it does incriminate social forces as the precipitating or reinforcing stimuli to the pattern which makes suicide possible.[29]

IX

The book *Aging and Leisure*, edited by Robert W. Kleemeier,[30] is replete with examples of the wide variation in the role of the elderly in our society as well as in other cultures. Robert J. Smith reports[31] that the Japanese with a strong Confucian influence exhibit a marked respect for the aged. He indicates that the older person is addressed with a title of greater respect than a younger person. He reports that at age sixty, which is the traditional age for Japanese retirement, a man is likely to turn over the leadership of his house to his eldest son. He explains that these persons are placed in a separate room or possibly in a separate house, and that the elders are employed in an advisory capacity. Although this implies respect and the rewarding of efforts of the elderly, I am not certain that this is true. Smith reports that grandmothers will stand on the bus so that their grandchildren can sit, and that in overcrowded public transportation no preference is given the elderly. This sounds very much like the United States. He also indicates that the death of an older person is not the occasion of a show of intense grief, as death for the ill and infirm is regarded as a welcome relief—both for the individual and for his family. It is my impression that this presentation does

[28] H. W. Gruhle, "Suicide in Old Age," *Zeitschrift für Altersforch*, 3 (1941), 21.

[29] Emile Durkheim, *Suicide* (New York: Free Press, 1951).

[30] Robert W. Kleemeier (Ed.), *Aging and Leisure* (New York: Oxford University Press, 1961).

[31] *Ibid.*, p. 95.

little to confirm the fact that life in Japan is for the older Japanese person equally rewarding or more rewarding than for the younger person, or that the older Japanese person is better off than the elderly American.

X

Medical and service professions are largely responsible for initiating and carrying out programs designed to improve or maintain the physical health and well-being of elderly persons. To construct and evaluate properly the effectiveness of such health programs, and then to appreciate limitations of the various methods of health assessment, we must have some knowledge of the major factors that influence health in all its aspects. Social and other factors play a role in the self-evaluation of health by elderly persons as contrasted with the assessment of health status determined by medical examination and evaluation. Maddox has made an important contribution to the reliability of self-evaluation of health.[32]

Maddox utilized data derived from a study of volunteer elderly subjects participating in a comprehensive longitudinal study of human aging. Objective health status, based upon extensive medical examination, was rated in terms of a five-point scale. A subject's health was assumed to be medically good if there were no symptoms of disease or, if the symptoms existed, he suffered no more than 20 percent limitation of his normal functioning. Subjects with limitations of 20 percent or more were considered to be in poor health. Self-assessment of health was determined from the response to the question "How do you rate yourself at the present time?" Intelligence as a factor was given consideration. Although the study included numerous psychological examinations, for the purposes of this study Maddox utilized the IQ determined by performance on the WAIS. In addition, consideration was given the attitudes and patterns of adjustment that were manifest in the psychiatric examination. Excessive preoccupation with health in the psychiatric examination was indicated as "high body concern." A count of symptoms or com-

[32] G. L. Maddox, "Self-Assessment of Health Status—A Longitudinal Study of Selected Elderly Subjects," *The Journal of Chronic Disease*, 17 (1964), 449-460.

plaints was obtained from the clinical medical evaluation. Morale was measured in terms of a Havighurst Attitude Scale, and level of activity was determined by an activity scale. Social placement factors were also included in the study. Considered were age, sex, race, alteration in work role, and social-economic status. Finally, the fact that health information was available to the patient was considered. Each subject had an opportunity by letter and personal contact to be informed of his objective health status as evaluated by the examining physicians.

The data from the original observations indicated that in 65 percent of the subjects there was congruity between self-assessment of health and the medical evaluation of the physical status. Incongruity of self-assessment of health and medical evaluation occurred almost equally regardless of the objective health status. In those subjects considered to be in good health, 31 percent were health pessimists, and of those with poor health, 44 percent were optimists. Thus, approximately one-third of elderly persons could not be relied upon to give an accurate self-assessment of their physical health. Subjects whose health was medically good and who had a realistic self-appraisal were likely to be older (that is, age seventy or above), to occupy a higher social status, and to maintain a high level of social activity. In those that deviated, it appeared that the younger subject was more likely to be pessimistic, while the older subject utilized denial and maintained an optimistic view. There was a sex difference; pessimism was more characteristic of women, in spite of the fact that the mortality rate favors the older woman. Also the pessimistic or hypochondriacal person was likely to have low morale, to be poorly adjusted to the environment, to report past and current periods of depression, and to express feelings of neglect.[33]

Three years intervened between the first complete study and the second longitudinal survey. At that time 76 percent of these subjects showed no change in their physical health status and 70 percent expressed self-health assessments congruent with physician's rating. These figures would suggest considerable stability in the health and self-assessments of the individuals included in the longitudinal study. This was not strictly true, since a shift took place. Of the subjects in the second survey, only 11 percent persisted in their faulty evalua-

[33] E. W. Busse, "Psychoneurotic Reactions and Defense Mechanisms in the Aged," *op. cit.*

tion of their health status. Two-thirds of these were persistent pessimists and one-third confirmed optimists. Over 18 percent of the total sample moved from a realistic to an unrealistic evaluation. Therefore, it is possible to speculate that self-assessments are idiosyncratic, have no common features, and are not predictable. This is probably not true. It appears that the persistent pessimist and the new pessimist were similar. The pessimist (hypochondriac) was likely to be a female of low social-economic status, with little change in her work role, younger and less socially active, with patterns of activity suggesting that they are not conclusive to a good adjustment. Clinical experience parallels these findings, characterizing the elderly pessimists.[34] In contrast, the persistent optimist was likely to be a male of somewhat higher economic status, with considerable relief from a demanding work role, and with suitable social activity. The optimist, that is, one who denies the existence of disease, was less likely to come to the attention of the physician until the physical disease had become so serious that it could not be denied. It is believed that both the health pessimist and the health optimist are medical problems requiring special attention. The self-assessment of health by elderly persons should be viewed with considerable caution, as psycho-social-economic influences are present.

Elsewhere in this book, Professor Henry, concerned with hospitals for the aged poor, expresses justified indignation and condemns the practices which degrade the patient and lead to the state of "depersonalization" (his term). Professor Henry's feelings are shared by many of us who have had experiences in institutions which supposedly provide care for the poor, the aged, and the chronically ill. The facilities, as well as the care offered by the personnel, are often shockingly inadequate. But to correct these conditions one must be concerned with the causes of such a situation. Inquiry reveals causes for which corrective measures are possible. Frequently attendants have not been sufficiently trained to recognize that their failure to perform certain tasks is not consistent with good health-care practices, but contributes to many serious complications which increase their work load. This, combined with the other legitimate concerns of Professor Henry, when understood by the attendants, can alter their behavior and attitudes.

Unfortunately, attendants are frequently selected from a low

[34] E. W. Busse, "The Treatment of the Chronic Complainer," *op. cit.*

level of society and do not possess the education, motivation, or capacities to provide the care that is necessary. Salaries are frequently too low to attract a better class of workers, and leadership is not present that will provide a reasonable priority list of tasks to be performed. Under these circumstances it is likely that the social conscious loading will give way to maintaining standards which are traditional and basic to the prevention and transmission of infectious diseases and to preventing accidents. Certainly it is possible to describe the facilities and personnel required to care for the aged poor in a humanitarian fashion. However, it is society that must decide whether it will make the efforts and sacrifices necessary, either by voluntary or legislative means, to make adequate care available.

It is also necessary for us to profit by the experience of individuals of skill and high motivation who have attempted to alter such adverse conditions by their dedicated and untiring efforts. It is of interest that such individuals can become victims of their experience. Personnel, exposed for long periods of time to appalling conditions that are beyond their capacity to change, often control their anxiety and distress by gradually excluding from their own awareness the existence of some very bad conditions.

BIOGRAPHICAL NOTE

EWALD W. BUSSE was born in St. Louis, Missouri, in 1917, and educated at Westminster College (A.B., Sc.D., hon.) and Washington University, St. Louis (M.D.). Dr. Busse, now J. P. Gibbons Professor of Psychiatry, is Chairman of the Department of Psychiatry and Director of the Center for the Study of Aging at Duke University. He is secretary-treasurer of the American Board of Psychiatry and Neurology and is the author of numerous scientific publications that are primarily concerned with psychosomatic disorders, problems of the aging and aged, and electroencephalographic studies. Publications include "Administration of the Interdisciplinary Research Team," "Pre-Senescent Electroencephalographic Changes in Normal Subjects," and "Criteria for Retirement: A Re-examination."

10

Personality and Aging — with Special Reference to Hospitals for the Aged Poor [1]

Jules Henry

I

This paper is based on a study of a large public institution for the chronically sick and aged poor, a cheap private institution for the same kind of patients, and a relatively high-priced hospital for those who are sick and aged but financially well off (not discussed here). The purpose of the study was to explore the effectiveness of skilled nursing care in restoring personality to hospitalized aged individuals. One group of skilled nurses gave care to the patients, while another group observed the general ongoing life of the hospital round the clock. What I have to say is based on the latter section of the study.

Since a very large proportion of the poor are aged individuals,[2] many of whom will end their days or at least spend a great deal of their terminal time in public institutions or very cheap private ones,[3] it is imperative to understand the nature of the peculiar institutional processes that make these last days, months, or years more miserable than necessary. Largely because of low budgetary allocations per patient, as in the public case, and also because of the necessity of

[1] Study supported by National Institute of Health (GN 5535).

[2] See Michael Harrington, *The Other America* (New York: Macmillan, 1962).

[3] For comparison of a public institution, a cheap private one, and a more expensive one, see Jules Henry, *Culture Against Man* (New York: Random House, 1963), Chapter 10.

realizing a profit, in the private case, such institutions suffer parallel inadequacies. Factual descriptions of such institutions can communicate to an audience their general dehumanizing characteristics, but theoretical analysis of the processes that generate them is also necessary in order to suggest points of entry for ameliorative action and to clarify the social dynamics of institutional inhumanity. Inhumanity is a strong inherent tendency in *Homo sapiens,* and in our culture it achieves its finest flowering among the lower levels of the population, because their inhumanity to one another—a common enough feature of the more refined dimensions of society also—is compounded by the inhumanity of the outer world to which they are especially vulnerable and often by the physical inability of the poor to take care of one another. The world's inhumanity to the aged poor and sick achieves a special form in public institutions; but it may be even worse in private ones run on a shoestring, where the pressure for profit may exacerbate certain features also present in public institutions. This paper concentrates on general theoretical considerations that cover salient issues having to do with organizational dynamics in both types of institutions, taking for a model a public one as representing the less extreme case. The reader will therefore bear in mind that usually what is said of the public institution may be true of certain private ones also, only "more so."

II

Sociology and anthropology have a traditional way of thinking about person and personality that derives from Emile Durkheim.[4] In this frame of reference "the essential element of the personality is the social part of us"[5] and a "person" is the embodiment of "all which represents society in us." If one looks in reverse at this idea of "representation of society in us," it becomes clear that a being in whom society ceases to be represented, in the broadest sense, can no longer be a person. If we view the idea of person from the standpoint of process, that is, of becoming a person, we perceive that all

---

[4] *Elementary Forms of the Religious Life,* trans. by Joseph Ward Swain (New York: Free Press, 1947). See especially pp. 269-272.

[5] *Ibid.,* p. 272.

events that relate or bind one to the social system can be called *personalizing*. It follows that everything that detaches him from the social system can be called *depersonalizing*. Thus in the theoretical formulation presented here, depersonalization refers to a social process, not to a psychic state. Meanwhile we are aware that, as Bird[6] has made clear, in psychiatry depersonalization refers "to . . . neurotic feelings of unreality." In this paper I do not use depersonalization in that sense.

III

Individuals are persons to the degree that they are attached to the social system—the complex of interpersonal and institutional relations. For example, in our culture, legitimacy, the social recognition of the attachment of a child to a family, an essential part of the social system, is acquired by a child born of a legal marriage and symbolized in the birth certificate. However, the marriage of the parents is actually the first jural act that binds children to the social system; the issuance of the birth certificate is the second. The child born out of wedlock is less attached to the social system and, by that token, less a social person than a legitimate child. Attachment of the individual to the social system is thus indicated by processes and/or events which bind him to and make him a member of it. The dependence of this binding on specific social events can be understood by examining the relationship in some societies between personalization—degree of membership in the society—and age. Common in anthropological reports are statements to the effect that in a given society infants are mourned or missed less than older children and older children less than adults. The failure of some societies to be deeply moved by the loss of infants or young children is structurally related to the fact that the latter make little or no contribution to the economy, but also to the circumstance that in such societies they have not passed through the ceremonials which attach them to the socioreligious system.

Personalization is measurable by the number and importance of

[6] Brian Bird, "Depersonalization," *AMA Archives of Neurology and Psychiatry*, 80 (1958), 467-476.

the processes an individual has gone through, and the socially significant symbols—a name, circumcision, taboos—he has acquired.
Among the Murngin of Australia[7] the boy moves through a series of
initiation rites, each one of which makes him more and more a
Murngin. In our society a middle-class child begins life with the acquisition of legitimate parents, a name, identification tag, blanket,
crib, and bottle. He moves on to spoon, high chair, and plate—material and ceremonial indicators of social status of children. Personalization of the child also involves acquisition of sphincter control, proper
sleeping and eating habits, succeeding in school, and so on. At each
point, as each process is completed and the symbol acquired, the
child's position as a personalized being is measurable by what he has
acquired and where he stands in the succession of ceremonials. He
struggles not so much to master the cultural tasks as to acquire those
symbols—"a child who does not wet," "a child who goes to school,"
"a man with a job"—which tie him to the social structure and compel
people to recognize him as a person.

It can be seen from the above that personalization involves not
only the acquisition of certain symbols and statuses, but also, in our
culture, a series of successes. By that token a person who fails or
who has lost the capacity to succeed is less a person, because he has
withdrawn from the success mechanism. Thus, just as the child who
still "has accidents" is not as much a person as the one who has mas-
tered his sphincters, so the old person who becomes incontinent loses
the right to personality. Children who fail in school may never become people at all; this is the experience of masses of slum children.
For such failure the culture destroys them by deprivation of income.
Since old people in our culture who have withdrawn or have been
displaced from the occupational system can no longer succeed or
fail, they are scarcely people at all—unless, of course, they can still
symbolize their past success by continued consumption capability.
In this way retention of consumption capability, even after having
withdrawn from the success machinery, is taken as adequate *quid
pro quo* for success, because through it, an indispensable service is
rendered to the economy.

The acquisition of certain symbols and successes compels society to recognize personality; thus such acquisition exerts a moral

[7] See W. Lloyd Warner, *A Black Civilization* (New York: Harper & Row,
1937).

force, even though existence of the latter may never be codified.[8] Similarly, the absence of the symbols and successes deprives one of moral force. A child who cannot control his sphincters cannot compel people to treat him as if he could, if for no other reason than that they are afraid of getting dirty. Anyone who puts people in danger of getting dirty loses personality. Yet something else is involved in the attainment and retention of sphincter control: it is a primordial demonstration of self-control and self-mastery. *Mutatitis mutandi,* loss of sphincter control in old age may dirty other people, and it demonstrates loss of self-control. A person who has failed or who has withdrawn from the success mechanism loses most of his moral force in the society. Even though he retains consumption capability it is difficult for people to listen to him, for he has lost the inherent moral force that accrues to one who still fights within the success system. Thus all who are still warriors in the war of success and failure are by that token more endowed with moral force than those who are not. Culture awards personality to those who fight its symbolic battles. Hence a child who is not yet in the economic system is less a person than the adolescent who is fighting.

Several factors make it clear that utilitarian notions such as survival or productivity have nothing to do with the moral force deriving from activity within the economic system. The first comes from those tribal cultures like Alor,[9] Kwakiutl,[10] and Trobriands[11] where there is a sharp division between the economics of prestige and the economics of essential production. In these cultures the honorific economic system has nothing to do with the essentials of life or mere biological survival, for it is occupied with the manipulation of largely unessential objects; it is expertise in, and initiation into, such manipulation that confers personality. On the other hand, if a man in these cultures does well at the economics of essential production only, he has no social personality. Furthermore, the

[8] Only when this is understood can the legend of Esau be understood by a modern; for Esau, having sold his birthright, had detached himself from the social system and ceased, thereby, to be a person. Having committed this enormous crime against himself, Jacob's businesslike swindling of Esau pales into insignificance.

[9] Cora Dubois, *The People of Alor* (Minneapolis: University of Minnesota Press, 1944).

[10] Ruth Benedict, *Patterns of Culture* (Boston: Houghton Mifflin, 1934).

[11] Bronislaw Malinowski, *Argonauts of the Western Pacific* (New York: Dutton, 1922).

women, though excellent at the production of essentials, are largely without honor. In our culture disdain for the old has less to do with their withdrawal from the economic system as a productive system than with their leaving the economic system that serves as an engine for generating personality.

The second set of factors derives from the realm of the voluntary work that is done without compensation by middle-class housewives in our culture. Many women find little satisfaction in such work because it is done without compensation. It is clear that what is missing in voluntary work is its lack of connection with the personality-conferring mechanism; any compensated job, regardless of how unessential it is, is more valued by such women than voluntary work, even though the latter is essential.[12]

In all cultures the nature of the attachment of an individual to the social system varies through time and is usually related to the economic and symbolic contributions made by him to the culture. Everywhere deference, access to goods and services, the ability to influence social decisions, the capacity "to be missed," and the right to control the disposition of one's own person emerge as criteria of "attachment" and, hence, of personalization. In the history of Western culture slaves have been the most depersonalized human beings, in the sense intended here, and close on their heels have come women and children.

IV

When we look at the position of the aged in different cultures from the standpoint of their economic and symbolic contributions to culture and from the standpoint of the criteria of attachment, we see a variegated picture. In contemporary village India, the aged man makes little contribution to the economy; yet since he is closer to the supernatural than the young man, and is therefore symbolically more important than the latter, he receives more deference than younger men and still has important influence on public decisions.[13] The same is true in most Australian tribes[14] and in traditional

---

[12] In this connection see Betty Friedan, *The Feminine Mystique* (New York: Norton, 1963).

[13] S. C. Dube, *Indian Village* (London: Routledge and Kegan Paul, 1955).

[14] Warner, *op. cit.*

China.[15] It is likely that in these cultures it is the close relationship of the aging man to the supernatural that tips the balance of life in his favor, for it is a common, though not universal, experience of the aged in cultures where they have no supernatural symbols attached to them to be neglected to the point where they are starved, treated with contempt, and even asked to commit suicide. Eskimo,[16] Siriono,[17] and Pilaga[18] are examples of cultures where contributions are made largely through techniques of physical survival—economic or military—and where, therefore, the aging person tends to decline rapidly into a "he won't be missed" condition.

Yet these functions cannot be considered apart from the concept of *centeredness*. The idea of centeredness derives from the answer to the question, "In any organization, whose interests are paramount?" Thus in the traditional public institution for the mentally ill, the staff's interests are paramount; in the contemporary university, the professors' interests are paramount and the students are merely a necessary condition for the staff's paramountcy. In Asiatic families the parents' interests were paramount—and in large areas of India still are—while in the contemporary United States the children's interests are paramount, and no parent who wants to retain respect in the community dare say, "I come first." Parent-centeredness or parent paramountcy, however, was the rule in traditional China and India for many centuries; along with it went extreme solicitude for the aged. In these circumstances the supernatural powers of the aged were a functional reinforcement of parent paramountcy. Neglect of the aged in contemporary American culture is thus basically caused by the disappearance of the tradition of parent-centeredness from Western culture. Eskimo, Siriono, and Pilaga, on the other hand, are not centered at all, in the sense examined here, but are highly individualistic cultures, where cooperative links are minimal. Thus extremely individualistic cultures may lack centeredness and also deal harshly with the aged. The Kaingang Indians of Brazil,[19] a highly cooperative society, live in about the same economic

[15] Martin Yang, *A Chinese Village* (New York: Columbia University Press, 1945).

[16] Mead, *op. cit.*, pp. 72 and 84 (Case 13).

[17] Allan R. Holberg, *Nomads of the Long Bow*, Institute of Social Anthropology, Publication No. 10 (Washington: Smithsonian Institution, 1950).

[18] Jules Henry, "Anthropology and Psychosomatics," *Psychosomatic Medicine*, 11 (1949), 16-22.

[19] Jules Henry, *Jungle People* (New York: Random House, 1964).

circumstances as the Siriono; but though they are nomads, hunting over a territory whose subsistence yield is often problematic, they carry their aged tenderly about in baby-carrying bands until the old die.

V

Loss of personality is accompanied by certain changes in social interaction, some more readily observable in one culture, some in another. However, all occur in our own culture; all serve to detach the individual from the social system, and all of them are, by that token, depersonalizing.

For the purpose of this paper, depersonalization has been defined as *the process of depriving an individual of the factors that attach him to his social system.* Where depersonalization occurs, in this sense, it is related to the declining economic and symbolic usefulness of the individual—as "usefulness" is understood in the particular culture.

VI

To the degree that one makes a contribution he will be readily contained within the social system, and positive social attitudes will exist toward him. When he ceases to make a contribution there is a tendency for the social system of which he is a member to expel him. Figure 1 presents in schematic form the movement of a typical male through a social system during his life span.

The model indicates that before birth the child is still at the outer periphery, although he is a member of a social system by virtue of being in his mother, who is legally married to his father.[20] As he grows older he moves toward its center where he commands most of the criteria of membership; and as he passes into old age, he declines toward the position of child. In our culture the aged, obsolete adult may readily fall below the status of an unborn, even an unwanted, infant (position 6), but in China and India the individual

[20] In Java the new-born would occupy position 7 on the diagram because he is a god. See Hildred Geertz, *The Javanese Family* (New York: Free Press, 1961).

FIGURE 1.   MODEL REPRESENTING THE MOVEMENT OF A TYPICAL
MALE THROUGH HIS PERSONAL COMMUNITY FROM IN-
TRAUTERINE LIFE TO DEATH AND THE HEREAFTER

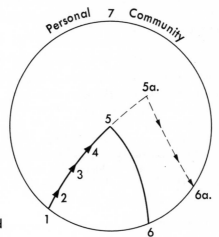

1. Prenatal period
2. Infancy
3. Childhood
4. Adolescense
5. Manhood
5a. Late-manhood and old age in traditional China and India
6. Point of decline to social and material death in our culture
6a. Decline to extreme old age in China and India
7. Posthumous spirtitual elevation in China and India

in late manhood and old age continues to rise in status up to the
peculiar, exalted, rather apart position of the aged. At any rate, this
is the ideal picture. Extreme old age places him somewhat in the
position of the demanding (child position 6a). The following from
the *Twenty Four Examples of Filial Piety*[21] illustrate the point.

[21] From Mischa Titiev and Hsing-Chih Tien, "A Primer of Filial Piety,"
Papers of the Michigan Academy of Science, Arts and Letters, 33 (1947), 261-
266.

Tale III: *Deer Milk Served to Parents*

There lived in the time of the Chou dynasty an extremely filial son named Yen-tzu. His father and mother were aged, and each was afflicted with sore eyes. They thirsted for deer milk, and to satisfy their desire Yen-tzu put on a deer skin and went deep into the mountains, planning to mingle with a herd in order to obtain some milk. A party of hunters saw him and were about to shoot, but Yen-tzu told them his whole story and was no longer molested.

Tale V: *Sleeping on Ice to Procure Carp*

In the days of the Chin dynasty lived Wang Hsiang, whose mother died when he was very young. His stepmother, Chu, had no love for him and spoke badly about him to his father. Consequently Wang Hsiang lost his father's affection.

During the winter season, when all was frozen, his stepmother had a desire to eat fresh fish, so Hsiang took off his clothes and slept on the ice, hoping to procure some. Suddenly the ice broke open and a pair of carp leaped out. Hsiang grasped them dutifully and took them home to his stepmother.

Tale VII: *Weeps Among Bamboos and Sprouts Grow*

In the kingdom of Wu lived Meng Tsung. His father had died when he was young, and his mother was aged and very sick. During the winter months she longed for a soup made of bamboo sprouts, but Tsung found no way to obtain them. Then he went to a grove, where he embraced the bamboos and wept. His filial piety moved Heaven and Earth, and all of a sudden the ground burst open and a few sprouts sprang up. Bringing them home, he cooked a soup for his mother; and when she had eaten it she found herself well.

Tale XIII: *She Suckled her Mother-in-Law Without Impatience*

During the time of the T'ang dynasty Lady Ch'ang-sun, great grandmother of Tsui Shan-nan, reached so great an age that she had lost all her teeth. Every day Shan-nan's grandmother, Lady T'ang, would make her toilet carefully, preparatory to entering the front hall, where she would suckle her mother-in-law.[22] By this means the venerable Lady Ch'-

---

[22] Since in traditional China daughters moved into their husbands' houses on marriage, the incoming daughter-in-law became a female child, subordinate and dutiful to her husband's mother, that is, her mother-in-law and symbolic mother. See Martin Yang, *op. cit.*

ang-sun, who was unable to eat solid food, lived in good health for a period of several years. At last, one day she became very sick; and as her old and young relatives gathered about her, Lady Ch'ang-sun said: "There is no way to repay your kindness, daughter-in-law, and I can only hope that your daughter-in-law will be just as filial and respectful to you as you have been to me."

In traditional China and India a parent's death places him among the revered ancestors in the realm of the supernatural (position 7), central to the society, yet at the same time at its outermost periphery.

Throughout recorded history, in the Judeo-Christian, Confucian, and Hindu traditions, supernaturalism, parent-centeredness, and consideration for the aged have formed one indissoluble complex. Loss of consideration for the aged is readily destroyed by attack on any of these components. Side by side with them has gone economic capability, playing an important, but perhaps not determining role. For example, though in traditional peasant China the father was treated with overt respect until he died, he suffered some decline in status as his economic functions were taken over by the sons.[23]

VII [24]

In our culture poor and aged persons who are unable to take care of themselves have lost the right to personality. From a functional point of view, the institutions to which they are relegated may be looked upon as mechanisms for depersonalization. In this section the process will be examined in detail.

Depersonalization through symbolic means. Here belong those acts which deprive a person of the symbols that represent attachment to the social system. Outstanding among them are its sign systems: communication in general, the personal name, exchange of positive and negative responses by some verbal or nonverbal device. When an individual is being depersonalized in our culture, people do not communicate with him; he is often addressed as "you" in-

[23] See Martin Yang, *op. cit.*
[24] After writing this section, it was pointed out to me that Erving Goffman had dealt with similar considerations in *Asylums* (Garden City, N. Y.: Doubleday, 1961).

stead of "Mr. Jones" (or "John"); since little account is taken of his wishes and he is deprived of communication, he does not have the opportunity to give positive or negative responses. In addition, people act as if he were not present; they talk about him in his presence as if he were not there.[25] It is thus apparent that while the sign system is a communications system, in human society—as probably in animal societies also—a more primordial function is to link a member to the social system.

Awareness on the part of others that one's body is part of a sentient human being, and that it is not just a thing, is another factor that contributes to one's sense of being a person. When one's body is rolled around in a bed like a log or merely transferred by hospital employees from one place to another without any indication that the employee is aware of its humanness, the human being enclosed in the body may well feel that he is being treated as an inanimate object. The handling of the body as if it were a thing—as if it were labeled "log" instead of "Mr. Jones"—is therefore included in the category of "depersonalization through symbolic means."

All these processes can be observed in hospitals for the aged poor.

Depersonalization through material means. In every culture, material objects are organized into a system I have called the "object system,"[26] which is a phase of the social system. Objects are organized in terms of (1) assignment to particular persons or groups, (2) certain standards of excellence, and (3) use.

Evaluation of an individual's attachment to the social system, and hence of his personalization, must therefore take account of whether he has the objects to which a fully personalized individual is entitled, whether the objects he has are of good quality in conformity with cultural standards, and whether the objects he has are being used for the purpose for which they were intended.

If a hospital patient has no personal accessories such as toilet articles, towels, and comb, if the surroundings are poor, and if, in addition, he is compelled to use material objects for purposes for

[25] This is documented in Chapter 10 of *Culture Against Man,* and it is paralleled in a striking way among the Pilaga Indians.
[26] See Jules Henry, "A Cross-Cultural Outline of Education," *Current Anthropology,* 1 (1960), 267-305.

which they were never intended (washing his face in a bedpan, using a commode for a chair, or a urinal for an emesis basin), then he is being depersonalized through material means.

Distortion in the use of material objects plays a peculiarly destructive role in this environment for two reasons: (1) A large number of the distortions that occur are of a degrading character, inasmuch as they compel the patient to utilize excremental utensils (bedpans, commodes, urinals) for purposes for which they were never intended. In this way a cultural taboo is repeatedly violated. (2) The unconscious confusion between face and buttocks, between mouth and anus, between saliva and urine is well known from the psychoanalytic literature. To the degree that the environment forces these on an individual, therefore, it presents him with an invitation to regression with all its appalling consequences.

However this may be, what one observes in such environments is the attenuation and even apparent disappearance, in some patients, of the capacity to experience disgust.

Depersonalization through attack on the shame and disgust functions. There is no culture without shame—the name we give to the feeling that comes upon us when we become exposed to public revilement for having broken a centrally important taboo. The universality of shame and its close relation to culturally central considerations suggest its adaptive significance. Since in our culture the paradigm of the shameful act is exposure of the genitals, it follows that when one is permitted to lie naked where he can be seen by anyone, he is no longer violating the taboo on exposure, because in certain respects he has ceased to be a member of the social system to which most members of the society belong.

However, exposure is merely symbolic of his having ceased to be of adaptive significance to the culture. Much less attention is paid to shame in institutions for the aged poor than in those for the more comfortably fixed, and in our research we never saw an exposed person in the latter, but they did occur in the former. The tendency not to permit shame to the sick and aged poor is simply one aspect of the generally degraded existence they lead. Parallel conditions can be seen in old-fashioned snake pits for the insane, where so-called regressed patients lie about in the cellar, naked and incontinent.

Disgust is the name given to the physical feeling experienced when confronted with foul material objects or foul behavior. Disgust often, though not always, is a spectator complement of the shameful behavior of another person. The symbol of the disgusting object is feces; in our culture a paradigm of disgusting behavior is the public violation of a socially central taboo, such as defecating in public, perhaps. At any rate, it is primarily the disgust function that gets defecation out of the house in human society; and it is the disgust function that makes feces on the body intolerable. Defecation out-side the house—usually quite far from it—and removal of feces from the body are two abiding characteristics of life in a human social system. A milder form of disgust is generated in our culture by an adult with his face smeared with food. Perhaps it symbolizes regression and is therefore frightening also.

If, then, a bedfast patient is permitted to lie in excreta, to lie naked and exposed to everyone's eyes, to remain with his face covered with food, it must impress on him, and on everyone, the fact that he is not part of the larger social system. Such actions provide the conditions for extreme regression, destroy the capacity to experience shame and disgust, and by that token remove the individual from the larger social system.

Thus, the capacity to experience negative sensations is just as important for attachment to the social system as the capacity to experience positive ones, for example, the sensation of prestige. Such considerations can be extended to all disadvantaged classes—Negroes, slaves, serfs, some servants, and so on—for they are often degraded below the capacity to experience shame or disgust. The function of the destruction of the capacity to experience shame and disgust is therefore to dehumanize and to make an individual docile and resigned.

Depersonalization through routinization and deprivation of individuality. In routinization all of certain groups of events in a social system are viewed as identical: all are considered to have the same material characteristics and to be governed by the same temporal sequences. It is the difference between serving each patient food which he selects and at hours chosen by him (nonroutine) and serving all patients the same food at the same time (routinization). All hospitals are highly routinized and, even in private pavilions, have relatively little capacity to deal with improbabilities—that is, chance, unusual, special events—in the system.

It is one of the properties of the personalized individual in our culture that he has a right to his improbabilities, that is, to peculiarities that distinguish him from others. In a sense his improbabilities are possessions, inalienable indicators of his self. To the extent that a social system recognizes these, he is a self; the social system, in taking account of his improbabilities, makes a place for him as an individual. In routinization—giving medications, taking temperatures, making beds in assembly-line fashion—a patient is deprived of his improbabilities, reduced to the level of everyone else, and treated like a thing; he is depersonalized.

In a rapidly changing society everyone has, by that fact, a right to his improbabilities; and the contrary push, to conform, is merely a brake on the rush of change. In a hospital for the chronically-ill aged poor, improbability must be eliminated because of the extremely parsimonious conditions under which the institution is conducted and, as has been pointed out, because the patients have lost the right to personality. Thus such institutions may give the impression of timelessness. In their vast reaches time seems suspended; the patients become like figures in a wax museum; it is as if a Piranesi prison, with its atmosphere of hollowness and detachment, had been actualized.

Depersonalization by deprivation of protection. Every social system must provide protection for its members. This is true not only because human beings need protection in order to survive, but because if protection is not provided the reverberations in the unprotected are "Nobody cares, I am nothing," and depersonalization and loss of the sense of self are stimulated.

In institutions for the aged poor, evidence of lack of protection include absence of control of pilfering, indifference on the part of staff to extremes of temperature (so that, for example, they will permit a ward to become extremely cold while not covering the patients), severe violations of medico-nursing aseptic techniques, and, of course, in the most depraved institutions, lack of food, water, and medical care. While such neglect threatens physical survival, the stress here is on the psychological meaning of such deprivation—the feelings that one is cast away, that one is nothing—and the ensuing dejection and apathy.

Depersonalization through inconstancy and distortion of the human environment. The self emerges in social interaction,[27] and most people require continuous reaffirmation of self through social interaction. Before self-affirmation can begin through social interaction, mutuality has to be established so that self-affirming feedback can occur. This requires constancy of association.[28] However, when there is constant change, the individuals with whom one becomes involved in the ongoing and necessary process of self-affirmation disappear. Since efforts to reestablish the interrupted process probably become increasingly painful, the individual tends to withdraw from social interaction and thus loses attachment to the social system. This is the line of speculation I have followed in attempting to understand what happens as a consequence of constantly shifting patients' beds, in attempting to understand why noisy ones whose beds are often shifted become quiet.

In the situations under discussion, inconstancy arises because patients are frequently moved from one part of the ward to another. As a matter of fact, if staff sees patients in vigorous interaction, one of them may be moved. This is a factor responsible for the low interactional rate and for the tomb-like quiet noted.

Just as constancy and continuity of human contact seem necessary to full personalization, so does corporal intactness; if one is surrounded by the blind, the deaf, the dismembered, and the incontinent, there is just as great a tendency to withdraw as if these persons were not there. One of the most powerful depersonalizing agencies is the inability to escape from such distorted people.

Depersonalization and staff-centeredness. All social systems embody a certain choice with respect to the direction in which energies

[27] See George Herbert Mead, *Mind, Self and Society* (Chicago: University of Chicago Press, 1934).

[28] Experiments have been done on animals deprived of social interaction. It is necessary to do similar experiments with animals whose society is constantly changed, but who, nevertheless, are not actually deprived of associates.

and sanctions shall be focused. We call our contemporary society child-centered. The cultures of traditional India and China were parent-centered. The concept of centeredness implies not only a mobilization of energy toward a group but a possible tendency to sacrifice the well-being of other groups to that of the central group.

Centeredness is a culturally determined perception that facilitates the mobilization of energies in favor of one group rather than another. In a hospital in which staff-centeredness prevails, the comfort and convenience of the staff tends to overshadow that of the patients, and thus makes a massive contribution to depersonalization. When the patients are poor and aged, that is, have already lost much of their right to membership in the larger social system, staff-centeredness is facilitated because no one is bound to center his attention on those already slipping out of the social system.

Staff-centeredness is expressed in a number of ways:

1. *Through routinization.* Routinization of functions occurs when the functions are performed in the simplest and most expeditious way. It means that the employee does not have to think about what he does or take any individual differences in patients into account. Communication is reduced to the minimum necessary to discharge the routinized and highly standardized functions. The emphasis is on smoothness and ease of repetition.

2. *Through the elimination of improbability.* To the extent that staff has to take into account the unpredictabilities of patients, their task is made more difficult. However, if all patients are calm and quiet, task performance is easier. The most powerful way of eliminating conflicts between patients is by moving them from one part of a ward to another.

3. *Through equalization of functions.* Perhaps the ideal in any task-performing organization is that all roles should be interchangeable, so that everyone can perform everyone else's task. Under such circumstances there is little to fear if an employee is absent or leaves, for anyone can do what he does. Interchangeability of roles can be accomplished by constantly rotating staff through all divisions, with the result that personnel rarely remain permanently on any division. Although this may be good for the performance of routine tasks, it creates an inconstant relationship between staff and patients, and thus contributes to depersonalization.

VIII

Social conscience loading (SCL) is the strength of the social feelings of right and wrong that attach to the commission or omission of any act.[29] Some acts can have a higher SCL than others. Thus, in our culture murder has a higher SCL than robbery; rape has a higher SCL than seduction. In hospitals cleanliness has a higher SCL than tenderness: a dirty hospital would excite universal anger and probably have its license revoked, but patients have been treated coldly in clean and efficient hospitals for generations, and the social conscience scarcely twitches.

In the situations of which I speak SCL plays an important role in depersonalization.

Social conscience loading and task visibility. Since in our culture the social conscience is readily aroused by dirt and disorder in a public institution, major effort falls on the performance of tasks of highest visibility: keeping the wards neat and clean. Specifically the following are emphasized: unlittered bedside tables; well-made beds; clean floors; uncluttered walls without pictures, calendars, or posters; removal of loose personal property like newspapers and books. Plaques and prizes may be awarded staff teams having the neatest wards.

Social conscience loading and medical supplies. To the degree that the social conscience can be affected by conditions in a public hospital, it will be more readily aroused by absence of medicines and dressings than by a shortage of washcloths, towels, tissues, or even soap. This is so because the social conscience is more readily aroused by death than by anything else. Furthermore, since guilt and feelings of respectability are important ingredients of the social conscience in our culture, the guilt and sense of offended respectability that follow upon the death even of inadequately medicated paupers readily stimulate society to take punitive action. On the other hand, it seems likely that requests for more washcloths, towels,

[29] See Emile Durkheim, *The Division of Labor* (New York: Free Press, 1933).

tissues, and soap might arouse the social conscience against "pampering" and against "making a hotel out of a public institution." Thus in our culture the social conscience is characterized by a polarity which emphasizes survival of the body and burial of the personality.

This being the case, funds are allocated first for materials having the highest SCL, and the amenities and accessories of life (the "pampering materials") tend to be absent or in short supply.

Social conscience loading, material culture, and status. In speaking of the object system, I pointed out that material culture is assigned to different groups in line with the status of the group. Thus boomerangs, *churingas,* and bull-roarers are not handled by women among Australian tribes because women have low status. In our culture a person who earns his money operating a drill-press is of lower status than one who operates a bookkeeping machine. In a hospital the supplies having the heaviest SCL—medicines, dressings and so on—are handled by the high-status personnel (h.s.p)—doctors and nurses—and the supplies having little SCL are handled by low-status personnel (l.s.p.). When funds are low, the supplies having the heaviest SCL are usually available, while the others tend to be in short supply. The effect of this is to depress the morale of the l.s.p. and contribute to *their* depersonalization, thus making a double contribution to poor patient care and hence to depersonalization. The shortage of supplies makes it difficult to do a good job of taking care of the patients, and the depressed morale of the l.s.p. contributes to their surliness in dealing with the patients.

Furthermore, the effect of short supplies in these materials is cumulative, for it may lead to hoarding, which in turn creates false shortages and throws the staff into collision; this is bound to affect staff-patient relations adversely. Meanwhile it should be borne in mind that since the things the l.s.p. handle have low SCL, l.s.p. can do little to remedy the condition. Thus the quality of patient care, and hence the extent of their depersonalization, is a complex function of the interrelation among supplies, their SCL, and the status of the persons manipulating them. The object system of the hospital is part of a status system, and both are related to the social conscience. The social conscience cares less about what the l.s.p. does with its low-status supplies than it does about what the h.s.p. does with *its* supplies. Meanwhile it is the l.s.p. who are in closest contact with the patients and manipulate the (nearly nonexistent) human amenities.

I have spoken previously of disgust and its relation to depersonalization. Here we may note that it is the l.s.p. who are compelled by their tasks to do most violence to their own disgust functions, for it is they who must clean the incontinent, wipe the excreta from the beds and floors, and empty the bedpans. Thus here, as well as in the object system, the forces of depersonalization operate on the personnel as on the patients. And here, as well as in the object system relations, the tasks of the l.s.p. serve to turn them against the patients, for the patients are the source of the attack on the disgust function of staff personality.

IX

A large proportion of the aged are sick and poor and thus likely to spend a good part of their remaining time in public or cheap private institutions. It is necessary, therefore, to understand the extent to which such institutions may destroy personality, in the sociological sense.

Individuals are persons to the degree that they are attached to a social system, and this involves the acquisition and retention of certain tangible and intangible symbols of attachment. In acquiring these symbols, individuals in all cultures go through certain processes and achieve certain statuses. Taken together these constitute personality, in the social sense, and have a moral force, in the sense that a person, by virtue of having acquired all necessary symbols and statuses necessary to attachment, has the power to compel deference to himself—in short, to be treated like a person. From a genetic point of view, personalization changes through time and varies as the individual acquires or loses symbols and statuses. In line with these considerations, it can be seen that the position of the aged—their degree of attachment to the social system—varies in different cultures.

The process of depersonalization, defined as the process of depriving an individual of the factors that attach him to the social system, has been studied in a very large public and in a large cheap private institution for the chronically ill aged. This deprivation of the individual of the components of attachment to the social system, of the components of social personality, includes depersonalization through symbolic means—essentially the generalized loss of communications possibilities and the negative handling of the body; depersonalization through material means—essentially the deprivation of the material amenities, the generally poor quality of the available material culture, and the use of material objects in a distorted way; depersonalization through extinction or violation of the shame and disgust functions; depersonalization through routinization and deprivation of individuality and protection; depersonalization through inconstancy and distortion of the human environment; and depersonalization through staff-centeredness. Finally, since society's interest in its poor, sick, and aged charges does not go beyond material things—including the medical—and the correct performance of tasks of high visibility, humane behavior by the caretakers is left to chance. Since the caretakers in such institutions are poorly paid, poorly educated, and overworked, they have little incentive to humaneness.

The ultimate consequences of depersonalization are mutual hostility, loss of social capabilities, and apathy.

BIOGRAPHICAL NOTE

JULES HENRY was born in New York City in 1904 and was educated at the College of the City of New York (B.S.) and Columbia University (Ph.D.). Mr. Henry, now Professor of Anthropology and Sociology at Washington University, has published essays in cultural anthropology, linguistics, and emotional disturbance, which accounts for the bulk of his publications. Mr. Henry's publications include *Jungle People*, a study of the Kaingang Indians of the highlands of Brazil; *Doll Play of Pilaga Indian Children*, a study of sexual and hostility patterns in Pilaga Indian children; and *Culture Against Man*, the last chapter of which is based on five years of study of old-age homes. He is past Vice-President of the American Orthopsychiatric Association.

11

The Social Meaning of Death and the Law

Kurt W. Back
Hans W. Baade

The consciousness of death, both of one's own and of one's fellowman, is one of the basic facts of human existence. The necessity of facing death, the need to explain and justify it in the order of things, has provided some of the principal motivation for man's development of the philosophy of religion and of a general understanding of his position in the world. Psychologists, psychoanalysts, and psychiatrists have found the reaction to death to be a crucial psychodynamic force. Since death is such a powerful factor in the life of the individual, the culturally dominant attitudes toward death in a society will be reflected in its structure, its institutions, and its laws. The attitude toward death as reflected in the society is also intimately connected with the general attitude toward the life cycle in its different stages. In many ways the position of the aged within a society will be but another aspect of the way in which the society deals with death.

I

Many students of the American scene agree that the predominant attitude of American society toward death is the complete denial of its presence and concomitantly a complete discontinuity of the dead with the living.[1] It seems likely that this position represents

[1] Cf. Herman Feifel, summarizing the main trend of nineteen articles in his collection, *The Meaning of Death* (New York: McGraw-Hill, 1959), writes in his Introduction, "Denial and avoidance of the countenance of death characterize much of the American outlook" (p. lxvii).

an extreme in human history and is the outcome of a number of congruent influences. First, the general trend of social development has been running in the direction of isolating death. Man is the only being who is conscious of his own death.[2] In preliterate societies the borderline between life and death seems not to have been as clear-cut as in later societies. The dead were still members of the tribe and considered active in many ways; hence, the living had to deal with them as members of the society. The complete break with the dead, as existing not at all or, at best, in a different sphere, is a comparatively recent phenomenon in human history. The gradual elimination of the dead from any relationship with the individual and the life of the society is in part an extrapolation of this trend.

Second, American society, with its conscious break with the past and its faith in the future and in future development, is less concerned with the continuity with past generations than are the more tradition-oriented societies. The ideology of deemphasizing the importance of ancestry, as shown, for instance, in the absence of inherited titles of aristocracy, places emphasis on individual achievement, on the use of one's individual life-span. This places death, one's own and that of others, outside the area of socially relevant events. Death comes to mean the end of influence and importance.

Finally, the actual facts of the situation in contemporary Western society make death a less immediate concern during most of the life-span than it is in other societies. Lengthened life expectancy means that the risk of death is low during most of life and increases only in later years. As has been shown in other chapters,[3] lengthened life expectancy is a minor factor in the proportion of the aged in a society; but it becomes a major factor if the proportion of one's life to be spent in old age increases. Further, the main causes of death in the adult ages are accidents and suicide. These are considered preventable and practically within the individual's responsibility. In other societies, death has been a regular event in youth; dying in old age has been the exception. Thus, we should not be surprised to find more concern with death at all ages in these societies. But it is possible in American society to be unconcerned about one's death for a great part of one's life.

[2] Jacques Choron, *Death and Western Thought* (New York: Collier, 1963), especially Chapter 1.

[3] Cf. Joseph Spengler in Chapter 2 of this volume.

Yet, with the banishment of the sort of death that is necessarily part of the human condition, death has assumed another aspect as an ever-present background of contemporary life: the usual, accidental, violent, or other unexpected form in which it presents itself. While the statement has often been made that present-day American culture denies death, the same statement has been made with equal truth that the consciousness of death is a principal part of the spirit of the time. Just as the principal cause of death during adulthood is accidents and other forms of violence, this kind of abrupt, absurd ending of the course of life has been an event to be recognized at any age. In addition, the increasing mass toll of two world wars and the threat of total extinction through nuclear war have helped to shape the background of much contemporary thought.

However, it is seldom directly expressed in the life of the individual or in the institutions of society. It does express itself in art, literature, and the fine arts, as well as popular art. It may well be that this ever-present violence in the mass media of entertainment is less a cause than an effect of the actual existing violence in a society that does not accept death as a normal course of events. Geoffrey Gorer has noted that the denial of natural death is the prudery of our age, while the increased presence of violent death, through war, concentration camps, and—more prosaic and ubiquitous—the automobile, has made death an aspect of mass fantasy. In consequence, death has become the pornography of present-day society.[4] Moreover, even in serious literature, literary critics have noted the preoccupation with death in much of contemporary work.[5] It seems that here, in this expressive phase, society acknowledges the fact of death, even its heightened presence, while so firmly denying it in other phases of the culture.

We may state, then, that the constellation of the role of death in contemporary society is a peculiar tension between denial of death (the relevant factor of everyday existence) and the intense threat of death in the background—not only of death but of total annihila-

[4] Geoffrey Gorer, "The Pornography of Death," in Stephen Spender, Irving Kristol, and Melvin J. Laskey (Eds.), *Encounters: An Anthology* (New York: Basic Books, 1963). Gorer refers to such examples as detective stories, westerns, spy stories, and horror comics.

[5] Frederick Hoffman, *The Eternal No* (Princeton: Princeton University Press, 1964), in which he traces the theme of death from *The Red and the Black* to *The Deputy*.

tion. One effect of denying death in the real world and placing it in the world of fantasy is the lack of research and social scientific writing on this topic. Death has been regarded as one of a series of taboo topics,[6] topics where there is some social hindrance on doing research. It seems no accident that in the psychoanalytic literature the writing of Freud on death that is most often quoted is an essay which he wrote in time of war,[7] and that death, although nominally one of the two main instincts in the psychoanalytic scheme, has been followed up little by psychoanalysts. Sociological and social-psychological work on death has been attempted; but much of it relies on literature for its argument,[8] again showing that here is the main realization of the consciousness of death. In investigating the social meaning of death and its relation to the aging person, we shall rely mainly on the formal structures of society, especially as they are expressed in law and its applications.

In order to focus our attention on the main questions related to the place of death in society, we can divide man's attempt to come to grips with this problem into two broad divisions. One is the attempt to conserve one's own life, seen in terms of the value placed on individual life within society. The second accepts the fact of death and attempts to achieve immortality in some way. We can follow Lifton[9] in classifying these attempts into four types. One is biological immortality—the continuation of one's own life in one's children and future generations. The second is belief in actual immortality, in individual ideology represented in religious or philosophical systems and shown especially in society in the ritual of dying, funeral, and bereavement. The third is the continuation of life through one's achievements, fame, or physical signs of survival. The fourth is a belief in con-

[6] Norman Farberow, *Taboo Topics* (New York: Atherton, 1963). Here research in death is classified with such topics as sex, suicide, homosexuality, parapsychology, and graphology.

[7] Sigmund Freud, "Thoughts for the Times on War and Death," *Collected Papers*, Vol. 4 (London: Hogarth Press, 1923), pp. 288-317; originally published in 1915. On the lack of follow-up, see K. R. Eissler, *The Psychiatrist and the Dying Patient* (New York: International University Press, 1955), p. 39.

[8] This is exemplified from the earliest papers on this topic, e.g., Howard Becker, "The Sorrow of Bereavement," *Journal of Abnormal and Social Psychology*, 27 (January-March, 1933), 391-410, to recent ones, e.g., Eissler, *op. cit.;* Feifel's anthology, *The Meaning of Death*, in addition to having two chapters on art, contains numerous literary references.

[9] Robert J. Lifton, "On Death and Death Symbolism: The Hiroshima Disaster," *Psychiatry*, 27 (August, 1964), 191-210.

tinuity of life and nature after one's death, the belief that the complex of connections to which one is attached in life does persist beyond one's death.

We shall proceed by examining each of the reactions to death in terms of their relation to the whole of society, and the problems which they bring up for the individual and the type of people he is in contact with. At the same time we shall raise the question of how society deals formally with these problems and what are the formal rules, the legal framework in which they relate to public policy. The following sections will deal with the legal aspect. Finally, we shall discuss how this legal framework surrounding death affects the position of the aged within the society.

II

The social consequences of the different possible reactions to death will depend on the basic stance people in the society take toward death. We might, therefore, inquire into the consequences for American institutions of the peculiar attitude in our culture of denying natural death while being conscious of it in its violent forms. The student of society can pose these questions in the general framework; in turn, these can be answered in terms of the current legal state of the society.

The great value given to life itself leads to strong social support for the protection of each individual life. Responsibility for maintaining life rests with professionals whose codes and laws are relatively circumscribed. It seems logical from our analysis of the high evaluation of life that the actions of a professional are rigidly determined, even to the extent of negating the free choice of a person who might prefer death to certain kinds of life.[10] This specialized function of a professional in the maintenance of life especially in dealing with the aged and infirm, is one of the means of separating the dying from

[10] Not everyone prefers a long life. In a recent national survey, only about half of the population wanted to live 150 years, with older people less willing to do so than younger people. Kurt W. Back and Kenneth J. Gergen, "Individual Orientation and Morale of the Aged," in Ida Harper Simpson and John C. McKinney (Eds.), *Social Aspects of Aging* (Durham, N. C.: Duke University Press, 1966), Chapter 19.

the rest of society.[11] Some of these measures are described in Chapter 10 of this volume.

Commitment of the aged and infirm is an alternative to accepting death or living with it. The question of commitment becomes an important problem under these conditions—in effect, proposing a legal death.[12] But euthanasia, imposing physical death, violates one of the widely accepted taboos, conscious taking of individual lives without intent to punish, and is not sanctioned under contemporary law. This question has been raised more and more frequently, and model laws have been proposed.[13] One of the most telling arguments against euthanasia is the fact that it readily lends itself to horrible abuses, examples of which have occurred all too recently.

However, this "wedge theory" (that permissions under circumscribed conditions are necessarily an entering wedge to unrestricted abuse) is questionable; moreover, it might also be applicable at the other end, namely, in committing excessive use of the society's resources for saving individual lives. At great effort and cost it is possible even now to save lives and even resuscitate the biological dead to a limited degree. An example is the sustained work of a large group of scientists over a period of months to save the life of the Russian physicist, Lev Davidovitch Landau.[14] He was biologically dead six times, but was eventually saved. From now on, is doing anything less for anyone else a form of euthanasia? On the other hand, medical advance makes it possible to maintain life for helpless and vegetative creatures, as well as for individuals whose life consists mainly of suffering. From both points of view, that technical means of maintaining life are not universally practicable and that prolonging life may not be an unmitigated good, the question of euthanasia arises anew in our society. It is thus not a legal problem until the aims of society are more clarified.[15]

[11] Barney Glaser and Anselm Strauss, *Awareness of Dying* (Chicago: Aldine, 1965).

[12] Thomas D. Szasz, *Law, Liberty and Psychiatry* (New York: Macmillan, 1963).

[13] Glanville Williams, *The Sanctity of Life and the Criminal Law* (New York: Knopf, 1957), p. 343. For an example of dignified euthanasia, see Lael T. Wertenbacker, *Death of a Man* (New York: Random House, 1957).

[14] Alexander Dorozynski, *The Man They Wouldn't Let Die* (New York: Macmillan, 1965).

[15] For a summary of the acceptance of some methods of euthanasia in primitive societies and conditions related to it, see Leo W. Simmons, *The Role*

We can approach the problem at the present time at the point where society has a more statistical approach toward death, namely in the control of death from accidents and violence. Ubiquity of insurance may be a sign of decreasing fear of sudden death and an increasing view of accidental death as a manageable risk. In contrast to the protection of life in the natural course of events, the laxity of safety legislation with regard to enforcement and control of the sale of guns is markedly negligent. Emphasis seems to be put on the individual responsibility for prolonging life, but society accepts little responsibility for collective violence. How does the law protect individual life to the greatest extreme, even while allowing anonymous death to occur?

Society can neither deny nor prevent death completely. It can deal with the fact of death in the four ways indicated above. Thus, the first question to be raised refers to the manner in which society deals with biological immortality. This question includes the way in which institutions and laws help or hinder a person's influence over his offspring. If the individual life becomes so important, influence of the deceased over other people is likely to decrease. With the lessening of influence of the extended family and increased mobility of the individual nuclear units, a direct necessity of action depending on an ancestor is likely to increase. To what extent does the law allow individual expression of biological immortality?

Secularization is also likely to reduce the influence of religion and philosophy in mitigating death. This is in fact a concomitant of the emphasis on the individual life-span. Society seems to have a certain ambiguity toward the ceremonial surrounding death itself. The traces of the dead are obliterated from everyday view. No longer are elaborately built tombs located at prominent places in the landscape, as the most famous buildings of previous times were, such as the Taj Mahal, or forming the center of villages, as in Latin America and Europe. Whereas two of the seven wonders of the ancient world were tombs, even memorials to the war dead tend now to become living memorials—auditoriums or recreation centers to be used by the living. Cemeteries, which used to form the center of villages next to the church, are generally situated outside of town and hidden from view. On the other hand, the ceremonial surrounding the indi-

of the Aged in Primitive Society (New Haven: Yale University Press, 1946), Chapter 8, and Appendix A, pp. 281-284.

vidual death, the funeral, is becoming more elaborate and expensive until the very extent of the influence of the funeral profession has become a matter of public concern.[16] As with concern for biological immortality, society's concern ceases after the reaction to the individual death passes. Halloween, the traditional holiday when society honors its dead by attending the graves, has become in American culture the time in which the future generations (the children dressed as ghosts) are paid off and mitigated.[17] How far has this attitude been reflected in the formal regulations of the society?

Control over the future is not only possible in terms of control of one's family, but relates to other works and achievements as well. Here we would expect the society oriented to individualistic achievement to protect the individual or even impose limitations. Society clearly makes it more difficult for a wealthy man to conserve his whole fortune for his family than to conserve it for a foundation bearing his name. But even here society places some limitations. Similarly, the right of authorship, invention, and appreciation of good deeds are preserved but limited by society. However, just as in the power over one's own offspring, society limits the power that a person might have had through other means or through society at large. Conditional bequests, for instance, can be set aside if they no longer fit the changing conditions. The recent suggestions by the Patman Commission to limit the life of foundations to twenty-five years shows a powerful trend of opinion within the society. How far does the current legal trend encourage or discourage a person's striving for immortality in this way?

Finally, we have stated as Lifton's fourth point the continuity of nature as a way for man to mitigate the impact of death. Lifton mentions this point especially as a means that is lost in contemplating nuclear war. In contrast with the other ways, it is not the means by which an individual can assure his belief in a modified but continued existence, but in which society and the natural environment can provide comfort by their very existence. Continuity of society by itself without any specific institutions can provide this means of surpassing death. For example, we can point specifically to a conservative tradi-

[16] Cf. the controversy aroused by Jessica Mitford's *The American Way of Death* (New York: Simon and Schuster, 1963). The same point had been made earlier in fiction (and attributed to denial) by Evelyn Waugh, *The Loved One* (Boston: Little, Brown, 1948).

[17] Richard Sterba, "On Halloween," *American Imago*, 5 (1948), 213-224.

tion in many fields, continuity of political institutions or organizations, and conservation of natural resources and buildings. What is the position of American society in this respect? What is the perspective for the forces of conservation and continuity within the society, and the influences which support them?

III

The above sociological survey of death in contemporary American society has raised five questions addressed to the law member of the team: (1) Why does the law protect individual life to the greatest extent while allowing anonymous death to occur? (2) How does the law help or hinder a person's influence over his offspring after his death? (3) How is the removal of the immediate symbols of death from constant public view reflected in legal institutions? (4) How far does the current legal trend encourage or discourage a person's striving for immortality through the creation of permanent charitable establishments? (5) How far does the legal order as such provide comfort in the continued existence of society as it was known to the deceased?

We approach these questions with some misgivings. The relatively high degree of specialization of the academic legal profession and our resulting lack of expert knowledge in at least some fields raise the proverbial danger of sounding knowledgeable to the uninformed and uninformed to the knowledgeable.[18] Furthermore, we seem to detect at least some traces of what has been referred to above as the social hindrance on doing research into topics considered taboo. As will be seen, this is the case in only some of the areas to be discussed; nobody will regard the specialist on estate planning (who would deal with questions 2 and 4 above) as disadvantaged, in either the academic or the more mundane understanding of that term. Nevertheless, it can be assumed with some degree of confidence that no legal scholar has gained eternal fame by writing a learned treatise on what is charmingly called the Law of Cadavers and Cemeteries; and no promising young teacher has made his mark by teaching "dead bodies." This itself may be of sociological signifi-

[18] This juxtaposition was inspired by Raphael Powell, "Good Faith in Contracts," *Current Legal Problems,* 9 (1956), 16-38.

cance; but it may also be merely due to such prosaic causes as natural aversion to gloomy subjects and lack of challenging jurisprudential problems in the legal regulation of the Dismal Trade.

For the sake of convenience, we will start our discussion with the bleak subject just mentioned (question 3), and thence move to the increasingly more challenging problems raised by question 1 and questions 2 and 4 (the latter to be discussed together). We will be able to make very few observations as to the comfort to be derived from the relative stability of the legal order; here, as will be seen, the academic lawyer is in a rather peculiar position.

1. Obscuring the symbols of death. *Hominem mortuum in urbe ne sepelite neve vicinitate,*[19] the second law of the Twelve Tables is said to have provided. But this rule appears to have fallen into desuetude even in Rome; it was not received into Anglo-American law. Quite to the contrary, English law provided until well into the nineteenth century that each person, except a felon, a heretic, or a suicide, was entitled to be buried on the consecrated ground of his parish churchyard, as of right and without charge. This was a rule of ecclesiastical law, enforced by ecclesiastical tribunals; it did not become part of American common law. Nevertheless, the practice of burial in churchyard cemeteries was brought to this continent by the early settlers.

The frontier contributed two new burial practices: the family plot and the public cemetery. The former was a portion of the homestead set aside for burial purposes. The latter, usually located at the outskirts of municipalities, became a necessity, because in many pioneer communities single men without relatives or even friends made up a substantial portion of the population.

The location of public cemeteries at the outskirts of cities was probably, at least initially, merely a reflection of land values. However, within the last century, cemeteries have been driven out of cities by legislation. The growth of urban populations and the attendant rise of land values overcrowded the churchyard cemeteries to the point where they became serious health hazards, causing water pollution and epidemics. Agitation for the legislative control of cemeteries was quite strong in England in the latter part of the eighteenth century. The English Act was passed in 1855; by now, all

[19] "Do not bury the dead in or near the city."

states in the United States have followed suit. The typical legislative scheme consists of the prohibition of the creation of new cemeteries in municipalities, coupled with local discretion to prohibit further use of existing facilities and the regulation of the creation of new cemeteries outside of municipalities.

Thus, sanitary legislation has closed the churchyard cemetery and driven new cemeteries out of town. The further attrition of pre-existing cemeteries within towns is primarily the result of two forces: rising land values and the need for public space. Legislation regulates but permits the liquidation of inactive cemeteries.[20]

As for the Dismal Trade, it has to some extent been barred from public view with the advent of zoning laws. Since undertaking is a business, it cannot be carried out in a residential area.[21] However, even in the absence of pertinent zoning regulations, undertaking establishments have occasionally been closed down as so-called nuisances where they were offensive to neighbors in residential areas. As was stated in a leading case,

> People of ordinary sensibilities whose homes are in close proximity to a place where dead bodies are received at all hours of the day or night, where the awesome business of embalming is conducted, where hearses come and go, where funeral processions assemble, where funeral sermons are preached and dirges sung, would be subjected to annoyances of a peculiarly depressing and aggravating character. Persons subjected to such constantly recurring incidents and dismal circumstances could not enjoy their homes in peace and quietude; the laughter and play of their children about their own dooryards would seem heathenish and unfeeling in such a doleful environment. Social and family gatherings in residences so placed would be a pathetic caricature of happiness and enjoyment.[22]

Although there also are authorities for the proposition that a properly run, modern funeral parlor is not a nuisance, the weight of authority still on the books and the lack of judicial sympathy evident from statements such as that quoted above combine to reinforce a natural tendency toward restraint of publicity in the undertaking business.

[20] See generally Percival E. Jackson, *The Law of Cadavers and of Burial Places*, 2nd ed. (Englewood Cliffs, N. J.: Prentice-Hall, 1950), Chapters 1, 5-7, and 13.

[21] *Ibid.*, pp. 454-459.

[22] Leland v. Turner, 117 Kan. 294, 297-298, 230 Pac. 1061, 1063 (1924).

2. The decision for accidents. *Navigare necesse est, vivere non est necesse.*[23] This inscription over the portals of a Bremen guildhall is a good summary of the law's approach to hazardous activities that are considered to be in the public interest. Theoretically, no less than four courses of legal reaction to such activities are available: (1) prohibition, coupled with penal sanctions; (2) safety regulation, enforced by penal or quasi-penal sanctions; (3) imposition of pecuniary liability toward the victims, possibly in conjunction with a scheme of compulsory insurance; or finally (4) *laissez-faire* or even the conferral of immunity from liability for harmful conduct.

It is true that the first alternative is seldom if ever adopted. The second and third courses are complementary, not mutually exclusive. The history of modern accident law is largely the record of the gradual displacement of laissez-faire by safety regulation and the expansion of civil pecuniary liability.

A lawyer surveying American developments in this area in the last century or so would hardly agree with his sociologist colleague that society accepts little responsibility for collective violence, or that it is indifferent to the problem of anonymous death caused by hazardous activity. In the first half of the last century, when railroads and industrialization began to cause drastic increases in industrial and traffic accidents, the situation was bleak indeed. The law afforded no remedy to the survivors for the death of their bread-winner, and even allowed a person's own personal injury claims to abate with his death. As the saying went, it was cheaper to kill a man than to scratch him. But even if the workman or traffic victim survived, his chances for recovery were slim. The three ugly sisters of personal injury law—contributory negligence, assumption of risk, and the fellow servant rule—each fatal to any recovery at all, usually managed to shield the party primarily responsible and at fault. There was, generally speaking, no liability without fault.

The change has been dramatic and swift, although perhaps not dramatic enough and certainly not swift enough. Lord Campbell's Act, enacted in 1846, provided remedies for wrongful death; its example was quickly followed by most American states. Today, every state grants some recovery for wrongful death, although a minority of states still imposes maximum limitations on recovery. Subject to increasingly less important exceptions, the personal injury claims of

[23] "Navigation is necessary; living is not."

the deceased are likewise preserved by statute for the benefit of his estate.[24]

By far the most important change has occurred in industrial accidents. Workmen's compensation, coupled with work safety regulations, has completely replaced the former law in this area. Its basic principle is a limited but speedy exclusive compensation for all injuries to workmen arising out of the course of employment. The imposition of the employer's liability without fault was justified by the thought that "the cost of the product should bear the blood of the workman." It is reasonably apparent that workmen's compensation legislation has not only achieved its primary objective of relief to the victims of the industrial production process, but that it has also substantially contributed to a decrease in accidents. Whether this is primarily the result of direct self-interest in reducing accident liability or mainly due to work safety regulations indirectly enforced by industrial accident underwriters is a matter of conjecture. But in either event, the conclusion that workmen's compensation legislation has significantly decreased the chances of anonymous death is inescapable.[25]

Outside of the employment relationship, the picture is not so clear. Liability without fault for hazardous activities (for example, dynamite blasting) is again on the march; and so is compulsory automobile insurance. Still, the increasingly serious problem of anonymous death through traffic accidents has not been brought under control. Here, what Professor Calabresi has called the "decision for accidents" is seemingly irreversible.[26]

It appears to be quite clear that driving automobiles will not be prohibited, and that neither the strict enforcement of driver qualification standards nor the improvement of roads and traffic safety devices will even come close to eliminating carnage on the highways. With prohibition out of the question and regulation promising only limited success, it is generally recognized that major improvement can come primarily in the area of civil liability.

[24] William L. Prosser, *Handbook of the Law of Torts* (St. Paul, Minnesota: West, 1964), Chapter 25.

[25] *Ibid.*, Chapter 15; Arthur Larson, *Workmen's Compensation*, Vol. 1 (Albany, N. Y.: Matthew Bender, 1952), Chapter 2.

[26] Guido Calabresi, "The Decision for Accidents: An Approach to Non-fault Allocation of Costs," *Harvard Law Review*, 78 (February, 1965), 713-745.

The two basic objectives of torts (civil damage) law are deterrence to potential offenders and compensation for victims. These aims are normally complementary; but especially in the field of private traffic accident law, it has become increasingly clear that there has to be a basic preference for either deterrence or compensation. Improving the victim's chances for recovery by eliminating the standard common law defenses will come close to, or result in, liability without fault, thus decreasing, although not necessarily eliminating, deterrence. Much more important, however, the guarantee of actual recovery from "guilty" parties by compulsory liability insurance will lessen the deterrent effect of civil liability.

The main deterrent against noncriminal harmful acts in road traffic is, of course, the danger to the person of the "offender." The presence of this built-in deterrent has made it easier for law reform efforts to concentrate on methods for the compensation of the victim. Here the main problems are the extent of liability, financial responsibility, and adjustment procedure. A number of plans for the increased protection of the victims of highway accidents are currently being discussed; and some progress toward this goal will in all probability be made.[27] But it seems clear that any such progress will not be primarily directed at further reducing the chances of anonymous death on the highways. Nevertheless, it would seem to be equally clear that this tendency is not expressive of relative indifference to anonymous death, but rather a consequence of a policy choice in favor of anonymous traffic victims.

3. Death, taxes, and public policy.

In the halls of University College, University of London, prominently displayed within a glass case, are the bones of the great legal philosopher, Jeremy Bentham. The skeleton is clad in the garments which the great man wore in life. A wax replica of his head is substituted for his skull. His bony fingers grasp the walking stick, which he called "Dapple." On the glass case is a typewritten extract from his will, stating that the

---

[27] In addition to the study cited in footnote 26, mention should especially be made of Walter J. Blum and Harry Kalven, Jr., "Public Law Perspectives on a Private Law Problem—Auto Compensation Plans," *University of Chicago Law Review*, 31 (Summer, 1964), 641-723; and of Alfred F. Conard et al., *Automobile Accident Costs and Payments: Studies in the Economics of Injury Reparation* (Ann Arbor: University of Michigan Press, 1964).

316 KURT W. BACK AND HANS W. BAADE

testator desired to have his preserved figure, on certain occasions, placed
in a chair at gatherings of his friends and disciples, for the purpose of
commemorating his philosophy. It is said that this direction is still observed at banquets in his honor.

Professor Simes, from whose lectures on "Public Policy and the
Dead Hand" the above quotation has been taken, goes on to observe
that he knows of no more vivid illustration of the influence of the
dead hand.[28] But the dead hand of Bentham rules only by sufferance.
The relevant portion of his will clearly seems precatory and hence
unenforceable; and in any event, public policy would bar its legal
enforcement.

Most testators, with or without the advice of counsel, would
prefer to pursue less bizarre objectives in disposing of their wealth.
However, the urge to control the conduct of future generations
through conditional or limited testamentary dispositions in favor of
natural persons and of charities is deep-seated, especially in Great
Britain and in the United States. No other legal system approaches
the solicitude of Anglo-American law for the last wishes of wealthy
decedents. There is as yet no definitive explanation for the patent
and substantial divergence between the common law and the civil
law in this area. The main factors appear to be greater transmissible
family wealth, a fading but unbroken feudal tradition in England,
and United States federal estate tax policy. The latter is usually regarded as the crucial factor in this country, for a tax that is levied
only on the estate of the decedent at the time of his death naturally
places a tremendous premium on schemes for the tax-free transmission of the estate to successive beneficiaries for limited periods of
time. Still, this explanation hardly suffices, for the federal estate tax
reaches only a small minority of the American population, and the
use of estate planning devices is much more widespread than the
incidence of this tax. (State inheritance and estate taxes are, on
the whole, not a significant consideration in estate planning.) Many
a practicing lawyer has frequently encountered the client of moderate wealth who distrusts his children's business acumen and wants

[28] Lewis M. Simes, *Public Policy and the Dead Hand* (Ann Arbor: University of Michigan Press, 1955), p. 32. The following discussion is based in
good part on this study.

to provide for his grandchildren; it is possibly this attitude that lies at the base of estate planning law in the United States.[29]

The interaction of succession, trust, and property law with the federal tax structure can perhaps be illustrated best by discussing a reasonably typical case. Suppose that T is a man of substantial but not extravagant wealth, a millionaire but not a magnate. He has a wife, three children, two of whom are married, and about five grandchildren. His fortune consists of a medium-sized manufacturing enterprise organized as a corporation (with himself the controlling but not the only shareholder), a carefully diversified portfolio of securities, a home and the usual personal property, and a substantial life insurance.

Ordinarily, T will wish to provide for his widow during her life, give something to his children, and leave the remainder of his properties to his grandchildren. He will be concerned with three more technical objectives: minimizing taxes, retaining family control in the factory, and preventing the dissipation of wealth until the ultimate objective is reached. T will also be likely to have several not so typical objectives. He might prefer one child or grandchild over the others. He might wish to perpetuate his name, his philosophy, or both by leaving some permanent symbol of his fame. Finally, he might have some more personal preferences and prejudices, and might want his offspring to marry his own kind of people.

With these objectives in mind, T will consult his business lawyer, only to be referred to a specialist in estate planning, possibly but not necessarily a member of the same law firm. This specialist is a person who has for some time devoted his energies primarily to advising clients in T's position, who has a sound knowledge of the

[29] Cf. Lawrence M. Friedman, "The Dynastic Trust," *Yale Law Journal*, 73 (March, 1964), 547-592, especially 547-551. Another explanation is offered by Wilbert Moore elsewhere in this volume: The combined effect of increased longevity and shortened generations is that by the time the surviving parent dies, the children are "probably well beyond the middle of their own careers." Therefore, Dr. Moore speculates, "it seems probable that lifetime distributions to immediate heirs are increasingly common, with posthumous transfers skipping a generation and running to grandchildren, who are at a more propitious stage of the life cycle to benefit from an inheritance." *Supra*, pp. 37-38. If increased longevity and shortened generations are relatively recent demographic developments, however, it seems likely that they merely (if substantially) reinforce a preexisting tendency to prefer grandchildren over children.

intricacies of property and trust law, who knows everything there is to know about federal estate, gift, and income taxes, including trends and likely future developments, and who is also rather well acquainted with business and investment practices. If he is of middle age, he is likely to have acquired most of this knowledge by individual research and practical experience. Most younger lawyers of the kind likely to be consulted by T will have had one or more courses in estate planning in law school (the better law schools have been teaching it for about a decade).

Counsel will probably advise T as follows: T is free to devise all of his wealth to the exclusion of any or all of his children or grandchildren, but he must make suitable provision for his wife. Unlike the civil law, American law (with the exception of French-derived Louisiana law) does not provide an indefeasible share (*légitime*) of the offspring in their parents' estate. The widow's share will differ from state to state, usually amounting to the intestate share which here would be a child's part, that is, one-fourth.

After having made suitable provision for his wife (which, incidentally, is tax-favored in that it will be taxed only at the widow's death), T can now dispose of his remaining properties at his sole discretion. He will be advised to employ two standard devices: the trust and the future interest. Together, they will enable T to create limited successive interests in his property, thus at once controlling its use and preventing its dissipation. In the instant case, standard advice would be the creation of one or more trusts for the management of the properties and securities, the income of which is to be paid to the children during their lives and then to the grandchildren.

Here the public interest in the alienability of property will impose some ultimate limits, known as the Rule Against Perpetuities and the Rule Against Accumulations. In misleadingly simple terms, the combined effect of these two rules is that the ultimate disposition of T's property cannot be postponed beyond ascertainable lives in being at his death, plus twenty-one years thereafter, allowing for all necessary periods of gestation. Thus, T could bequeath the income from his estate over and above the widow's share to his children for life, then to his grandchildren for twenty-one years, and then distribute the estate to his surviving grandchildren. He could also create life estates in his grandchildren living at his death, but not in grandchildren born thereafter. Such interests would be "remote" and void.

Now, by skillful utilization of trusts and future interests, T can postpone the ultimate disposition of his estate for about eighty years (the youngest grandchild in being at his death may still be *en ventre sa mère* and live to be ninety, but that is an outside possibility). He can lay down binding rules for the management of his properties for this entire period, and he will have postponed another federal estate tax (but for his wife's share) for almost a century.

During this period, T can also attempt to govern the personal lives of his descendants. He cannot, of course, force them to behave in certain ways, but he can punish them for not conforming to his wishes by providing for the termination of his munificence. Again, the law imposes some limitation. Some conditions are treated as illegal and void as against public policy, for example, an obligation not to marry at all. But T can provide, for instance, that a grandchild shall forfeit his share if he marries before reaching a certain reasonable age or if he fails to marry within the family faith.

Although thus permitting the dead hand to rule the future, the law is still somewhat hostile to the whole technique. Until recently, courts were generally willing to strike down estate plans merely because in some quite unlikely contingency they might violate the Rule Against Perpetuities—without waiting to see if such violations actually occurred. Professor W. Barton Leach has coined a series of expressions for the more extreme of these cases, for example, the Mysterious Gravelpit (it might not be exhausted within ascertainable lives in being plus twenty-one years); the Fertile Octogenarian (he might still have children); the Precocious Toddler (he might already have children); and the Sluggish Executor (he might not probate the will within eighty years).[30] In a similarly hostile manner, courts have dealt harshly with personal conditions. They have disregarded religious practice or upbringing clauses as vague and, above all, generally assumed, in the absence of clear indications to the contrary, that void conditions were mere conditions subsequent. This means that with the void condition eliminated, an unrestricted

[30] For discussion and illustration (including appropriate Steinberg cartoons from *The New Yorker Magazine*), see Jesse Dukeminier, Jr., *Perpetuities Law in Action. Kentucky Case Law and the 1960 Reform Act* (Lexington: University of Kentucky Press, 1962), pp. 9-14.

bequest will normally be enforced unless the contrary is expressly specified.[31]

Still, it would be premature to describe the policy and trend of the law as hostile to the dead man's rule. In the area of perpetuities, at least one consideration strongly militates in favor of reducing the period available. There will be a substantial demand for public lands in the next decades, primarily for road construction and the like. The condemnation of land subject to a sophisticated estate plan is extremely cumbersome and time-consuming. It should therefore be thought that the Rule Against Perpetuities should be tightened up, not relaxed;[32] but the opposite has happened. Largely as a result of Professor Leach's efforts, courts and legislatures are increasingly adopting the so-called wait-and-see approach, finding a violation of the Rule only when it does occur, not where it merely might. Some states have also by statute chosen the so-called *cy pres* solution, which does not treat provisions violative of the Rule as void, but merely cuts them down to the permissible period. It is as yet hardly possible to discern a dominant trend, but better opinion seems to be that the classical Rule, with wait-and-see and possibly *cy pres* safeties, will be available for some time to come.[33]

Now, suppose that after having consulted his tax tables, T's lawyer comes to the conclusion that it will not be possible to preserve the bulk of the estate intact. In order to pay estate taxes, some assets will have to be liquidated. Here, the lawyer will suggest a scheme that realizes T's desire to keep the factory in the family as well as his fond hope to erect a permanent monument to himself. This scheme almost suggests itself because any bequest to a charity is excluded from the decedent's properties for estate tax purposes and gifts to charities are not subject to the federal gift tax.

Donner et retenir ne vaut,[34] an old French legal maxim says. Estate planners know otherwise. T will be advised to provide for his widow by leaving her the bulk of his nonbusiness properties, retain-

[31] A good recent summary is John J. Murphy, Jr., and James S. Parkhill, Jr., "Conditional Bequests and Devises," *Boston University Law Review,* 42 (Fall, 1962), 520-546.

[32] Robert N. Cook, "American Law Reform: Legal Co-Ownership, Dower, and Courtesy," *Duke Law Journal,* Fall 1960, pp. 485-523, especially pp. 497-501.

[33] W. Barton Leach, Jr., "Perpetuities: Cy Pres on the March," *Vanderbilt Law Review,* 17 (October, 1964), 1381-1390.

[34] "You cannot give and retain at the same time."

ing enough readily convertible assets to pay anticipated estate taxes on the rest (as already mentioned, the widow's share, up to 50 percent of the estate, is taxable only at her death and taxable to her, that is, at substantially lower rates unless she is independently wealthy). He will then reorganize his business by dividing stocks into two classes of voting common and nonvoting preferred, with the latter constituting as much in value as he desires to give to charity. Now, either by testamentary devise or by *inter vivos* gift—preferably by both to ensure the soundness of the scheme—he will transfer the bulk of the preferred stock to the T Foundation, a charity organized for the purpose of pursuing T's pet social objectives and, incidentally, perpetuating his fame. He will allocate the voting stock and the remaining property, including enough liquid assets (e.g., life insurance) to pay the now greatly reduced federal estate tax, to the trusts set up in favor of his children and grandchildren. Thus, everybody will be happy. The widow is taken care of, the taxes are paid, children and grandchildren are suitably hamstrung and provided for, the family retains control of the business, and T's fame is kept in living memory—in perpetuity, no less. For the Rule Against Perpetuities does not apply to charitable foundations.

This brings us to the subject of foundations. By now, it has become clear why the number of foundations had risen to over 15,000 by the end of 1963, with total assets of over $14 billion. After the Fords showed the way, those in the relatively modest position of our hypothetical manufacturer-dynast-philanthropist T have followed suit.

Curiously enough, a foundation can be set up without much difficulty, either as a charitable trust or as a corporation. No prior investigation or government approval is necessary for this purpose. In about half the states, the attorney general has statutory powers to enforce charities; a few states have also recently created government commissions for the supervision of charities. It is still somewhat uncertain whether in the absence of statutory authority the donor, the general public, or even the attorney general has standing in this area. In any event, as Professor Austin Wakeman Scott observes in his leading treatise, "Both in England and in the United States the Attorney General is charged with many duties which have nothing to do with the enforcement of charitable trusts. The result has been that, in the absence of statutory changes in the law, the enforcement of charitable trusts is bound to be more or less sporadic."[35] Thus, it is still true today that as a practical matter, there is no real subsequent government control of foundations, with one exception, presently to be mentioned. Consequently, the "monohippic" foundation, typically a corporation consisting of the donor as president, his wife as vice-president, and his lawyer as secretary, has become a favorite pastime of middle-range businessmen.

The one control extant today is the federal tax system. A foundation that does not qualify as an exempt charity under this system will be economically useless, if not worse. Consequently, great care is taken to meet the qualifications listed by the International Revenue Code. A tax-exempt corporation must be "organized and operated exclusively for religious, charitable, scientific, testing for public safety, literary, or educational purposes, or for the prevention of cruelty to children or animals."[36] It cannot, of course, distribute profits; nor may it unreasonably accumulate income. Unless it is a church, it may not engage in an unrelated business activity, although its investments can and as a rule do consist of participations in business. And insiders may not engage in self-dealing, such as obtaining low-interest loans for their private businesses.

It may now seem to T that all of this is sufficiently tame and easy to comply with, since all he has to fear is an occasional Treasury audit. He might therefore be tempted to tailor the foundation exactly to his own philosophical views.

His lawyer will almost certainly advise T that this would be most unwise. For a man who plans in terms of centuries must take future developments into consideration, and it seems quite unlikely that the present situation will continue. Especially after Representative Patman's investigations have brought this matter into public focus,[37]

---

[35] Austin Wakeman Scott, *The Law of Trusts,* Vol. 4, 2nd ed. (Boston: Little, Brown, 1956), p. 2754. In connection with the above, see especially two studies by Professor Kenneth L. Karst, "The Efficiency of the Charitable Dollar: An Unfulfilled State Responsibility," *Harvard Law Review,* 73 (January, 1960), 433-483, and "The Tax Exemption of Donor-Controlled Foundations," *Ohio State Law Journal,* 25 (Spring, 1964), 183-221.

[36] Internal Revenue Code of 1954, section 501 (c) (3).

[37] Recent discussions include John E. Riecker, "Foundations and the Patman Report," *Michigan Law Review,* 63 (November, 1964), 95-140; and Jan Z. Krasnowiecki and Alexander Brodsky, "Comment on the Patman Report," *University of Pennsylvania Law Review,* 112 (December, 1963), 190-208.

thoughtful observers are agreed that the policing of charities by the federal tax law alone is intolerable in the long run. It seems almost inevitable that a substantive state or federal regulatory law of foundations will develop, and that this law will ultimately distinguish between various degrees and kinds of charities in accordance with their public utility, granting a differentiated scale of tax and other benefits to each class.

Furthermore, there is some likelihood that the enforcement of foundation law will be substantially tightened. The Internal Revenue Service has already greatly stepped up the number and intensity of its audits.[38] But it seems likely that in the future there will be enforcement through actions of state agencies acting in the public interest. This will especially be the case where the aims of a charity are narrowly conceived and have become impracticable or socially undesirable. Here, the so-called *cy pres* doctrine already offers some guidance. It signifies that where a charitable purpose becomes impracticable and there is both a valid bequest and a general charitable intent, courts have power to direct the employment of the funds for another, presently practicable, charitable purpose as closely in line with the donor's intent as may be.[39]

It seems reasonable to expect that the *cy pres* doctrine will be generally recognized and liberalized in such a way as to apply to all charitable gifts, with impracticability determined in accordance with the public interest as it may be from time to time. This will mean that charities will become "socialized." After all, they have been established largely by funds which otherwise would have become public through the incidence of taxation; and it can be assumed with some degree of assurance that the public will eventually act in one way or another to protect its basic interests.

However, T can probably be advised with some assurance that his charitable contribution will not be "nationalized," that is, drawn into the anonymity of the public treasury and transformed into fungible state property bearing no trace of the donor's personality and ideals. Individual and individualistic charitable giving is, at least if controlled as discussed above, entirely compatible with the

[38] See Mortimer M. Caplin, "Foundations and Government: Some Observations on the Future," in F. Emerson Andrews (Ed.), *Foundations: 20 Viewpoints* (New York: Russell Sage Foundation, 1965), p. 15, especially pp. 16-17.

[39] Edith L. Fisch, *The Cy Pres Doctrine in the United States* (Albany, N. Y.: Matthew Bender, 1950).

welfare state, and probably a vital protection of pluralistic society against bureaucratic uniformity. As was written by a great champion of the welfare state and a great North Carolina chief justice:

> While Mr. Carnegie's assertion that "To die rich is to die disgraced" cannot be sustained, those rich men should be remembered with honor who devote some part of their estate to widen opportunity and enjoyment for the public. In death, as in life, those who have accumulated large estates should have regard "for the spears of Judah and the archers of Benjamin"—that solid mass of men who have lived in poverty or struggled through life on small means, yet whose law-abiding spirit has protected the property of those who have made large accumulations of wealth, in safety and untroubled by the spoiler. Not to do this is to fail in their reasonable duty to the community and to defeat the just expectations of the public.[40]

There is no reason why these rich men, if they are wise enough, should not continue to be honored in the future.

4. The government of the living by the dead. *Es erben sich Gesetz und Rechte wie eine ewge Krankheit fort,*[41] says Mephistopheles in Goethe's *Faust*. Ever since the mechanics of the creation of rules of law have been de-mystified and openly discussed, it has become commonplace to think of law as perennially lagging behind the needs of society.

This seems a dangerous generalization. When law was largely customary, it necessarily had to lag behind societal developments, for only that custom became law which was followed because of popular belief in its binding nature. But legislation, now by far the most important source of legal rules, made its debut as the weapon of absolute monarchs and their advisers for social "revolution from above," and recent history is replete with examples of legislation shaping rather than following customary community standards. Common examples are the legislative output of the French Revolution and the reception of Western law in various non-Western countries, for example, Swiss law in Turkey. Another, more recent illustration is the abandonment of tolerance for regional divergencies by the dominant legal order of a country, such as the enforcement

---

[40] Walter Clark, C. J., in Wachovia Banking and Trust Company v. Ogburn, 181 N.C. 324, 331-332, 107 S.E. 238, 242 (1921).

[41] "Laws are inherited like permanent diseases."

of the political rights of Negroes in what used to be called the Deep South.

Still, there can be little quarrel with the basic proposition that stability and relative immobility are inherent characteristics of the legal order, and that they are, on the whole, at least as significant as the utilization of the monopoly of legitimate force for reform purposes. Consequently, a society's attitude toward law is necessarily ambivalent: the legal order is valued primarily because of the stability that it implies, while legislation is a welcome tool for peaceful social change.

The attitudes of the legal profession toward the legal order show the same ambivalence, only thinly disguised under conciliatory slogans like "Rule of Law and Peaceful Change." Generally speaking, the legal profession tends to be conservative—partly in response to the attitude of the more profitable potential clients, but perhaps equally if not primarily because the familiar is preferred over the unknown. After all, every significant piece of legislation *pro tanto* repeals existing legal knowledge along with preexisting inconsistent law.[42]

Of course, a number of practicing lawyers, including several of the more outstanding members of the profession, are actively engaged in law reform and in advanced social engineering by legal devices—setting up new foundations, organizing transnational business empires, and the like. Still, for the very reason that much of their success depends upon their easy familiarity with the governmental power structure, they instinctively prefer to remain out of the limelight.

The sum total seems to be that the practicing bar is generally, if not universally, conservative, and that a common attitude toward the relationship of professional activity and the legal order to the life hereafter is a collective pride of having stood, not anonymously perhaps but certainly not very publicly, in the common-law tradition.[43]

[42] A recent study has documented basic conservatism of the legal profession. Walter O. Weyrauch, *The Personality of Lawyers: A Comparative Study of Subjective Factors in Law, Based on Interviews with German Lawyers* (New Haven: Yale University Press, 1964).

[43] This tradition has been eulogized in a famous song by the late Karl N. Llewellyn, reproduced in Karl N. Llewellyn, *The Common Law Tradition: Deciding Appeals* (Boston: Little, Brown, 1960), pp. 398-399.

This attitude is shared by a number of legislators with legal backgrounds, some judges, and a few law teachers. But although there is no reason not to respect and admire the competent conservative craftsman of the law at the bar, one is tempted to regard such legislators as lazy, such judges as mediocre, and such law teachers as deadwood.

Since the law needs motion as a necessary complement to repose, those whom society enables and empowers to supply that motion have to live up to their obligations or face public condemnation. But legal change and anonymity are no longer compatible in an age where the process of the creation of legal norms is de-mystified and directly subjected to the political power struggle. The legislator must accept some anonymity for various reasons, if only because Congress cannot pass enough significant bills associated with only one or two sponsors' names. Still, there will be the occasional Fulbright Act and Taft-Hartley Law. The remaining legislators will have to see satisfaction in a job well done and, at least on the federal level, more fully documented for posterity than almost any other socially significant activity.

This leaves the judges and the teachers. Obviously, although we all know that judges not only find the law but also make it, their contribution to the evolution of the legal order has to be more gradual and more circumspect; at the same time, it will be more definitive. It seems beyond doubt that a truly great judge, one who does not merely state or settle points of law but writes truly creative judicial opinions, is motivated to some not inconsiderable extent by the conscious or subconscious wish to reach immortality in this manner.

Clearly, the great legal scholar will have similar motives, whether or not he is conscious of them. The differences between the scholar and the judge in this regard are that the professor is accountable only to the republic of scholars of his and succeeding generations, and that his contributions can change the law merely by persuasiveness, not by authority.

We may well conclude the above, somewhat discursive and speculative remarks by quoting from one who has achieved immortality:

Learning, my learned brethren, is a very good thing. I should be the last to undervalue it, having done my share of quotation from the Year

Books. But it is liable to lead us astray. The law, so far as it depends on learning, is indeed, as it has been called, the government of the living by the dead. To a very considerable extent no doubt it is inevitable that the living should be so governed. The past gives us our vocabulary and fixes the limits of our imagination; we cannot get away from it. There is, too, a peculiar logical pleasure in making manifest the continuity between what we are doing and what has been done before. But the present has a right to govern itself so far as it can; and it ought always to be remembered that historic continuity with the past is not a duty, it is only a necessity.[44]

IV

Because of the decreasing mortality in younger ages, the period of old age has become singled out as the one concerned with death. We seem to be taking the concept of the life cycle seriously, as well as expecting that normally everyone should reach the end of the cycle. This relation to death and preparation for it becomes one of the permanent roles of the aged, and we can ask how the peculiar relation of the society to death makes execution of this role easy or difficult.

First of all, the separation of death from the normal life of the society reinforces the general tendency of the society to separate the aged. The aged are concerned with one aspect of life that society does not like to be reminded of. Therefore, society does not like to be reminded of the aged. In turn, the aged accept as a primary duty the prolongation of their own lives, and to do so under any conditions. Therefore, preoccupation with death, funerals, and burial is considered to be morbid. The continuity implied by viewing death as a necessary event and preparing for it is to be avoided. Thus, society makes concern about death a function of the aged and at the same time tells the aged not to be concerned.

The most striking example of this conflict is exemplified in the discussion of family law. Orientation toward the future of the society conflicts with the idea of the dead hand lying on future generations, and the loss to society by entailment limits the application of such devices. However, from the point of view of the individual, the question of action and projection into the future does become important.

---

[44] Oliver Wendell Holmes, Jr., "Learning and Science," (1895), in *Collected Legal Papers* (New York: Harcourt, Brace & World, 1921), pp. 138-139.

An old person is more likely to use the power which he has in present-day society than in earlier periods. When aging and dying are considered to be part of the normal continuity of generational succession, the person can take the general arrangements of transfer of property as a matter of course. If the tradition of the society stressed the life of the individual and placed a premium on future orientation, then the fact of estate planning would become more prevalent although more difficult. The value which an individual can put on himself depends not only on his position in the succession of generations, but also on what he can do to show his influence for the longest possible time.

Western society has always put great emphasis on legitimacy of successsion, both of political power and economic goods. At the same time, the rapid obsolescence of the individual because of rapid social and technological change leads to individual discontinuity between generations; skills or wisdom cannot be transmitted.[45] In this situation reliance on influence through estates or publicity, through foundations and bequests, becomes of great importance to the aging individual, but society circumscribes this power.

The same kind of conflict with emphasis on individual life and future orientation on the one hand, and the relegation of the function of death to the aged is shown in other spheres. As all the visible signs of death are taken from any easily accessible place, it is hard for the aged to prepare for the act of dying itself. For the larger part of society death is merely envisioned as an abrupt, catastrophic event, caused by either individual violence or general destruction. There is little concern with making death natural, and nothing is done for the older person to help him view it in this light. Thus, the standard for the aged is to emulate the young and to engage as much as possible in similar activities. Only when the aged person cannot participate in activities of this kind is he allowed, or forced, to stop accepting the standards of the younger generation.

Thus we find that the attitude toward death held by the majority of the society is frequently accepted by the aged person too. This forced orientation for the future makes him deny death, although sometimes it may become difficult for him to do so, and makes him plan individual actions which may have great consequences for the future. Thus the society removes the sense of death and tries to pre-

[45] This volume, Moore's chapter.

vent the influence of death on the person as long as he lives. He is compelled to stay active and to ignore, as far as he can, impending death. The aged in this society become a symbol of delaying death and simultaneously of its inevitability.

BIOGRAPHICAL NOTES

KURT WOLFGANG BACK was born in 1919 in Vienna, Austria, and was educated at the Universities of Vienna and Geneva, New York University, the University of California at Los Angeles, and the Massachusetts Institute of Technology (Ph.D.). He was a research associate at Columbia University, the University of Puerto Rico, and the University of North Carolina, and is presently Professor of Sociology and Medical Sociology at Duke University. The scope of his inquiry encompasses research conducted in experimental social psychology, large-scale social survey, demography, and general methodological problems. His most recent publications include *The Family and Population Control* (with R. Hill and J. M. Stycos); *The Control of Human Fertility in Jamaica* (with J. M. Stycos); and "A Social Psychologist Looks at Kinship Structure," in *Social Structure and the Family: Generational Relations.*

HANS W. BAADE was born in Berlin, Germany, in 1929, and was educated at Syracuse University, the University of Kiel, Germany (Dr. iur.; Privatdozent), and Duke University (LL.B., LL.M.). Now Professor of Law at Duke University, he has published a number of studies on international and comparative law. From 1961 to 1965, Mr. Baade was the editor of *Law and Contemporary Problems*, a legal periodical published by Duke University. He also serves on the Board of Editors of the *American Journal of Comparative Law* and is a member of various professional organizations in this country and in Germany.

INDEX

Accidents, decision for. *See* Decision for accidents

Accidents, industrial, 314

Aged: assets, 216-217; average income, 54; and chronic illness, 263; and credit, 226; defined, 158; economic relief for, 73-74; and health insurance, 217; health of, 217; and housing, 218; income level, 216; median income, 55; number of, 2-3, 222; and policy postulates, 196; political power of, 107; and power, 90-112 *passim;* and responsibility, 214; and social activities, 218-219; societal attitudes toward, 267-268; societal role, 268-269; and suicide, 275-276; unemployable, 73; and use of health facilities, 270-272; values of, 96-97

Age distribution: and fertility, 27-29; and mortality, 27-28

Age grading, 30-33; and education, 30; and employment, 30-31; and married women, 31; and military, 31; and older persons, 32-33

Agencies, private, 98-99. *See also* Institutions; Philanthropic system

Age-specific fertility, 51

Aging: defined, 43; as disengagement, 129-132; and health, 261-262. *See also* Collective aging

Aging and Leisure, 276

Aid for Aged, 100

Aid to Dependent Children, 202-203

Alcott, Mrs. Bronson, 203

Alleviative programs, 159, 162-164, 188

Alor tribe, 285

AMA, 99, 104; and hospitals, 106

American Association of Retired Persons, 99

Anderson, W. H. Locke, 74 n.

Annuity, 151, 179-182; benefit levels, 182; deferred, 179; immediate, 179; joint-and-survivorship, 182; single life, 181-182; variable, 177, 193

Arrow, Kenneth, 190

Assumption of risk, 313

Australian tribes, and aged, 286

Baade, Hans W., 17-18, 329

Back, Kurt W., 17-18, 329

Banking, and housing, 226

Barone, Enrico, 67

Becker, Howard, 132

Bentham, Jeremy, 315-316

Bird, Brian, 283

Bismarck, Otto von, 199

Blue Cross, 105-106

Bossard, James H. S., 199, 200

Boulding, Kenneth, 189, 191, 195

Bowlby, John, 260

Browning, Robert, 42

Brumberg, R., 71

Burial practices, 311-312

Business, and aged, 92, 98

Busse, Ewald W., 15, 280

Calabresi, Guido, 314